ALSO BY JON T. COLEMAN

Vicious: Wolves and Men in America

HERE LIES HUGH GLASS

HERE LIES HUGH GLASS

———◆———

A MOUNTAIN MAN, A BEAR,
AND THE RISE OF
THE AMERICAN NATION

———◆———

JON T. COLEMAN

AN AMERICAN PORTRAIT

HILL AND WANG
A DIVISION OF FARRAR, STRAUS AND GIROUX
NEW YORK

Hill and Wang
A division of Farrar, Straus and Giroux
18 West 18th Street, New York 10011

Distributed in Canada by D&M Publishers, Inc.
Printed in the United States of America
First edition, 2012

Portions of chapter 4 were previously published in Jon T. Coleman, "Animal Last Stands: Empathy and Extinction in the American West," *Montana, the Magazine of Western History* 55 (Autumn 2005): 2–13; and in Jon T. Coleman, "Killed Him a Bear: Wildlife and the Man," *Environmental History* 16 (July 2011): 408–12.

Library of Congress Cataloging-in-Publication Data
Coleman, Jon T., 1970–
    Here lies Hugh Glass : a mountain man, a bear, and the rise of the
American nation / Jon T. Coleman.—1st ed.
        p.   cm.—(An American portrait)
    Includes bibliographical references and index.
    ISBN 978-0-8090-5459-6 (cloth : alk. paper)
    1. Glass, Hugh, ca. 1780–ca. 1833.   2. Frontier and pioneer life—West (U.S.).
3. United States—Territorial expansion—History—19th century.
4. Pioneers—West (U.S.)—Biography.   I. Title.

F592.G55C65 2012
978' .02092—dc23
[B]   2011036617

Designed by Jonathan D. Lippincott

www.fsgbooks.com

1   3   5   7   9   10   8   6   4   2

FOR ANNIE

CONTENTS

AUTHOR'S NOTE

In the coming pages I tell a story about a man famous for nearly being killed by a grizzly bear in the Rocky Mountains in 1823. There's not much left of this man. He contributed one letter to history. He spoke to people, but the writers who tracked him through twice-removed conversations only disfigured him further with their literary ambitions, calling him America's Odysseus, a laughable honorific for a working-class guy whose major talent, accident proneness, made him more Homer Simpson than Homeric. Undocumented, the man disappeared into his surroundings. That's why I picked him. I'm a historian of culture but also of nature, animals, landscapes, biomes, and habitats. Environments intrigue me as much as people.

The story of Hugh Glass and his environments calls into question the central conceit of biographies: that individual human lives tower above all else. Unlike Jesus, Attila the Hun, or Benjamin Franklin, Glass remains almost wholly lost in time. His predilections, his appearance, as well as his opinions are unknowable. His work as a hired hunter rendered him barely visible. Even his saving grace, the regional authors who seized upon the stories of western workers remade by nature to secure national fame, did so for their own purposes. Stripped of his past, his personality, and his individuality, Glass surrendered the lead role in his own drama. He shared the bill with the environments that claimed parts of him.[1]

Glass arrived at the same end as most. Ordinary people tend to vanish. Birth certificates, parish records, and tombstones mark their existence, but the memories, the tastes, the passions, and the individual flourishes, all the hiccups in form, carriage, and delivery that separate one mortal pilgrim from another, erode quickly. Style may be the most perishable substance on earth. Hugh Glass was an ordinary man with exemplary style, and glimmers of his humor and his rebelliousness have withstood the ravages of grizzly bears, hard labor, and literary abduction. Yet the information that has survived evokes as much loss as satisfaction. Forever incomplete, he is a reminder of the deletions awaiting us all.

What follows is more a missing-person report than a biography. But instead of cursing the holes in his paperwork, I intend to plumb the absences surrounding Glass. The gaps in the record open onto his environs, they made him an American environmentalist of a sort. A vocalist rather than a writer, Glass didn't produce a memorable tome—a *Walden*, *A Sand County Almanac*, or a *Silent Spring*—but he contributed to American environmental thought in his own way. Glass withstood a posse of consumers—the fauna, bosses, and literati out to swallow him—and his staying power leads the history of American environmentalism in new and unsettling directions.[2]

Indeed, Hugh Glass reverses the emphasis and order of the phrase. Instead of highlighting individual thinkers contemplating the nation's environmental practices and values, he shows how groups of Americans used the violently altered bodies of working-class hunters out West to define their nation. Instead of American environmentalism, Glass serves up environmental Americanism. By stressing the relationship between the environment and nationalism, his story underscores the links between marginal people laboring in far-off places and the rise of American exceptionalism. Americans looked to the outskirts of their society and their population centers to define their nation as unique and chosen for greatness, and Hugh Glass, a hunter physically transformed by nature on the country's frontier, surfaced as a bit player in a nation-building drama. His ordeals rooted environmental history in the thick of early-nineteenth-century American history.[3]

Americans, of course, were kidding themselves when they imagined that environments created exceptional nations. Neither born nor planted, nations rise and fall on the words, thoughts, and deeds of people. Families, homes, regions, religions, classes, genders, races, and ethnicities bolster and erode national identities. To placate crosshatched loyalties, nation-builders biologized and sanctified the nation, binding it together with myths that suggested the polity had both earthly and otherworldly origins. In 1839, John L. O'Sullivan, the writer, party activist, and coiner of the phrase "manifest destiny," cobbled together these origin myths in his essay "The Great Nation of Futurity." God, he wrote, had selected the United States to "smite unto death the tyranny of kings, oligarchs, hierarchs, and carry the glad tidings of peace and good." O'Sullivan pleaded with American artists to turn away from Europe, ancient Greece, and Rome for instruction and inspiration. Writers especially should look at their own continent to find the "vigorous national heart of America." The nexus of the nation thrummed in "the wilderness," where "the great masses—the agricultural and mechanical populations"—worshipped at the "sacred altars of intellectual freedom." This, O'Sullivan wrote, "was the seed that produced individual equality, and political liberty, as its natural fruits, and this is our true nationality." God had entrusted America's awesomeness to the grunts in the sticks.[4]

Hugh Glass, who died six years before O'Sullivan published his essay, would have been surprised that he and his coworkers were founding a nation when they stripped the hides off beavers in the Rocky Mountains. No one mistook their camps for altars, and not all the laborers in them were equal, free, or American. A motley crew gathered in the camps: African American slaves, mulatto freemen, Indian men and women from many tribes, various white Americans from states like Missouri, Illinois, Virginia, and Pennsylvania, French-speaking contract workers (*engagés*) from St. Louis, Mexican nationals, Canadian voyageurs, and British fur company proles. Hunting in the West mingled races, genders, nations, cultures, and languages. It was an unlikely birthplace of American futurity. Yet, for some nationalists, the riffraff laboring on the political, geographic, and social fringes manifested America's genius.[5]

I will follow Glass—hunt him if you will—through three environments. But I warn you: Glass didn't experience them neatly in a row, and neither will you. His cultural, social, and nonhuman environments washed over him as overlapping waves; his battered form will churn to the surface only every so often.

Books, authors, and readers made up Glass's cultural environment. In 1825, James Hall, a semiprofessional regional author stationed in southern Illinois, latched on to Glass and published a story about his exploits in a Philadelphia literary magazine. A judge and lawyer, Hall resembled other aspiring writers in the towns along the Mississippi River and its tributaries. These men hoped to create a market for western American literature, a niche that would allow them to quit their day jobs as clergymen, missionaries, lawyers, bankers, clerks, and printers. They looked to the nation's hinterlands to find distinctly American source material, and they wrote about the violence done to and committed by frontiersmen.

Bondage and rivers animated Glass's social environment. Recruited on the wharfs of St. Louis, Glass belonged to a working population that moved up and down the Mississippi River and its feeder streams. Some of these workers sold their labor for wages, but only a minority. Most workers weren't free. Black slaves, wives, children, apprentices, soldiers, servants, and prisoners received little or no remuneration for their work, and they faced state-sanctioned violence if they disobeyed their masters. Still, many did rebel. Advertisements in newspapers throughout the watershed offered bounties for returned runaways. Rivers connected masters to international markets. They made owning slaves and contracting servants profitable. But the waters transported disgruntled workers as readily as furs, whiskey, hemp, and salted pork. Rivers underpinned and undermined the labor system that mixed coerced and free labor, and as fur companies tried to move this system up the Missouri River and into the Rocky Mountains, bosses and workers constantly renegotiated the terms of their service.

Animals were the central players in Glass's nonhuman environment. As a hunter, Glass followed, observed, and killed deer, elk, antelope, ducks, bears, raccoons, coyotes, and wolves. Bison robes and beaver pelts drew him west; horses and mules carried him there. The meat of all beasts, including horses and dogs, sustained him. His relationships with Native Americans, his employers, and his coworkers revolved around animal fur and flesh. He wore the skins of animals, ingested their tissue, and acquired their status. To many observers, western fur trappers looked, smelled, and were no better than animals. Hunting stories often transposed hunters and their quarry, and this reversal of identity underwrote the hunters' nationalistic potential.

The physical transformation of laboring bodies promised the emergence of a national body. Environmental Americanism brought a measure of fame to an obscure hunter and his environments. Environmental Americanism taught a nation to take pride and pleasure in catastrophic workplace injuries. Environmental Americanism valorized white male survivalists, editing women and people of color out of the nation's origin stories. Environmental Americanism converted multicultural, multiracial (including multiple versions of blackness and whiteness), multigendered, and multinational fur hunting expeditions into the seedbeds of a unified white male American identity.

Then again, perhaps the missing parts of Hugh Glass can help me salvage an alternative past, one that blends humor and rambunctiousness to upend expectations rather than certify destinies. We'll see. Glass rose from the grave once; he might have another round in him.

HERE LIES HUGH GLASS

INTRODUCTION

Hugh Glass nearly ended his days as meat. In August 1823, a female grizzly bear attacked him. She caught him as he scrambled up a tree, slicing a gash with a fore-claw from scalp to hamstring. She bit his head, punctured his throat, and ripped a hunk from his rear. The bear tore him "nearly to peases," and actually swallowed a few mouthfuls before Glass's associates shot and killed her. Expecting his hunter to die soon, Colonel Andrew Henry bribed two men to wait and bury the body. The expedition traveled on, and after six days the death watchers left, too, abandoning their comrade, who was still sucking breaths through a punctured trachea. Unable to walk, subsisting on insects, snakes, and carrion, an enraged Glass crawled and hiked two hundred miles to Fort Kiowa to kill those who had left him to die.[1]

In his line of work, Glass had witnessed countless gaffes, wrong turns, crack-ups, breakdowns, and mortal blunders. The inability of his employers to transport men, goods, and pelts safely scarred him; poor logistics etched his skin. William Ashley, Andrew Henry's partner, Missouri's lieutenant governor and a general in that state's militia, hired Glass in 1823. This was Ashley's second winter recruiting workers. The previous year, he contracted one hundred hunters and two crews of French-speaking boatmen. The Upper Missouri River seemed ripe for a big haul; fur prices were on the rise, and four St. Louis trading companies hustled to acquire the financing, goods, and labor they needed to cash in on the shifting hat fashions in the eastern United States and Europe. Ashley and Henry's outfit hit the Missouri first, but the river struck back. A tree limb snagged one of their keelboats and sank it.

Glass missed this first catastrophe, but there were plenty left for him. On Ashley's second expedition, he survived a brutal attack by the Arikaras. Seventeen hunters died in the fight; a bullet blew a hole in Glass's leg. Glass participated in the retaliatory campaign under Colonel Henry Leavenworth. Neither shocked nor awed, the Arikaras—their strategic position as middlemen in the fur trade being undermined by the Americans, their access to horses and bison being checked by the Sioux—closed down the river. Ashley moved his goods and hunters to horseback.

Grizzly bears gathered in the thickets along river bottoms in the summer months to gorge on berries, roots, and carrion. The mounted fur hunters rode into their larders. Grizzly bears, then as now, see poorly, and humans approaching downwind easily spooked them. Some bears reacted by charging and clamping down on intruders' heads. Following a skull-cracking bite, they released their prey and tried to seize the torso near the hip. If successful, they dragged their victims to a secluded location for ingestion.

Glass escaped this fate, but even after his epic crawl brought him to safety, he couldn't avoid repeated injury. He acquired another gun, a new set of clothes, and negotiated passage on a pirogue headed up the Missouri to find the men who had abandoned him. The crew included Glass and five French-speaking *engagés*. When they reached the Mandan villages, the Mandans' new neighbors—the Arikaras—attacked them. Four of the *engagés* died. Glass escaped after two Mandan warriors dragged him off the killing ground. That night, he snuck out of their fortified village and began the three-hundred-mile hike upriver to Fort Henry.

It took him thirty-eight days to reach the men who had left him months before. At the fort, Glass confronted Jim Bridger, one of his betrayers. The other, a man named Fitzpatrick, had slipped past him on the Missouri. Glass forgave Bridger, a young and inexperienced hunter, but only after lecturing him on wilderness ethics. Then Andrew Henry handed him a reason to turn around and head back downriver to get Fitzpatrick. Henry needed to contact Ashley, and Glass and four other hunters volunteered to deliver a package of letters to Fort Atkinson.

As the spring thaw filled the streams, the men constructed bullboats. They stretched buffalo hides over willow-sapling frames to create impromptu transportation that resembled giant peanut-butter-cup wrappers. In these they floated downriver until they spotted an Indian village. The inhabitants seemed friendly. They waved the Americans ashore, helloing in Caddo. The hunters thought they were talking to Pawnees, but Arikaras spoke Caddo as well. The smiles and peace-pipe offerings were a ruse. Glass sensed the ambush and bolted for the river. His companions followed, but the Arikaras picked off two of the slower runners. Glass hid behind rocks and "sallied forth" at night. A fifteen-day walk brought him again to Fort Kiowa, where he caught a boat to Fort Atkinson to deliver the mail and get his revenge.[2]

The West tore some bodies up. To a degree, Hugh Glass anticipated and accepted the abuse. The place was supposed to change people— make them wealthy and substantial, or at least give them a scar and a story to tell. Like their forebears, nineteenth-century Americans be- lieved that landscapes and climate determined physical health. Wet- ness, dryness, heat, and cold interacted with the body's liquid humors—yellow bile, black bile, phlegm, and blood—and imbalances in these fluids led to illness. Many American doctors bled, blistered, and purged their patients in the hopes that, by readjusting fluid levels, they could cure them. Environments invaded humans at the same time hu- mans invaded environments, making travel into new territories worri- some. As a laborer, Glass understood the physics of these dual invasions more intensely than tourists, doctors, or medical philosophers. The bear's assault was an extreme instance of nature's penchant for remodeling la- boring bodies. Rivers, forests, and prairies strengthened muscles and burned calories. Labor changed how workers looked and felt. Poling a keelboat, sowing a field, felling a tree, or tracking a bear might build bod- ies, wear them down, or tear them apart.[3]

A division of labor organized fur-hunting expeditions as it did other gang or crew jobs in early-nineteenth-century America. Men and women joined together to accomplish a task, and their focused activity left scant time for the production or preparation of food, clothing, and equipment. The workers depended on others to satisfy their basic needs as they raised barns, transported cargos, served in military campaigns, built roads, and picked cotton. Ashley and Henry provisioned their employees (they shipped some food and designated hunters to "make meat" for the rest of the crew), freeing them to concentrate on killing animals and accumulating pelts. Theoretically, the Americans would thereby outstrip Indian hunters, the traditional suppliers of hides for the American and European market. Indians traded skins for guns, ammunition, garments, tools, ornaments, and alcohol, but they stopped hunting when they fulfilled their material desires and food production demanded their attention. With a supply line stretching from the Rocky Mountains to St. Louis, New Orleans, Boston, New York City, and points beyond, the Americans would reap the profits Indian hunters left swimming in the streams.[4]

Distance and impotence ruined these plans. The fur companies could neither provision nor protect their expeditions. Workers communicated their unease with these failings in tales of starvation, abuse, exposure, and endurance. Through their greed and incompetence, bosses—the stories implied—exposed laborers to outrageous hardship. Hunters disrobed, swam rivers, and ran barefoot marathons to escape human and animal enemies. They lost their bearings in wastelands. They froze. They roasted. They bruised and bled. They ate bugs; bugs ate them. Bears mashed their skulls; wolves disemboweled their corpses. The West was dangerous and unpredictable. While similar to the gang labor arrangements in the East, the fur-trade expeditions seemed exotic for the horrific punishment they visited on workers.

Still, when viewed from the right angle, the hunters' injuries could look adventurous. The wreckage of the fur trade roused imaginations. Newspapers celebrated the expeditions, and regional authors reworked the disasters to suit the nation's mythology. The injuries and accidents of the fur trade became the badges of environmental Americanism.

Hugh Glass's tussle with the bear slipped out of the West quickly. In 1824, Glass told someone at Fort Atkinson about his ordeals, and that unknown gossip (or, perhaps, chain of gossips) passed the saga to a lawyer with literary aspirations. James Hall had been trolling for "scraps of history, reminiscences of noted men, incidents of the chase and of border violence" along the rivers connecting Ohio, Illinois, and Missouri for a number of years. In addition to having a successful law and political career, including stints as an Illinois district attorney, circuit judge, and state legislator, Hall collected and published frontier histories and legends. Attracted to the "romance of real life" and the potential of the West to supply American heroes of Herculean proportions, he found Glass irresistible. He wrote the story down and published it anonymously as "The Missouri Trapper" in the Philadelphia literary journal *Port Folio* in March 1825.[5]

Hall pulled the hunter into a literature of geography, race, gender, and nationalism that prefigured (and rejiggered) Frederick Jackson Turner's frontier thesis. In 1893, Turner codified the alchemy of personal transformation and wilderness travel in his famous essay "The Significance of the Frontier in American History." On the frontier, new arrivals stepped from railroad cars into bark canoes. They stripped off their smoking jackets and spats and put on hunting shirts and moccasins. They slept in log cabins, planted corn with sharp sticks, conversed in whoops, and took scalps "in orthodox Indian fashion." The frontier overwhelmed their civility, turning them into brutes. In time, the men crawled out of the muck, rebuilt their societies, and reclaimed their respectability, but the journey changed them. They acquired the independence and democratic spirit that distinguished rough-hewn Americans from delicate Europeans.[6]

For Hall, Glass's body resembled the one that would later enthrall Turner: he was an environmental American. Place (the backcountry, the frontier, or, in Glass's, case the West), nature (the woods, the wilderness), and gender (manhood) intermingled to breed a new human. "The privations" Glass "manfully endured" ushered him into the "hardy race" of "American woodsmen," whose ranks included heroic individuals like Daniel Boone and a crowd of regional stereotypes. Hall described these men in *Letters from the West*, a compilation of his frontier writings published in 1828. In it, Glass's broken form appears as a prop in a grand drama of national rebirth that revolved around bodies.[7]

Letters from the West opens with another torso. As a boy in Philadelphia, Hall's narrator, a traveler who will grow up to describe the American frontier in letters sent home to an unnamed relative in the East, spots "the brawny limbs and sun-burnt features" of a visitor from Kentucky. Mounted, armed, and dressed in animal skins, the westerner made the city dwellers he passed on the street look like "butterflies of fashion." As chic as corn pone, the woodsman's clothes and physical appearance were simple and easily read. His "face" communicated his spirit, his "look" certified his "disdain for control," and "his movements" recalled his "habitual independence of thought and action." While urbanites cloaked their identity in gaudy and interchangeable costumes, the West had fused the Kentuckian's outer and inner self such that he wore the truth on his skin. He was "one of the progenitors of an unconquerable race."[8]

In Hall's West, nature hammered away older regional identities and national loyalties. Englishmen, Frenchmen, New Englanders, New York "Hollanders," and "high-minded, luxurious" southerners worked together to build farms, communities, and governments. They plowed fields, erected homes, and wrote laws in a spirit of liberty. This labor changed their physiques—they grew bronze and brawny—and unchained their persons. In Europe, some men were born free; in America, the West "bred" freemen. This was a curiously masculine form of reproduction. Male bodies rubbed against a region and produced new male bodies that were stronger, freer, and truer. Still, even as Hall lauded the woodsy spectacle of men begetting men, he kept his distance. The narrator witnessed and chronicled his countrymen's rebirth, but he didn't experience this transformation himself.[9]

Hall's scribe shared westerners' "locomotive propensities": he moved with them, but he didn't move like them. The journeys of woodsmen like Glass or the Kentuckian toughened their muscles and "burnt" their skin as well as tested their moral fiber. Hall's narrator avoided wholesale physical renovation by traversing the West with one organ: he was a roving eyeball. To him, the region was "a scene" and an "enchanting picture" rather than a proving ground, a worksite, or a home. By limiting his involvement to sightseeing, Hall stepped back from the darker implications of the transformations he chronicled. The backwoodsmen's prolonged engagement with wild nature may have liberated and purified them, but it also rendered them suspicious. What kind of man is created by hacking trees, shooting beasts, and fighting Indians? If these men represented a "new race," were they still white? And what about their disfigured bodies? If being an American entailed feeling the jaws of a grizzly bear close around your skull, then who longed to join such a club? Once scarred, how many woodsmen traveled the short distance from seasoned and ornery to broken and demented?[10]

Turner shared Hall's concerns. He admired the manly products of frontier, but he couldn't stand parts of them. He found their bodies particularly repellent. His thesis moved westerners through space and time. The canoe carried men back to the wild, the savage, even the prehistoric. The analogy reached deep: frontier men looked, behaved, and thought differently. It's a wonder then, with all these alterations, that the men's bodies stayed constant. Turner's metaphor implied root transformations while his examples skated on surfaces. He represented fundamental change with costumes, customs, and fashions. The one body that did undergo an alteration remained offstage: the owner of "the scalp" the frontiersmen had removed in the orthodox style. Turner is famous for making Indians disappear from history, but he also erased the bodies of the males he wanted to see turned from dandies into democrats. Where were their tired muscles and their bushy beards, their gritted teeth and their hungry bellies? Turner's frontier has none of the raw physicality that has attracted the aficionados of masculine vigor to real and imagined Wests for more than two centuries. The bodies and stories of fur hunters like Hugh Glass help explain Turner's reluctance to touch the corporeal.

Americans looked to the West and to nature for origin stories and distinguishing traits. They broke free from their European past by imagining their costumes changed, their bodies transformed, and their spirits unchained. Yet these dreams of renewal were stalked by nightmares of loss, retrogression, and dismemberment. Cultural interpreters like James Hall and Frederick Jackson Turner developed strategies to keep their visions of nationalism from degenerating. Hall founded his America on bodies and voyeurism, Turner on costumes and nostalgia. Hall's readers gazed out at frontiersmen from safe observation posts in the East, while Turner's looked back at the frontier as it passed into history. Both audiences cheered the physical wreckage of conquest, but they recoiled from the teeth and the claws, the bullets and the fires, the blizzards and the famines, and especially the body-shaping labor that made back-woodsmen into ideal Americans.

The distressed males on the country's geographic margins surfaced in nineteenth-century American literature as ambivalent icons. They promised to invigorate and to democratize, to teach a nation to love freedom and to tell the truth. But at a price. Bears took their limbs, Indians took their horses, and colleagues took their rifles and left them for dead. The West was a swindle as well as a stage for masculine regeneration. The easterners who became mountain men may have radiated authenticity, but when they spoke and wrote, people scarcely believed them. Their words proved as untrustworthy as the region that carved their flesh.[11]

The truth vexed mountain men. They traveled through vast sections of the West, at times searching purposely for furs, at others merely wandering lost. They viewed South Pass, visited the Great Basin, sailed the Great Salt Lake, trudged to California, and encountered thousands of people and beasts. They knew the region better than anyone back East; they had expertise to show off and to market. Yet their inability or refusal to write about their experiences diminished their potential as heroic reporters of conquest. Writing well and wooing publishers were the keys to cultural dominance in the nineteenth century. Thus, Meriwether Lewis, William Clark, Zebulon Pike, Stephen Long, and John C. Frémont discovered the West for the United States through the power of their literacy (or, in Frémont's case, through the authorial might of Jessie Benton Frémont, his wife and ghostwriter).

Western fur hunters fell into a shadow of history cast by the journals and reports of their literate superiors. But they weren't wholly silent. They described the region and passed along news about its human and animal inhabitants. Up to 25 percent of them produced written journals or memoirs. Their stories, however, lacked clear authorship. Officers and gentlemen attached their good names to their work, underlining their sole right to discovery as well as the veracity of their information. Their status, honor, and character backed their words. The trappers' stories that made it into print suffered from a deficit of authority. Many came with coauthors who transcribed, edited, and sometimes embellished the material. The narratives often seemed fantastic and contained elements of folklore—repetitive plots, humorous and exaggerated situations, and stock characters. Many of the stories were remnants of a collective oral culture, inventions of working people trading stories around a campfire, and they contrasted sharply with the explorers' scientific and militaristic narratives.[12]

Hugh Glass spoke his epic, and the method of communication he chose put him at odds with the standards of veracity of both his society and our own. Although he was literate, next to none of his writing exists. (A single letter, a condolence note sent to the family of a friend killed by the Arikaras, survives.) Much of the information regarding him has been garbled through numerous translations. Take, for instance, the tale about Glass's pre-bear adventures as a Gulf Coast pirate. The source for this story was an Ashley trapper named George C. Yount. Glass supposedly told Yount about his capture by the New Orleans pirate Jean Laffite sometime in the 1820s. Yount then retold the story to the Reverend Orange Clark, a Harvard-educated writer, in San Francisco in 1851. Glass's pirate history not only had to pass through the faulty memories, shifting agendas, and differing assumptions of an aging mountain man and a Boston Brahmin but also through Yount's wife, who disapproved of her husband's fur-trading past. All of these vectors of distortion worked on the story, chewing up Glass's background much like the bear gnawed on his behind. In the end, neither story nor man was pristine or coherent.[13]

Scant, slippery, and unbelievable: as a historian, these are not the words you want associated with your source base. Compared with the giants of early western American history (Jefferson, Lewis and Clark, Frémont, Ashley, and the Chouteau family of St. Louis) or with his famous hunter colleagues (Jedediah Smith, William Sublette, Robert Campbell, and Jim Bridger), Hugh Glass was an undocumented nobody, an empty vessel.[14]

Yet peering into voids can be instructive. The paucity of data that obscured Glass created an opening for poets, novelists, screenwriters, and actors to fill him with whatever imaginative content they liked. Among the multitude of Glass retellings, three of them stand out as not only the best known but the most illustrative of the tale's journey through American culture: John G. Neihardt's 1915 epic poem *The Song of Hugh Glass*, Frederick Manfred's 1954 novel *Lord Grizzly*, and Richard Sarafian's 1971 film *Man in the Wilderness*.

Neihardt's Glass remains a hero and exemplar of American toughness and freedom. Hall would recognize this hunter. So would Turner; both he and Neihardt peddled in nostalgia. In 1915, epic men like Glass, Jedediah Smith, Mike Fink, and Crazy Horse no longer strode the earth, and the poet lamented their passing. Frederick Manfred took hold of Glass for more personal reasons. He identified with the hunter and reveled in the bear tale's symbolism of masculine regeneration. In his novel, the she-bear gives birth to a new man when she tears into Glass. He awakes alone in the wilderness, naked beneath the hide the death watchers stripped from his tormenter and placed over his body. The blood from his wounds has dried, and the bear skin clings to the scabs. Barely alive and nominally human, he crawls toward civilization and, as he heals, regains his footing as a man. In the march to Fort Kiowa, Glass reenacts his growth from infancy to adulthood as well as the rise of his bipedal species. But he does so by himself. He's reborn parentless and matures friendless; he's lost his home and his country. He is the ultimate outsider.[15]

Born Frederick Feikema in 1912, Manfred abandoned his old name and his strict religious upbringing in rural Iowa for the sensual and natural West he created in his writing. He drafted mountain men and Native Americans as allies in his rebellion. They both stood against the onslaught of American civilization, and the novelist stood with them.

Cast out of society, set free from the constraints of religion, capitalism, and hair clippers, Hugh Glass had all the makings of a hippie, and he flowered into full counterculture glory in the film *Man in the Wilderness*.[16] To avoid paying Manfred and other Glass dramatists, the screenwriter, Jack DeWitt, altered the historical record. Glass appears as "Zach Bass," and DeWitt rechristened Andrew Henry (played by John Huston) "Captain Filmore Henry." It's unclear what he gained by calling Henry, a formidable guy by most accounts, Filmore. The change reflected a lurking silliness that plagued the entire movie. The bear mauling and Bass's struggle to survive are wrenching to watch, but the revenge plot veers into odd territory when DeWitt and the director, Sarafian, decided to make Filmore the captain of an actual boat as well as a beaver-trapping expedition. His employees push an enormous wheeled ship across the West while Bass hunts them down. The arklike contraption does add a dash of *Moby-Dick* obsessiveness to the payback storyline, but the overall effect is baffling.[17]

The reviewer for *The New York Times* thought the film a "pretentious bore," and while he considered the person playing Bass "a fine actor," he reported that the film made him look more like "Rasputin pulled through a meat grinder" than a leading man. And the actor? That would be Richard Harris, the British thespian who late in life donned the robes of Albus Dumbledore in two Harry Potter movies and decades before that made Western historians squirm with his portrayal of John Morgan, the adopted white Sioux Indian, also known as A Man Called Horse.[18]

Cultural history can entertain and instruct, but I can't pretend that *Man in the Wilderness* merits a vigorous mulling over just because my grizzly man inspired it. An antiauthoritarian avenger, the Bass character does represent a twist in the Glass legend. However, movies featuring long-haired western outsiders played in many theaters in the early 1970s. The same year the bear bit into Richard Harris on screen, Warren Beatty established a brothel in a frontier boomtown and fell in love with his partner, an opium-smoking madam. The artistic subversion in Robert Altman's *McCabe & Mrs. Miller* trounced *Man in the Wilderness's* psychedelic gore.[19]

By itself, the long, strange afterlife of Hugh Glass in literature and B-movies cannot support a book. But the countercultural pose he struck in the 1970s hints at a line of inquiry from which one might hang. Richard Harris's Bass was scarred and furious, and this depiction rings true given the shards of evidence Glass and his fellow hunters left behind. A bear did tear up Glass's body, and several observers commented on his poor attitude. Nature remade him; anger propelled him. But drove him to what? To murder?

Fort Atkinson: Glass arrived on foot at the military post after his hair-breadth escape from the Arikara ambush that swallowed his bullboat companions. He delivered Henry's letters and asked around for Fitzpatrick, the man responsible for his abandonment and the theft of his gun. As it turns out, the deserter had joined the army. According to the legend, the grisly hunter confronted the private, dressed him down, and then let him go. No fists flew, no guns exploded; he punished Fitzpatrick with words. Hugh Glass walked hundreds of miles, lost all his belongings and suffered numerous assaults, to administer a tongue-lashing? Forgiveness is nice, but Glass had a great deal of emotion and moccasin leather invested in this moment. Why was he satisfied with a verbal exchange? His choice seems so unwestern. Words don't end Westerns; bullets and body counts do. Western heroes and villains can't solve their problems with lectures, negotiations, or apologies because the genre demands their blunt inarticulateness. Western men express themselves physically; they have no other choice. Their bodies define them as men, as western, as free, as truthful, as white, and as American. Why does the Glass legend, a story launched by nature's growling reconstitution of a human body, conclude with talk?

I long for a corpse. I want Glass to pull the trigger, to skewer Fitzpatrick with a buck knife. Talk recedes into history like smoke on the wind, but dead army privates, they generate records: news articles, investigative reports, letters from relatives, court testimony, perhaps even a confession. A killer Glass would be such a help; the book would write itself. I'd structure it like a murder mystery, the text rolling backward from Glass's trial to his tussle with the grizzly bear. A meditation on conquest, the West, and human and animal violence, it would tingle with emotion, plumb the depths of a tortured soul. The documents would crack Glass wide open: he would explain his ferocious desire to live, why he pursued the men who betrayed him with such zeal, and what he pondered as he trekked through the wilderness alone. The trial records would be his memoir, giving him the chance to interpret his traumas and obsessions.

Alas, Glass and most of his fur-hunter colleagues talked amongst themselves, with no stenographer to record their prattle. While I yearn for them to shut up and scribble, to author revealing diaries on nonacidic paper, ziplock them in plastic bags, and store them in humidity-controlled, sunlight-free environments, I respect their commitment to gab.

In most versions, the Glass legend ends with spoken words. Talk was his revenge. Glass and the string of chatterers who developed his legend unleashed their spoken words on the pack of explorers, politicians, journalists, artists, publishers, and readers who would appropriate them in the name of race, truth, nation, democracy, manhood, and conquest. The pack embellished and fabricated. They told stories about Indians and bears, violence and nature. They crafted spectacular and goofy personas, and through their outlandishness, they staked a claim to the West and the nation that reflected their intelligence and their marginality.

Hugh Glass died in 1833, killed at last by the Arikaras. Three years before this final body blow, the mountain man encountered an American doctor on the Santa Fe Trail. The doctor's wagon company employed Glass to hunt meat for them. The doctor kept a journal and later wrote a memoir recalling his western travels. Glass, he remembered, looked old and beaten down. The geriatric hunter liked to drink; his money disappeared in bars and bottles. The old man told the physician about the bear and displayed the scars on his back. They were all he had to show for his years in the West.[20]

An obscure and impoverished man, Glass entered history through a grizzly bear's mouth, and his journey from anonymity to minor celebrity opens new sightlines on the interplay of culture, labor, nationalism, and nature in the American conquest of the West. Before they could possess the region, Americans had to imagine themselves into it. They crammed their myths, ideologies, cartographies, literatures, and sciences into a space already filled with Native, French, British, and Spanish conceptions. Neither empty nor wild nor even west (Mexico considered areas their northern frontier, and many different Native groups claimed large portions as their homes), the space generated imperial rivalries, territorial struggles, and ideological competitions. As recent arrivals in the embattled zone, the Americans suffered. The place starved and maimed them, but not because of its essential savagery. Rather, the West seemed out of control to the Americans because, for most of them, it was out of *their* control. Grizzly bears commanded the river bottoms, Indians owned the horses, Mexico possessed California and New Mexico, and the British dominated the Columbia River country. French-speaking fur traders knew the Missouri River and its Native inhabitants better.

None of these groups agreed with Americans' designation of this place as their West. Why would they? Ignorance, weakness, and incompetence repeatedly steered the newcomers toward disaster. Hugh Glass's accomplishments as a pedestrian and a survivalist reflected his and his countrymen's helplessness.

The Americans, however, brought with them an idea that continually revised their fortunes. Environmental Americanism created a race of men who absorbed punishment, recasting catastrophe as progress, infirmity as toughness, terror as resolve. Their physical transformations naturalized collective power and exceptionalism. For hunters like Glass, however, being tagged a "new race of man" was a mixed blessing. Environmental Americanism got them on the grand stage of nationalism, but audiences' suspicions of men remade by nature turned the heroic drama into a freak show and con game. Some fur hunters calmed these doubts in published memoirs and reminiscences with narrative techniques the historian Ann Fabian has termed "devices of authentication." They leaned on the status and authority of obviously upright citizens. Preachers, doctors, and army officers vouched for their sincerity. A nonwriter, Glass eschewed these literary devices, but he and his colleagues wielded others. They entered the contest for the West and the nation armed with sharp wits and poor attitudes.[21]

PART I

ORIGINS

ONE

THE METAPHYSICS OF HUGH HUNTING

Hugh Glass strode into history upright and proud, a skilled gunman answering a want ad that promised adventure. Or he staggered into view, drunk, smelling like befouled dog. Either entrance works.

In the winter of 1823, Glass answered William Ashley's call for one hundred men to travel to the Rocky Mountains. Ashley placed an ad in the St. Louis newspapers and sent recruiters into the city's "grog shops and other sinks of degredation." Like most turning points in Glass's life, this one frustrates clear description. There's no person here—no brain to weigh options; no spirit to desire money, fame, or a change of scenery; not even a stomach to fill with pork and whiskey. The news of the expedition reached Glass; he joined.[1]

His absence from the written record confirmed his status as a regular guy. Ordinariness hid him in the crowd of working-class males who farmed, mined, boated, hunted, and soldiered along the Mississippi River and its tributaries in the early nineteenth century. These men washed onto the docks in Pittsburgh, Cincinnati, St. Louis, and New Orleans looking for wages and entertainment. Sometimes they drank too much and gouged out each other's eyes, but in general they led lives of unremarkable toil.

Except that's not exactly true. The workers of the Mississippi drainage inspired plenty of words. People noted their behavior and especially their bodies. Some heard and retold their stories. Yet all this print, while bountiful, said little about the interior life of individual persons. Two sorts of writers described the West's laboring population; they both snatched workers' bodies for their own purposes, neither caring overmuch about the psychology of their subjects. The first, the semiprofessionals, seized upon western working males to sell copy back East. These literati had a taste for boatmen and backwoodsmen, and they often turned them into dumb, violent, and gleeful stereotypes. The second group of authors encouraged readers to actually nab working bodies. The composers of runaway advertisements, court documents, arrest warrants, and public warnings detailed the physical appearance, the behavioral quirks, even the speech patterns of some laborers. With divergent audiences and goals, these authors crafted a literature that split workers in two: they jettisoned personality in favor of metaphysics and physiques.

The semiprofessionals transported workers into the realm of abstraction where they became hollowed-out regional types, masculine icons, and racial metaphors addressing such heady concerns as nationalism, truth, faith, charity, and reason. The subscribers for runaway ads undercut the personhood of laborers in the opposite direction. They stuck to the physical, describing scars, skin color, haircuts, and crippling injuries. Neither type of author gives me what I want: the opinions and motivations of one worker, a hunter named Hugh Glass. But their words are all that's left of the men and women of his class, the grog-shop compatriots with whom he shared his life. And the words we are left with underscore the problems, the confusion, and the unrest the laboring classes created for their masters, employers, and would-be chroniclers. The snatchers did not descend on these people because they were easy marks. On the contrary, it was the workers' unruliness—their tendency to run away, assume false identities, fib, and make fun of their superiors— that made them the targets of literature.

The authors William Ashley and James Clyman stood closest to Glass in the months before he embarked for the West. Ashley composed the words that attracted his labor, while Clyman described the social timber of the men who responded to the ad, headlined "For the Rocky Mountains."[2]

The year before, in 1822, Ashley crafted a differently worded advertisement for the St. Louis newspapers. Instead of a geographic location—the Rockies—this one opened with a reference to character:

TO
Enterprising Young Men
    The subscriber wishes to engage ONE HUNDRED MEN, to ascend the river Missouri to its source, there to be employed for one, two or three years.—For particulars enquire of Major Andrew Henry, near the Lead Mines, in the County Washington, (who will ascend with, and command the party) or to the subscriber at St. Louis.
    Wm. H. Ashley[3]

"Enterprising Young Men." The phrase exuded optimism, action, and reward. It captured the democratic zest of territorial expansion in Jacksonian America. In the West, vigorous youths could seize the wealth and stature denied them in the East, where rich and powerful men clogged cities like Philadelphia, New York, Pittsburgh, and St. Louis. Farther west, in unplanted space, little men could still grow big with enough enterprise.

    The 1822 advertisement attracted several historic employees, Jedediah Smith, Mike Fink, and Jim Bridger among them, and, years later, it drew the attention of several historians. The ad surfaced in biographies of mountain men as well as studies of St. Louis and the fur trade. Historians zeroed in on the idea of "enterprise." To many, the phrase unlocked the trappers, revealing their place in early-nineteenth-century America. As young men of enterprise, they typified rather than defied their times. However oddly dressed in animal skins, they sought money, titles, property, political appointments, loving wives, and manly reputations. They were small businessmen, bourgeois capitalists, more like store clerks and stockbrokers than white savages.[4]

    A convincing argument. But then why did Ashley drop such an appropriate and telling phrase when he wrote the 1823 ad that attracted Glass? The "For the Rocky Mountains" notice made no mention of youthful go-getters. Instead of "Enterprising Young Men," Ashley simply wanted "hunters." The shift in terminology may have reflected the lessons he had learned during his inaugural year in the fur trade. The previous spring, he and Henry lost ten thousand dollars' worth of trade goods and supplies when a tree branch sank their keelboat. The craft was named the *Enterprize*, and its loss hurt. Ashley needed to round up another hundred men in 1823 so that he could reverse their fortunes. Given his straits, the word "enterprise" may have depressed rather than buoyed the general. It no longer suited the business of killing animals for their pelts in the Rocky Mountains.

His word choice may have reflected other lessons as well. In 1823, Ashley knew his labor pool better than he had the year before, and experience may have taught him that "hunter" would attract more employees than "Enterprising Young Men." The chance to shoot animals ranked high in Jedediah Smith's reasons for joining Ashley in 1822. He wrote in his journal that he engaged "to go . . . as a hunter," and as the party worked its way up the Missouri, Smith was pleased that Ashley "kept [him] constantly hunting to which I was no means averse." Tracking game freed Smith from the "dull monotony" of moving the boats upriver and "enabled [him] to enjoy the full novelty of the scene."[5]

The idea of hiring St. Louis men to hunt was largely untested, mainly because the United States government barred Americans from hunting in Indian territories. Prior to Ashley, Manuel Lisa tested (and violated) the law; he contracted and transported workers up the Missouri to trap, but most fur trade outfits continued to acquire their hides from Indian hunters. Thomas Hempstead, the managing partner of the rival Missouri Fur Company, didn't think highly of Ashley's plan. He watched Ashley's party leave St. Louis in 1822. The men appeared "untried and of evry description and nation." They looked disorderly, and Hempstead predicted that they would "leave in a mass" once they reached the mountains. Workers, especially fur trade employees, needed discipline. They couldn't exercise their independence and scatter under duress. Insubordination during an Indian attack or a starving winter killed people and dampened profits. "This kind of business of making hunters," Hempstead warned, "will take time and much trouble."[6]

Hempstead spoke as a boss. From the workers' perspective, hiring on as a hunter carried enormous benefits. Foremost, as Smith hinted, the title offered some protection from the crushing labor of the boatmen. The Missouri roughed sailors up. The river pushed millions of tons of Rocky Mountain sediment toward the Gulf of Mexico. The particles altered the water's appearance. In contrast to the Mississippi's gun-barrel blacks, oily greens, and contusion blues, the Missouri wore a palette of browns, and these hues signaled trouble. The suspended dirt made the river "a monotonous and crooked stream." Grit collected in bars and bent the current into horseshoes and S-curves. The river deposited the sediment and then cut into it, producing the stream's distinctive high banks, which tended to break off and crash into the water in mammoth hunks.[7]

To move up the Missouri, boatmen unfurled sails and unpacked oars. They jammed poles into the sandy bottom and pushed against the current. When all else failed, they "cordelled." Fastening a "long cord" to the ships, they jumped out, waded to the banks, and walked the vessels toward the Rocky Mountains. Cordelling stunk, and the hunters avoided it whenever they could. James Clyman watched the towing of Ashley's boats in the spring of 1823. "A slow and tedious method of assending swift waters," he reported. It's unclear whether, like Jedediah Smith, Clyman escaped this chore completely. Ashley had hired crews of "St. Louis gumboes" to man the keelboats, but Clyman's description of cordelling suggests that more than French-speaking bodies were needed to move the craft. "It is done," he wrote, "by the men walking on shore and hauling the boat." The men—the workers—hauled the craft. The hunters belonged to this category. They were hired hands; people called them "Ashley's men." Clyman insisted on the separation of "hunters" and "boatmen," but the labor requirements of hauling goods upriver eroded such distinctions.[8]

The cordellers battled the Missouri's energy, and to move against the current, they required the constant replenishment of their own energy stores. The boats carried food, and Ashley supplemented these calories with wild game. Rather than keep track of seventy armed men scattered throughout the wilderness, Ashley offered the daily task of hunting along the banks to a small number of gunners. Not all the men who had signed on as "hunters" in St. Louis escaped into the brush and cottonwoods each morning. Ashley never intended for all his "hunters" to hunt all the time. Once they arrived at the Yellowstone River, every man could wreak havoc on the local fauna; before then, only a few won the privilege. Jedediah Smith drew the job consistently because of his skill and trustworthiness. An honest man, he wouldn't use the opportunity to abandon the expedition and seek his own fortune as many of Ashley's hires did. Smith's character made him a smart choice for the job.

Yet while integrity freed Smith from the towlines, hunting did not necessarily produce righteousness. In 1823, James Clyman witnessed a hunt in which the "Missourie Boats men" participated. One evening, only weeks out of St. Louis, strong winds forced the expedition off the river. The men camped on the bank and fanned out into the country-side with their guns in search of meat. They brought back "Eggs Fowls Turkeys and what not" and roasted the morsels late into the night, tak-ing care "to burn all the fragments." The next morning the reason for the cremation of the guts, heads, necks, and other refuse showed up. The neighboring farmers "came in hunting for [their] poultry." Ashley let them search the boats, but they found no incriminating carcasses. The expedition traveled on, and as the boats turned one of the river's sweeping curves, a favorable wind kicked up. Ashley ordered the sails opened. A shower of cooked pigs and chickens fell on the decks.[9]

Clyman told this story to reveal the "character" of the boatmen in contrast to the hunters. In his mind, the tale constructed an ethical rampart between the honest and the conniving workers engaged in the fur trade. The boatmen pilfered other people's animals instead of hunt-ing wild, un-owned ones. Unlike the Americans, the "Gumboes'" race and national allegiances were hard to pin down. The boatmen signed less generous labor contracts than the hunters. Were they freemen or slaves? Most damning in Clyman's eyes, they frequently disobeyed their American bosses, and their insubordination endangered and em-barrassed Ashley's more upstanding employees. Yet even as he tried to distinguish himself and other workers from the rascal "Boats men," Cly-man's anecdotes and asides often undermined his typology of laborers. As in his description of cordelling, Clyman's language slipped easily from the specific to the general—from "Boats men" to "the men." Both sailors and hunters took part in the sporting chase that devolved into a raid on chicken coops and hogpens. The sails filled with pork butts and drumsticks incriminated the boatmen, but all the men contributed meat and watched the previous night's suspicious cookery. If rectitude defined the hunters, why didn't they put a stop to this shameful business?

Clyman knew why not. Ashley had sent him into the St. Louis bars to collect these people. He was the one who labeled the establishments where he found them "Grog shops and sinks of degredation." The day the expedition left St. Louis, he recorded the excitement as keelboats shoved off and the men fired a "swivel" for the crowd gathered on the shore. Scanning the faces on the decks, he shook his head: "a description of our crew I cannt give but Fallstafs Battallion was genteel in comparison." Hugh Glass stood on the deck, and his appearance did nothing to change Clyman's opinion of the men.[10]

"Falstaffs Battalion." Was this Clyman's reference, or did it originate with the gaggle of children, grandchildren, collectors, archivists, editors, and typists who rearranged, amended, and clipped his papers? Any one of them could have inserted the Shakespearean tidbit into Clyman's mouth in order to quench the audience's desire for a Western. It was a cutting remark. The portly knight and his criminal gang mocked serious men. Falstaff's pretensions made him laughable and sad. But who was reaching above his station in the Clyman narrative—Clyman for turning his life into literature, or the men he observed on the keelboat for posing as hunters?

Falstaff's and Prince Hal's cavorting on an Elizabethan stage may seem distant in time and tenor from a group of Jacksonian trappers floating on a boat deck in the middle of the Missouri River. Yet the Falstaff quip, whoever made it, raises the question of the proximity of life and literature in the early American West. If a later addition, the reference fits a pattern of artists inserting the bard into cowpoke operas and shoot-'em-ups. In Western novels and films, Shakespearean actors often stood for effeminate civilization. The scene is cliché: a stagecoach disgorges a troupe of players in a boomtown filled with false-fronted buildings, painted ladies, and taciturn males. The actors jabber endlessly, and their hammy dialogue reminds the audience of classic Western opposi-tions: nature versus culture, savagery versus civilization, masculine ver-sus feminine, action versus language, history versus literature.[11]

John Ford inserted a Shakespearean actor into *My Darling Clemen-tine*, his 1946 retelling of the OK Corral legend starring Henry Fonda as Wyatt Earp and Victor Mature as Doc Holliday. The thespian Granville Thorndyke arrives in Tombstone with his troupe and is promptly kid-napped by the dastardly Clantons. Earp and Holliday go in search of the actor and find him in a saloon, half drunk, surrounded by guffawing men. The Clantons force Thorndyke to recite Hamlet's "To be, or not to be" speech while teetering on top of a poker table. He has made it halfway through when Ike Clanton, the patriarch, orders him to shut up: "That's enough, that's enough. You don't know nothing but poems." Holliday intercedes, ends the humiliation, and asks Thorndyke to continue. He does until alcohol and fear cloud his memory. He looks to Holliday for the lines, and the consumptive gambler finishes the speech, punctuating the final "thus conscience does make cowards of us all" with a rattling cough.[12]

Doc Holliday is a genre buster. He's a cultured gunslinger, a card-sharp with a sheepskin. Educated in Boston as a dentist, he has studied the mysteries of the human body; thus he knows the tuberculosis in his lungs is about to eat him alive. This awareness demolishes the Victorian reserve that kept most middle-class physicians out of the ranks of violent Western heroes. Undamaged gentlemen didn't reside in towns like Tombstone. They didn't blow holes in their enemies with sidearms or self-medicate with gallons of whiskey. They certainly didn't cohabit with "Apache" women named Chihuahua. In *My Darling Clementine*, Holliday indulges in all kinds of transgressive high jinks: he's a wheez-ing Hamlet perched over the abyss with a six-gun, a shot glass, and a multicultural lover. A doomed figure, he can mix regions, races, and classes. He's a mongrel, a mutant who will saunter into the OK Corral but not out of it. Like the Clantons, he does not belong in a West with settled boundaries.

Holliday won't challenge Earp for supremacy or threaten the

civilization symbolized by the porcelain schoolmarm, Clementine. His diseased lungs imprison him on the savage and dying side of the frontier even as the bloody spittle he coughs into his handkerchief gives him permission to break the rules of the genre. He can quote Shakespeare and shoot people. An oxymoron, Holliday confirms the rightness of placing Shakespeare and the West in opposing camps.

But what if we read literature and history differently? Perhaps the Falstaff quip belonged to a West more like Holliday's than Earp's, a West where life, labor, and literature merged.

In Clyman's West, wordsmiths stalked laboring men. James Hall belonged to this clique of bookish predators. He fed on the working underclass along the Mississippi River to satiate his writing ambitions. In 1855, Evert A. Duyckinck, the editor of the *Cyclopaedia of American Literature* and alpha male of New York City letters, asked Hall, then a Cincinnati bank president who had quit his law career, his judgeship, and his regional journalism for the comfort of small finance, to submit a short synopsis of his Western publications. Duyckinck expected paragraphs; Hall sent him nine folio pages. In a sense, Hall rendered himself transparent when he replied with such cringeworthy eagerness to the request. The document tracked his movements through his cultural environment, relaying his coordinates along the food chain that clicked into place when predators like Hall targeted hunters like Glass to impress bull publishers like Duyckinck.[13]

Born in Philadelphia on August 19, 1793, James Hall seemed headed for urban anonymity, hidden in the crowd of big-city lawyers, until the War of 1812 singled him out and pulled him west. He joined the army and fought along the Great Lakes in the battles of Chippawa, Lundy's Lane, and the siege of Fort Erie. Following the war, he entered the U.S. Navy and traveled to the Mediterranean as part of Commodore Stephen Decatur's expedition during the Second Barbary War. He returned to the United States, took a post in Newport, Rhode Island, and found trouble. In 1817, the navy court-martialed him for negligence and insubordination. Hall pivoted west to shake this unpleasantness. He left the navy, he wrote to Duyckinck, not with his tail tucked between his legs but rather "with great ardor and hopefulness of spirit, and energy of purpose." He headed to Pittsburgh and then Shawneetown, Illinois, for a fresh start. He would rise up with the flood of Americans breaking over the Appalachians.[14]

The West seduced Hall, rousing his "romantic disposition," his "thirst for adventure," and his "desire to see the rough scenes of the frontier." The way he responded to his bewitchment said much about him, his profession, and social caste. Spurred to the heights of romantic titillation, thirsty for a wild, new existence, Hall opened a legal office and started a newspaper. He slurped the marrow of life by doing paperwork. Words distanced him from the western environment. He observed and reported the alterations the country induced in his frontier brethren, but he stood above them, unchanged.[15]

Appointed a circuit attorney, the public prosecutor for ten Illinois counties, in 1821, Hall began passing judgment on the farmers, boatmen, and mechanics whose labor enmeshed them in the backwoods. The denizens of the rivers and forests, he wrote, came in two varieties: rogues and regulars. The rogues inhabited the counties bordering the Ohio River and used the flow of boats and people to camouflage their nefarious activities. They ran in packs, counterfeited money, stole horses, and shifted jurisdictions. They established border enclaves where "they could change names, or pass from house to house, so skillfully to elude detection—and where if detected, the whole population were ready to rise to the rescue." Upstanding backwoodsmen formed "regulating companies" to thwart the rogues and their wandering identities. Hall adjudicated. He hovered above the fray, listened to both sides, and delivered justice to the classes of humans hip deep in the muck.[16]

That's not to say he didn't find these people entertaining. Hall began writing Westerns and shipping them to Philadelphia for his brother John Elihu Hall's *Port Folio*. He submitted dozens, and in 1828 he collected the bunch in his first book, *Letters from the West*. About the time *Letters* came out, Hall—after seven years roaming as a prosecutor and a circuit court judge—settled in Vandalia, Illinois. He practiced law and edited two publications: the *Illinois Monthly*, a fiction magazine, and the *Illinois Intelligencer*, a weekly newspaper. He also entered politics and secured the post of Illinois state treasurer. His literary résumé bloomed. *The Western Souvenir* followed closely on *Letters from the West* in 1828.

Legends of the West appeared in 1832, *The Soldier's Bride* and *The Harpe's Head* in 1833, and *Tales of the Border* in 1835. "In all of them," Hall told Duyckinck, "the design was to exhibit American life, in the most of them Western life and adventure; and so intent was I upon the faithful portraiture of western life, that I curbed my fancy, and hardly did justice to myself in the management of the materials, which are rich."[17]

Critics initially praised Hall's creations, especially their western roots. At last, declared the reviewer for the *Literary Cabinet and Western Olive Branch*, the region had brought forth a western author writing western stories for western readers. Hall did indeed achieve literary fame, but he also acquired a reputation for fast and sloppy work. His brother objected to his careless plots and warned: "you do not prune enough—you have too many adjectives ushering in the substantives." In his zeal to rise with the country and create a unique western and American art form, he beat the themes of national exceptionalism and natural nationalism to death; to keep his name in front of the public, he often resorted to self-plagiarism. People began to poke fun at "the judge" and his Westerns. In 1828, an anonymous poet for the *Hesperian* magazine imagined a conversation between Hall and a cow:

ON JUDGE H_____'S LAST WORK ABOUT THE WEST
A Dialogue Between the Judge and His Cow

Judge. My cow__why stand idle there?
Not walking, eating, drinking,
Where I, within my easy chair,
Laboriously are thinking?

Cow. Dear Judge, I do the same as you;
I also *ruminate*—
And so, to-day the cud I chew
Which yesterday I ate.

Judge. I grant the likeness; I, my dear,
Make new *books* out of old,

And sell again, the present year,
The work I last year sold.

But tell me, does the cud *improve?*
Is its strength a winner?

Cow. On no, dear sir! But like your works,
It's always getting *thinner.*

To become the spokesman for his region, Hall published with more vigor than good sense. However, both his neighbors and his eastern audience lost confidence in him as the novelty wore off through repetition.[10]

The merit of the criticisms leveled at Hall concern me less than the simple fact that so many were critical. James Hall took himself and his western project very seriously. So have subsequent readers of his texts. Hall championed American aggression. He belonged to the chorus of regionalists who deployed literature to knit new territories into the nation. To him, the assimilation of the West defined the greatness of the United States. Writing about the West thus rose above other literary endeavors. Publishing was a selfless, patriotic act. He concluded his letter to Duyckinck with a tombstone inscription fit for a soldier as much as a wordsmith: "I have written to and for my country. My subjects are all American, and they are treated in an independent American Spirit. If there is an American Literature, I hope to have a place, however humble, in it. If there is no American literature, I am nobody." A cantor of conquest, Hall thought his words fulfilled the righteous destiny of the United States.[19]

But nations are arguments rather than settled facts, and Hall's patriotic overproduction encouraged attacks rather than acquiescence. Instead of bowing in silence before the altar of his mythic frontier, Americans laughed, and their derision hinted at the place of semiprofessional regionalist authors in the literary food chain that coalesced in the Mississippi River Valley at the midpoint of the nineteenth century. The judge was a bottom feeder; fiercer beasts swam above him, and they took chunks out of his reputation. One of Evert A. Duyckinck's best friends was such a predator, and following his movements through the cultural environment that nurtured Hugh Glass and popularized his injuries reveals the diversity of opinions in the Mississippi habitat. The discourse of conquest, of western exceptionalism and natural nationalism, emerged from tooth-and-claw competition, not in a triumphant echo chamber. The authors of Westerns labored to separate East and West, civilization and savagery, literature and history, but other writers unsettled their work, pointing out the hilarity of their constructions.

Herman Melville drew a bead on St. Louis and the rivers that converged near it in the 1850s. He based *The Confidence-Man: His Masquerade* (1857) on material borrowed from western newspapers and regional authors. He targeted western icons and sensibilities. His protagonist was a predator, as were most of his victims. Hunters hunted hunters throughout *The Confidence-Man*. Melville's literary habitat differed markedly from Hall's when he first published "The Missouri Trapper" in 1824. By the 1850s, newspapers, pamphlets, magazines, and telegraph lines knit the United States together. A "communications revolution" transpired between 1824 and 1857 as the infrastructure and consumer demand for information ballooned. The unspooling lines of communication made territorial acquisition possible. People living in Missouri could see themselves as part of a nation because print stretched the boundaries of their imagined communities. Melville's novel reflected the growth of communications; he pillaged books, newspapers, and magazines for satirical fodder. Yet while the production and consumption of words increased, most American writers continued to struggle to earn a living. Melville lampooned the West and Western authors, but he resembled Hall in at least one way: both men were hungry for artistic recognition and respect.[20]

Geographically, *The Confidence-Man* floats away from Hugh Glass. Rather than a keelboat inching up the Missouri, Melville's steamer, the *Fidèle*, churns south toward New Orleans. The story opens waterside in St. Louis on April Fools' Day as a stranger, dressed all in "cream-colors," boards. A shape-shifting devil—perhaps the Devil himself—he will wear eight disguises before midnight and talk a series of victims out of their credulity and their cash. He pleads with them to give him their "confidence," to trust in appearances, charity, capitalism, nature, medicine, money, friendship, the Bible, and the essential goodness of humankind.[21]

Hunting appears early in the novel. In the third paragraph, Melville describes a crowd gathered around a placard near the captain's office. The sign announces a bounty for the capture of "a mysterious imposter." As the crowd gawks, petty crooks ogle their watches and wallets. One criminal tries to sell another a money belt for protection, while still another hawks pamphlets containing the "lives" of famous Mississippi outlaws. These legendary bandits, Melville reports, were a generation of wolves, and their extermination opened space for small-time foxes to multiply.

The list of stalkers did not stop with the pickpockets. In chapter 2, Melville launches into a group ship portrait. He's mimicking Thomas Bangs Thorpe here. The author of many popular western stories and books, Thorpe included a roll call of regional types in his 1841 riverboat/backcountry tale "The Big Bear of Arkansas." He loaded a paddle wheeler with planters and merchants, gamblers and bishops. "Men of all creeds and characters, Wolvereens, Suckers, Hoosiers, Buckeyes, and Corncrackers, beside a 'plentiful sprinkling' of the half-horse and half-alligator species of men, who are peculiar to 'old Mississippi.'" Melville follows Thorpe's lead, populating his steamer with "natives of all sorts, and foreigners; men of business men of pleasure; parlor men and backwoodsmen." But then he tosses his template overboard. Instead of distinct types, the passengers merge into one. They become "farm-hunters and fame-hunters; heiress-hunters, gold hunters, buffalo hunters, bee-hunters, happiness-hunters, truth-hunters, and still keener hunters after all these hunters." The *Fidèle*, a ship of fools, is also a nest of raptors.[22]

And the archest of them all was Melville. He combed through newspapers, literary journals, travel logs, almanacs, and regional compendiums for source material. He snatched the confidence man in 1849. That July, the New York City police arrested William Thompson for stealing a "gold lever watch." It was hardly news that a petty criminal had lifted a watch in New York City, but Thompson's method grabbed headlines as well as artistic imaginations. Dressed as a "gentleman," he approached his victims like an old friend. He joked with them, patted their backs. After establishing a rapport, he sprung his trap. He queried, "Do you have confidence in me to trust me with your watch until to-morrow?" To demonstrate his trust in a fellow gentleman who seemed sincere, the dupe turned over the watch. Thompson walked away with several time-pieces until one victim, Thomas McDonald, spotted him on the street and called the cops. They tossed the grifter into jail and requested that others so defrauded report to the prison and "take a view" of the "Confidence Man."[23]

Thompson reminded Melville of other contemporary hucksters. He disliked the empty-headed optimism peddled by mid-nineteenth-century natural philosophers, philanthropic reformers, free-will preachers, utopian schemers, potion salesmen, western boosters, and sideshow barkers. All of these posers begged for an audience's confidence, and Melville satirized them mercilessly for offering sunbeam-and-butterfly versions of Christianity, market capitalism, democracy, and national expansion. Original sin had stained the human soul and guaranteed as unattainable perfection in this world. By pretending otherwise, all "truth-hunters" became suckers.

The confidence man executed his creator's revenge, stalking a series of characters deluded by excessive hopefulness. Yet while he loosed Satan upon fictionalized versions of Americans whose ideas bugged him, Melville himself felt preyed upon. He considered dedicating the book to the victims of the Spanish Inquisition. Melville could sympathize with tortured heretics; he had suffered book reviewers. Presbyterian ministers applied the screws to his South Sea adventure novels *Typee* (1846) and *Omoo* (1847) for their explicit depiction of Native sexuality as well as their portrayal of Christian missionaries as cultural wrecking balls. By the time he published *Moby-Dick* (1851) and *Pierre* (1852), some of his critics wondered if he had gone insane. He certainly had gone broke. *The Confidence-Man* represented Melville's last shot at writing a money-making and popular yet still artistically ambitious novel. But it didn't sell. He never published another. The confusion over victims and predators extended to Melville's self-perception as an author.[24]

At numerous spots in the novel, Melville adopts the hunting style of the confidence man. In chapter 14, he exits the narrative and addresses his readers directly. He's trying to soothe doubts about the "consistency" of his characters. Why do the personalities on this boat vacillate between extreme confidence and deep "discontent"? Surely this is a writing flaw. Not necessarily, responds the author. Look to "divine nature"—plenty of self-contradictory creations reside there. Take the example of the Australian "duck-billed beaver." If nature can produce such a divided animal, why can't you embrace my similarly inconsistent inventions?

In this passage Melville satirized novelists who broke the fourth wall of their texts to sweet-talk their audience, readers who shackled artists with their rigid expectations, and philosophers who looked to animals for insights into human nature. The duck-billed beaver finished the joke. The beast raised the issue of credibility and nature. Nineteenth-century Americans struggled to believe in platypuses. Even stuffed specimens tested their confidence. Beaked, egg-laying aquatic mammals that stabbed foes with poisonous spurs jutting from their hind legs, platypuses made P. T. Barnum's fake "Feejee" mermaid seem tame and reasonable.

With the weird beaver, Melville joked at the expense of the Transcendentalists. For him, those who found cosmic reassurance in ponds and woodchucks were as bad as those who located abundant hope in the Bible. The nature-loving philosophers would not escape the confidence man. Yet before he loosed his sinister alter ego on barely disguised stand-ins for Emerson and Thoreau, Melville steered him into a discussion with a human bear. The "Missouri Bachelor," Pitch, was natural man, a hunter who had taken on the appearance of his prey. He represented the special American amalgamation: the unique being created when European males exposed themselves to western wilderness. He embodied the vigor and newness of the young nation, and given Melville's satirical impulses, he wasn't quite right.

Pitch butts into the novel while the confidence man, disguised as a herb doctor, swindles a sick old man. "Yarbs, yarbs; natur, natur," Pitch growls; "yarbs and nature will cure your incurable cough, you thinks." Covered in animal skins, he appeared both earthy and extraterrestrial. He wore a raccoon cap, "raw-hide leggings," a "bear's skin" coat, and a scraggly beard. He was "ursine" and therefore a target of sport. Yet the double-barreled shotgun he carried signaled murderous inclinations. Half sub-merged in nature, he knew how the "Dame" worked, and he didn't place much faith in her.[25]

The novel's fiercest doubter, Pitch was one of Melville's platypuses. He looked backwoodsman and talked backwoodsman, but he had grown suspicious of nature while his colleagues remained wild and simple. As a regional type, he didn't make much sense. He dressed like Hawkeye, but he owned a plantation. Insubordinate servants were his nemeses, not bears or panthers. He wanted to distance himself from people, but he sought refuge in technology instead of the wilderness. His life's goal: the replacement of duplicitous workers with machines. All these contradic-tions served Melville's farce, but Pitch does more than amuse. His downfall reveals how literature might participate in territorial conquest, how novels might aid a predatory nation.

Americans told Westerns to distort their past, to justify their aggres-sion and their thefts, to erase or incriminate their foes. It's hard to overstate the genre's selfishness. Westerns fixed the world in the invaders' gaze; only the perspective of the people facing "west" mattered. The tales mulled the price of violence, but they contemplated the horror of pull-ing the trigger rather than the destruction caused by the bullet. Natives, both human and animal, lost their homes, their lives, and their skins, yet the Westerns pondered their tormentors' suffering. The invaders' pain incited revenge. Western heroes lashed out with the righteous anger of the victimized. Still, anxiety tugged at these victors' tales. The West's violence scarred American bodies and psyches. After incorporating the region into the body politic, would this place nourish the republic or make it sick?

Melville boded ill. Near the end of their battle of wits, Pitch barks at the confidence man: "All boys are rascals, and so are all men; my name is Pitch; I stick to what I say." The Devil replies with a sartorial observa-tion. Why are you dressed in the "skins of wild beasts" on such a warm evening? I contend that your "eccentric" rawhide leggings, bear coat, and ring-tailed cap reflect "the equally grim and unsuitable habit of your mind." Pitch's outfit didn't reveal his innermost being. Rather, his attire represents an "eccentric assumption, having no basis in your gen-uine soul, no more than in nature herself." Your clothes disguise you, the

Devil declared, and you can change them, just as you can change your mind.[26]

This reasoning "softened" the backwoodsman like an earthquake reduced some soils to jelly. Knocked off his foundation, Pitch collapsed in a hurry, and the speed of his fall evoked Melville's notes on "inconsistency." A planter cloaked in "skins," Pitch was an unstable concoction. His clothing marked him as a hunter, but he hadn't gunned down varmints for his togs. He earned the signifiers in battles with underlings, the thirty-five snotty servants he had imported from around the globe. His abuse of them made him a skeptic, and his clothing symbolized this mistrust. His duds advertised his naturalness, his rejection of humanity. But Pitch wore lies. He had discovered the truth "all boys are rascals; and so are all men"—from bodies he had purchased and placed between him and nature.

Through Pitch, Melville argued that the West was just another costume Americans could wear. Because Pitch believed in the lie that his appearance reflected his innermost being, he could be fooled by an analogy. He put too much faith in metaphors suggesting a correspondence between two unrelated things—like green corn and servant boys, or bear coats and cynicism, or truth and "thrashing-machines." Pitch wanted his animal-hunter clothes to correspond with his truth-hunter heart. He trusted in this analogy, and when the confidence man sniffed his devotion, he jumped him. This was all very funny, for Pitch was an analogy for the stickiness of correspondence, the idea that two divergent things could be glommed together with the linguistic glue of metaphor. But analogies required belief, and leaps of faith on the *Fidèle* landed you in the Devil's clutches.[27]

The expanse of continent passing starboard to Melville's New Orleans–bound steamboat was a hunting ground for correspondence. Literati scoured the West for analogues, capturing bears and beavers, high plains and lofty mountains, Natives and frontiersmen. They grabbed them and turned them into whatever they wished—God, Satan, nature, nation, whiteness, capitalism, manhood, benevolence, depravity. The entire region could be taken in this manner. Writers imagined the

West reborn as East. Americans would civilize the place, force it to correspond to the landscapes and the ways of living they knew and liked best. Literature manifested the nation's destiny through analogies.

Melville didn't invent this idea. In 1845, *The American Whig Review*, a New York literary journal, published Charles Wilkins Webber's "Metaphysics of Bear Hunting." The satire tells the story of a fallen eastern dude, a cynic and an atheist, who journeys to Texas to commune with "the vicious, the desperate, the social and civil Outlaws . . . gathered there." In the company of a squad of Texas Rangers, he sets out for the San Saba hills to kill bears. There things go wild. The dude loses his mates, a bear nearly kills him and a friend, and some Comanches steal his horse. Near death, starving and delirious, he crawls to a "mott," an oasis of trees in the ocean of scrub, and finds religion. It turns out, God is a squirrel, a large meaty one. The dude shoots and devours God raw while basking in the "sublimity of mercy."[28]

Stripped of its metaphysics, Webber's bear hunt imitated the writings of the army of American regionalist authors stationed along the Mississippi River and its tributaries. Their Western stories migrated east into newspapers, literary journals, almanacs, and travelogues. This was the crowd who discovered (invented) Daniel Boone, Davy Crockett, Mike Fink, Sut Lovingood, Simon Suggs, and Hugh Glass. They popularized the misadventures of laborers and scofflaws—hunters, flatboatmen, Indians, slaves, and robbers. Their fun could be remarkably grim. While under the employ of William Ashley, Mike Fink shot a comrade in the head when playing a game with a tin cup. Fink and the man took turns placing the vessel on their heads for the other to knock off with a bullet, until bruised feelings ruined the entertainment. Angry at his friend for a slight, a stolen lover, a pilfered whiskey bottle (reasons vary according to the storyteller), Fink "missed."

This level of comedy was unsuitable for a highbrow publication like *The American Whig Review*. Webber acknowledged this. He equated the West with vulgarity, and he used the region's uncouth savagery to ridicule eastern intellectuals. The West's nastiness made the region ripe for metaphysical transfiguration. What better place to view God's—or the Transcendentalist Oversoul's—mysterious power than a landscape filled with loathsome beasts and savage men? If Thoreau and Emerson spotted "sermons in stones" and "homilies" in trees, then religious epiphanies acquired while murdering a bear or a squirrel truly deserved to be labeled "miracles."[29]

Analogy converted Western vice into evidence of the divine, and while Webber poked fun at natural philosophers with a bear/God hunt, Melville sharpened the idea of metaphysics into a shiv. Following Pitch's losing battle with the confidence man dressed as the "Philosophical" labor agent, the hunter and the Devil fought one last time. This time Satan wore the garb of the philanthropic "Cosmopolitan," and Pitch beat him. He stuck to his misanthropy despite the Cosmopolitan's best efforts to lure him to trust, love, and confidence. In the aftermath, as the grumbling Pitch wanders out of the novel into his "solitude," a passenger walks up to the Cosmopolitan. "Queer 'coon, your friend," he says. "Had a little scrimmage with him myself." Pages later, we learn the man's name. He's Charlie Noble, another, lesser confidence man, a fox about to tangle with the wolf. Before the two criminals trade lies in the ship's saloon, however, they try to comprehend the backwoodsman. What made him despise humanity? In an attempt to explain Pitch, Noble brings up the story of John Moredock and the metaphysics of Indian hating.[30]

The petty con man's tale requires some stage setting. Noble didn't just tell a story; he told a story about another storyteller, a familiar one—the lawyer, judge, and Hugh Glass biographer James Hall. As a child, Noble heard Hall tell the history of American Indian hating. He remembered that Hall spoke with diligent care, as if he wanted to etch his words on his listeners' brains like an ink quill etched letters on a page. Hall explained how backwoodsmen came to loathe Native Americans with such purity and how one frontier soldier, Colonel Moredock, almost reached the pinnacle of "Indian hatred." Charlie Noble recalled every detail, and as he spoke, the confidence man could almost hear "the Judge."

As can we. Melville nearly plagiarized an essay on Indian hating that Hall published in several venues in the 1830s and '40s. Melville added some flourishes to signal his comic intentions. (His backwoodsmen, for example, surf the incoming tide of civilization, while Hall's merely drown in it.) But Hall's "history" and Melville's chapter shared a hero, a structure, and a quandary: Why did the West and nature, those wellsprings of truth, God, democracy, manliness, and American uniqueness, also spew forth generations of rabid, heavily armed bigots?[31]

According to Hall, the pursuit of animal flesh defined the western community. A "passion" for hunting lured some men (and their families) out of the East and brought them into conflict with Native Americans. This settler population grew "peculiar."[32] They moved constantly to find game and keep ahead of agricultural settlements, and they fought continually to preserve their access to unowned "hunting grounds," areas Indians considered their "ancient heritage."[33] Life on the frontier warped backwoodsmen, but Hall extended the torque of nature beyond firsthand contact with wild places, animals, and men. The American hunters loathed Indians even after the Indians had left. Generations learned to despise Natives from stories. "From the cradle," children heard "horrid tales of savage violence." They sat rapt on grandparents' knees and imagined "horses stolen, and cattle driven off, and cabins burned." They ingested so many stories that hate became "part of their nature." Anecdotes did to them what the Indians and the wilderness had done to their fathers and mothers.[34]

Hall granted stories tremendous power. The West toasted, broke, and perforated some famous white male bodies, but the Western—the narrative reconstruction of their violent deconstruction—could transform anybody. The portability of Westerns, their tendency to migrate back east in gossip, newspapers, and literary journals, presented Hall with a problem. How could he tell stories about Indian hating without creating a nation of Indian haters? If Westerns altered listeners' very "nature," how could easterners resist the West's ugliness?

Hall distanced his readers from the place. He pushed backwoodsmen to the nation's margins and quarantined them out of earshot of philanthropic ideas. Alone in the forest, the hunters talked only to themselves. They lacked news and books. They never spoke to learned outsiders. Thus, they heard only "one side" of Native Americans, the "war-whoop" side. Civilized readers, Hall's audience, had encountered other imaginary Indians. They met noble savages in plays, novels, philosophical tracts, and most spectacularly in the literature and the speeches of charitable reformers. These counter-Natives inoculated Hall's customers. Their exposure to noble savagery made them suspicious of one-sided haters. The backwoodsmen piqued the curiosity of civilized persons. Odd specimens, they raised questions. How did the West and nature create such people? Hall offered Moredock.

Born on the Illinois frontier, Hall's John Moredock learned race hatred as a child. Indians tomahawked his father, his stepfathers, and, in a final ambush, his mother and siblings. The last of his family died on the banks of the Mississippi River on their way to the French settlements at Vincennes. They would have been among the first "whites" in the area, according to Hall. "The sole survivor of his race," Moredock took up Indian hunting. For a year he stalked the group that murdered his family and destroyed all thirty members of "the lawless predatory band." Following these deaths, he "resolved never to spare an Indian," and he roamed the Illinois woods, watching, pursuing, and slaughtering human beings.[35]

A bloodthirsty fiend, Moredock in Melville's hands revealed his spectral creepiness. Traveling through the wilderness with his father, a young Charlie Noble happened upon a cabin. A man greeted them and pointed out a gun and powder horn on the porch. They belonged to the famous Colonel Moredock, the man said, and their owner was asleep in the cabin's corn loft. The man requested that Noble and his father keep their voices down. Moredock had been out tracking Indians the previous night. Desperate to see the famous backwoodsman, Noble snuck into the cabin and climbed the ladder to the loft. Poking his head through the trapdoor, he spied Moredock's bedding, a clump of wolf hides, but the scene looked wrong, more sylvan than human: "I saw what I took to be the wolf-skins, and on them a bundle of something, like a drift of leaves; and at one end, what seemed a moss-ball; and over it, deer antlers branched; and close by, a small squirrel sprang out from a maple-bowl of nuts, brushed the moss-ball with his tail, through a hole, and vanished squeaking." Moredock, if he existed, had melted into forest.[36]

According to Hall, the knack for disappearing into nature belonged to the "Indian-hater *par excellence*." Like all frontiersmen, the "Indian-hater *par excellence*" swallowed bloody stories with his mother's milk, but then an event—an attack upon himself or his kin—turned ordinary ire into a monkish devotion to wrath. He renounced his family and friends, plunged into the wilderness, and never came back. The hunter vanished from culture. Hall couldn't speak about him; the "Indian-hater *par excellence*" had no "biography." The predator worked beyond the reach of "news." The specter of the perfect bigot perturbed Melville's "Judge Hall." The judge, reported Noble, with typical Melvillean comic understatement, was "not unaffected" by the prospect of anger and wilderness turning American pioneers into killer racist ghosts.[37]

It was impossible to tell a story about a man who had disappeared into nature, but Hall could talk about Moredock, a "diluted Indian-hater." Moredock escaped into the woods, yet he returned to civilization on occasion. Indeed, by Hall's account, he stayed long enough to run for office. Voted a member of the Illinois Territorial Council, he declined to stand for governor, though many friends urged him to do so. The historical James Hall explained his demurral as a matter of fact. Moredock simply "refused to permit his name to be used." Melville elaborates: Moredock rejected higher office because he could never sign an Indian treaty, as governors were wont to do, and he knew his hunting habit would take him from the capital during legislative recesses. It wouldn't be right for the state's leading citizen to be seen "stealing out now and then . . . for a few days' shooting at human beings." Indian hating sometimes required men to temper their ambitions, to give up "the pomps and glories of the world." Like religion, Indian hating demanded piety.[38]

In the metaphysical looking glass, Moredock's devotion to rage and murder looked like perfect Christianity. Racism endowed him with a deep suspicion of humanity. He looked at Indians and witnessed sin and devilry. He hunted Satan without mercy and bigotry washed him clean. In his "diluted" form, he could return home, to whiteness, and be a nice person, a loving friend and father, a trustworthy democratic representative. Moredock's disappearance back into civil society signaled his disappearance from the novel. Melville drops Indian hating and the backwoodsmen, and proceeds to hunt down other American icons. Readers and critics have puzzled over Melville's metaphysics-of-Indian-hating interlude in the middle of *The Confidence-Man*. Melville celebrated noble savagery in his South Sea novels, and he criticized American writers like Francis Parkman for disparaging the "Indian character." He revered Indians and defended them as children of the same God. Yet, through analogy, he turned Moredock into a hero. The killer was the only true believer in *The Confidence-Man*. He's kidding, of course, but it's hard to know when to laugh.

I've come a long way from Hugh Glass. As far as I know, he resembled none of the hunters in Melville's satire. From the perspective of social history, Glass confirmed the distance between history and literature. After telling his bear story, he stepped back into the anonymity of the fur trade's labor pool. Imaginary backwoodsmen tramped elsewhere with the aid of regional authors trying to sell stories to an eastern audience. The captive of James Hall, Glass the American Odysseus surfaced in Philadelphia. While the laboring Glass struggled to earn a living as a trapper, his analogue crawled through literary journals and newspapers. Hall's Glass foreshadowed another of his creations—Moredock. A violent event transformed both into obsessed hunters of people. They both exemplified western rage, how wild nature drove some Americans mad.

Traversing the distance between fact and fiction, however, isn't as easy as the embrace of one and the rejection of the other. Regional authors labored to create the illusion of a *far* West. They distanced the place and its residents from the East, the nation, and civilization. They valorized men remade by nature, but they also isolated them.

Melville harpooned the far West. Human depravity spanned every divide, collapsed the largest space. Sin united East and West, black and white, the savage and the civilized. Americans had no right to treat Colonel Moredock as a metaphysical curiosity from an exotic frontier when they elected an Indian hater president. Andrew Jackson didn't disappear into leaves and moss balls. Neither did Hugh Glass. The literati cast Glass away, but he always staggered back. Crossing distances was his specialty. Real people inhabited the physiques that writers nabbed for metaphysical purposes, and they battled employers, owners, commanders, party leaders, and literati for the right to use their bodies as they pleased. James Clyman wrote only a few lines about Hugh Glass. Glass, he reported, "could not be re[strained] and kept under Subordination." He "went off the line of march one afternoon and met with a large grissly bear."[39] The encounter that rearranged Glass's body and dragged him into literature began with an act of defiance: a hunter, sick of military discipline, veered off course to find sport and adventure in the wilderness. Or a disgruntled worker stamped into the bushes grumbling about lines and bosses and places where bosses could shove their lines.

Either works.

TWO

BORN TO RUN

No one really knows where Hugh Glass came from, but when people imagine his life before he met the bear, they see him on the run. The trapper, Napa Valley pioneer, and performance artist George C. Yount delved deepest into Glass's past, and he spied a pirate. Before he killed animals for funds, Yount reported, Glass labored at sea. Around 1820, the "notorious" pirate Jean Laffite captured his ship off the coast of Louisiana and gave him and his crewmates a choice: join or die. "Oui," answered Glass; he took the job and swore an oath of allegiance to Lafitte. Alas, he enjoyed neither raping nor pillaging, and his kittenish behavior alarmed the other criminals. Lafitte ordered him executed, but minutes before his henchmen could decorate their cutlasses with Glass's guts, he and another man escaped into the swamps and marshes near what would become Galveston, Texas.[1]

They wandered north for weeks until a band of Pawnees captured them. The Indians tied Glass to a tree, roasted his friend (not in the funny way), and were about to insert slivers of pitch pine into his feet and commence his immolation when he offered them a bag of vermilion he had hidden in his shirt. The chief accepted the gift and released him. Glass traveled with the Pawnees as an adoptee for nearly a year. (Native groups sometimes—rarely in the case of adult men—adopted captives into their communities to replace killed relatives.) He learned to hunt bison, grizzlies, and beavers, and in 1822, when the Pawnees visited St. Louis, he took his leave of them. He bummed around town for "some eight to ten months," then hired on with Ashley.[2]

Another origin story repeats the themes of bondage and flight;

careers tossed off and personas taken up. In 1795, a twenty-year-old apprentice named Hugh Cook Glass ran away from his master, the Pittsburgh gunsmith Henry Wolf. He stole two items: his body and a continental rifle. The body measured five foot six or seven; smallpox scars marked the skin. Glass had "short black hair" and a "darkish complexion." Wolf surmised that his servant was headed downriver and would try to pass himself off as a journeyman gunsmith. He offered sixpence reward for his return.[3]

The truth of these stories matters less than their coincidences. Whether as a sailor or an apprentice, to reach the West and the bear, Hugh Glass first had to free himself. To gain his liberty, he ran, fibbed, bartered, bushwhacked, and pilfered. He retailored his appearance and his occupation. He adopted the strategies of runaway apprentices, indentured servants, slaves, soldiers, and criminals. Advertisements to catch these escapists filled the St. Louis newspapers read by the likes of Glass and his hunting associates as they lounged around the docks waiting for their keelboats to be outfitted. The ads supply a primer in the history of work, appearance, and bondage in the Mississippi Valley in the 1820s. In an era before mug shots and fingerprints, authorities monitored their subordinates' entire beings. Masters remembered the precise hue of slaves' skin, and the location and curvature of their scars. Craftsmen observed their apprentices' hairstyles. Militia captains listened for accents and verbal tics among the rank and file. Bosses noted missing teeth, limps, and split lips. Sheriffs discerned manners and recalled deportments. Along with their clothing, laborers' bodies defined and often betrayed them.[4]

Work along the Mississippi River and its tributaries in the early nineteenth century left marks, and authorities kept track of them. Their oversight depicted laborers in a manner far different than the one conjured by the literati. Runaway ads, public warnings, and court records came no closer to the actual personalities of working people than the stylized portraits of backwoodsmen. Yet, whereas the regional authors valorized (and Melville satirized) bodies remade by nature, the overseers' literature documented how work, landscapes, and physical punishment inscribed and imprisoned some people. It was hard to tell whether overseers or landscapes altered laborers more. Whatever the source, authorities used the evidence to keep servants in the yoke. Runaways could flee the lash, the plow, the oar, the forge, the bayonet, the shovel, or the cordell, but they couldn't escape their own flesh.

On March 16, 1823, John Hanna, a tailor's apprentice in St. Louis, ran away from his master, Richard Milligan. Two days later, Milligan posted an ad in St. Louis's *Missouri Republican*. Milligan promised a twenty-dollar reward for his servant's return. To aid the capture, he offered a physical description of two young men: Hanna and Nathan B. Starr. As Milligan worked through the details of age, build, and dress, a story emerged. Starr, aged "18 or 19," had resided in Milligan's household with the tailor acting as his "guardian." An "old offender," Starr "enticed" Hanna to run away with him. Starr's body announced his bad character: he had "a manly appearance, rascally inclined, visage slim, complexion light." By contrast, Hanna was "a stout robust lad," a valuable worker. Milligan would give only "one cent" for Starr's apprehension, and he refused to pay any charges the scoundrel might accrue while on the lam. Both Hanna and Starr wore blue coats and gray-striped pantaloons. Last seen in a canoe on the Mississippi River, they were most likely headed for Ste. Genevieve, Natchez, or New Orleans. As was custom, the editor of the *Republican* forwarded the ad for reprint in the newspapers in the towns along their flight path.[5]

    The aims of Milligan's runaway notice differed from most. He wanted to find one underling and lose another. The ad welcomed Hanna home while breaking ties with Starr. In return for his labor and obedience Milligan had promised to teach Hanna a trade; he offered the "lad" a pathway from servitude to independence. As Starr's "guardian," Milligan's obligations are harder to pin down. Starr lived in the tailor's household, but he didn't seem to share in Hanna's professional training. He was worth less than Hanna, and his "visage" indicated his market value. Skinny, fair, and rascally, Starr wore his insubordination like a second skin. But what did a tendency toward rascality look like in 1823?

    That was Milligan's problem: a rascal appeared to be a young man in a blue coat and gray-striped pantaloons steering a canoe into the current of the Mississippi River. Rascality looked like Starr and Hanna and

countless other workers who cut ties with their masters and took to the water in search of fun, money, independence, and a better labor contract. At a glance, employers couldn't tell rotten workers from faithful ones. They dressed, spoke, and behaved alike. They flowed into one another, moving up and down the rivers that knitted Pittsburgh, Cincinnati, New Orleans, Lexington, St. Louis, and Natchez into a global market of goods and people.

Markets delighted and tormented masters like Milligan. Such men welcomed the transmutations of capitalism—the spectacle of forests cut into farms, beavers trimmed into hats, pigs smoked into hams, corn distilled into bourbon—but they drew the line when their human property or contracted servants sought refuge and rebirth in the exchange economy. Capitalism might reduce some people to commodities, but slaves and apprentices couldn't be allowed to profit from their status as sentient, roaming merchandise. They couldn't be allowed to peddle themselves. In order to keep their human property and servants from disappearing into the fog of the Mississippi River and free-market capitalism, masters had to give their laborers an identity without raising pesky questions about the justice of their confinement. The newspapers and their runaway ads helped. They identified workers through their bodies, stripping them of their anonymity while preserving their alienation.

In 1820, Antoine Soulard wrote an advertisement intended to nab a runaway called Alexis. Thirty years old, six feet tall, in possession of an "erect nature," Alexis escaped Soulard's St. Louis plantation with two coats: a "white blanket capote" and "a blue jacket." He usually wore a hat but went without a handkerchief. His French and English were "very broken"; so, too, was "one of his front teeth of his upper jaw." When Alexis spoke, Soulard reported, he held "down his head." These tips would aid an interrogator who spotted a black man with a hat and no handkerchief, and they robbed Alexis of his primary bargaining tool—his voice. To pass as a freeman, he might change his clothes and work on his pronunciation. He might even learn to look people in the eye when he addressed them. But, given the state of dentistry along the Mississippi wharfs, he'd still have a kink in his smile. More than any other bit of information, the jagged fact of that missing tooth enslaved him.[6]

The ads gathered physical quirks and piles of clothing. In 1825, Joel Starky wrote to recover Tom, his "negro man." Twenty-three, five foot eight, "well made," fluent in conversation, Tom could "read and write a little," and he limped. One of his "heals was less than the other, from a burn or frost bite." Tom traveled with two of his sisters, Patsy and Jude. Patsy was "low and heavy built"; Jude skinny. Her slender frame carried two distinguishing features: the toes on both of her feet were "considerably cramped," and a carbuncle the size of a "partridge egg" bloomed from one of her wrists. In another St. Louis ad from 1824, a Kentucky master demonstrated his remarkable familiarity with his slave's wardrobe. Five foot six with a "yellow complexion" and a checked handkerchief on her head, Rachel absconded with "two black crape dresses, two calicoe, one white cambric, one hemp linen, one linsey, one white made flannel under dress, two calicoe patched quilts, one red cotton shawl, one three cornered silk velvet shawl, and other articles not remembered." A white man in "a blue coat and white pantaloons" had "persuaded" Rachel to leave Kentucky. A mole dotted one of her seducer's "dark" cheeks.[7]

The extent of Rachel's laundry list suggests that her clothes represented more than costumes to be changed to avoid detection. Her master wanted to keep these valuable garments off the market. If he had given them to Rachel, he wouldn't want his generosity to finance her escape. But, if these were presents, why did he give her so many? Why did a slave woman possess five dresses, an underdress, two quilts, two shawls, and more? Perhaps she was his seamstress; more likely she was his concubine. The Kentucky master acted more like a cuckold seeking revenge than a capitalist seeking a wayward laborer. He offered one hundred dollars for the capture of the white man; fifty for the return of Rachel. The wardrobe list may have been a swipe at the beauty-marked lothario. It reasserted the Kentucky master's claim to Rachel's body and reminded her and her companion that they carried his tokens in their luggage.

The runaway ads invite speculation. They hint that amid the most unequal and odious power relations human beings were still capable of mixed emotions and surprising behaviors. Take, for instance, the most prominent physical feature mentioned in the ads: skin color. Runaways came in shades more subtle than black and white. "Negros" could be "black," "very black," "yellow," or "sallow." Yellow or sallow signaled the lightness of the African Americans' skin. The "dark complexions" of so many of the runaway apprentices and deserting soldiers indicated that whiteness moved on a sliding scale as well. In 1828, the master cabinet-maker William Grimsley purchased a notice in the *Missouri Republican* offering a twenty-dollar reward for the return of his apprentice Edward Lesseiur. Nineteen, standing five foot six, Lesseiur was "of dark complexion." Yet, while dusky, his skin was pale enough for a bevy of freckles. Edward Lesseiur and Rachel from Kentucky moved in a world where black slaves took white lovers and white, "much freckled" carpenters' apprentices looked "dark" when they ran away.[8]

The case of the "negro man named James" highlights the murkiness of race, freedom, and sentiment along the Mississippi. In 1822, authorities in Scott County, Kentucky, published a notice warning "the public" from Lexington to New Orleans not to buy James. He wasn't a slave. Upon his death, James's former master, Phillip Patton, had instructed his heirs to free "the boy" when he reached the age of twenty-one. On January 4, 1822, James, a blacksmith working in the household of William Fant, "obtained a certificate of freedom from the clerk of the Scott county court." He gave the certificate to Fant for safekeeping. On February 18, a gang of kidnappers broke into Fant's kitchen and stole James. Authorities believed that the robbers were headed for New Orleans, and they asked people along the river to notify the Scott County court if they saw James so that they could send him the paperwork to "free himself from the clutches of the unmerciful band of kidnappers."[9]

Part of me yearns to interpret the James episode kindly: Fant cared about the young blacksmith, and the authorities were outraged at the thought of kidnappers stealing and marketing a free person. In this view, friendship and justice overcame racism; white people in an epoch and a region marinated in bigotry rallied to protect the liberty of a black former slave. My cynical self reads the ad differently. There's little doubt that Fant and the officials felt bad for James and wanted him freed, but the fate of the young blacksmith was not their primary concern. The first line of the ad signaled their intentions—"beware of purchasing a negro man named James." They sought to protect the downriver consumers of human property rather than the human being consumed. White citizens needed to keep nefarious gangs from kidnapping free blacks and selling them to safeguard the integrity of the slave market. How could masters trust in their investments when, at any moment, a clerk upriver might produce a slip of paper and nullify the transaction? The authorities in Scott County publicized James's troubles to sustain white people's confidence in their system of bondage.

The runaway ads documented the cruelty of this system. In 1826, Martin Ruggles sought to restrain Sam, his escaped slave. Fond of whiskey and an experienced miner, Sam had a "little yellow" complexion, a "thick" build, and "short, thick, hard hands." "Several marks of the whip" notched his back. Daniel Bennet slipped away from his owner in 1820. A "likely, fierce looking fellow," with polite manners and talented with the fiddle, Bennet bore "scars on his forehead, over his left eye, and the scar of a burn below his left elbow—and a few marks of the whip on his back." Other runners carried scars from cut lips and cigar burns. Bob, an "old offender," from Florissant Township, St. Louis County, repeatedly ran away from his master Alexander Stuart. Bob's physique drew few stares. He looked "ordinary"—"very dark, full face, broad shoulders, hair cut very close." Crippled fingers gave Bob away; several were noticeably "disjointed." Of course, accidents left marks and bent digits as well as malevolence, but in an atmosphere filled with swinging fists and cracking whips, it's naïve to think that fate alone twisted Bob's fingers. His disfigurement served his master too well, offering him details to feed the newspapers whenever Bob "offended."[10]

In the ads, the brutality of slavery mingled with evidence of unremitting toil. Landscapes and workplaces—rivers, forests, plantations, mines, shops, and smithies—shaped laboring bodies. So worn down were some runaways that fast movement no longer seemed possible. Manuel sought to escape his St. Louis owner, A. F. Delauriere, in 1828, despite being forty-eight years old, "lame," and "remarkably knocked kneed." Randolph, a skilled blacksmith and cooper ("very handy with tools of all kinds"), left his master William Baker in St. Louis County and crossed the river into Illinois. Bacon supplied a lengthy physical description. Randolph had "a sallow complexion"; he was "built stout and bony," with "a sharp chin covered with beard." A small gap separated

Randolph's upper teeth, and he was "intelligent when spoken to." But if a captor truly wanted to identify him, he would ask Randolph to walk away: "when walking away his feet appear to wind and his toes approach each other very acutely." His awkward gait limited Randolph's effectiveness as a fugitive.[11]

Advertisers seized on odd details and indelible features to keep their underlings from vanishing into the Mississippi River economy. Scars, funny walks, gapped teeth, white hair, shy demeanors, gray-striped pantaloons, and cotton underdresses became ammunition for those seeking to monopolize the benefits of mobility. Masters, owners, bosses, and military superiors wanted certain goods, people, capital, and information to move like foam on a swift current. Their problem was that blacks and whites, the free and the enslaved floated equally well. They bet that data could fly faster than servants, and they trusted that specificity would conquer the fluidity that both enriched and enraged them.

Authorities along the Mississippi endeavored to bind workers in place—to both a geographic location and a station in a social hierarchy. Their fixatives included the courts, lynch mobs, contracts, jails, corporal punishment, slave patrols, and newspapers. They retained and publicized the details of their laborers' bodies and appearance in order to brand them with an identity difficult to alter or hide. To acquire these bits of leverage, they watched. To labor along the Mississippi was to be appraised, to be monitored and memorized. Oversight gave workers an audience, and many learned to play to it.

Timothy Flint surveyed the West and its laborers. The prototypical semiprofessional regional author, Flint traversed the river system from Pittsburgh to New Orleans, looking for employment as a missionary, a clergyman, and a teacher. He never found a job that would support his wife and family, but he did accumulate enough "adventures" to fill a book. Published in 1826, his *Recollections of the Last Ten Years, Passed in Occasional Residences and Journeyings in the Valley of the Mississippi* contained numerous descriptions of workers. Teamsters, boatmen, sailors, farmers, hunters, and slaves caught his gaze and captured his imagination. They told this wide-eyed son of a Congregationalist minister wild and sexy stories, and he believed them. Flint wrote his *Recollections* to launch a literary career, but he accidentally preserved some workers' responses to their surveillance.

Like the literati and those who advertised runaways, Flint didn't investigate the depths of laborers' psyches. Like them, he cared mainly about their bodies. Flint studied workers' physiques to understand how western nature created a new race of men, an obsession he shared with other regional authors. Flint's own body sparked his interest. He left his home in Salem, Massachusetts, in 1815 to heal. New England's cold winters had made his body "miserable," and he hoped that "in a milder climate and a new order of things, I might regain my health and cheerfulness." Like most early-nineteenth-century Americans, Flint believed in humors. He assumed that the Mississippi River countryside would flow into him. He braced for the heat swells, cold snaps, noxious gases, thunderstorms, and morning breezes. He prayed that the climate would improve his humors, but a change in scenery in 1815 could as easily ruin a body as invigorate one.[12]

Flint, for the most part, got ruined. But it wasn't heat, humidity, dew, fog, or an ill wind that nearly did him in; a bug bit him. Malaria-infected mosquitoes thrived in the stagnant pools and hot weather of the Lower Mississippi Valley. The disease found Flint in St. Charles, Missouri, just as he returned from a missionary trip to Illinois. He had been sickly in New England, but this was a fiercer beast. The first day, he couldn't get out of bed: "I was prostrated in infantile weakness." By the third, he suffered "paroxysms of derangement." On the fourth day he could no longer recognize his friends, and he began speaking in tongues. While he had no idea that insects and microscopic parasites caused the disease, Flint had been briefed on the symptoms. People sick with the "ague" or "bilious fever" suffered from recurrent cycles of high fevers, sweats, chills, and shakes. Most fell ill in summer or autumn, and endured bouts of swelling, pain, and "enfeeblement" for months. After a time, if the victim survived (and most did), the symptoms abated. Locals along the river called the loosened grip of malaria "seasoning." A seasoned person belonged in the West; their fluids better matched their environment.[13]

The protozoan *Plasmodium* cared nothing for its host or its host's medical theories. Mobile, blood-pumping animals tended to attract more mosquitoes than rotting corpses, and *Plasmodium* needed a ride to its next body. It spent the flight tucked in the guts of insects completing a vital stage in its life cycle. The parasite had evolved to maim but not kill the majority of its vertebrate hosts: Timothy Flint was worth more enfeebled than dead. Although intimate on a cellular level, Flint and *Plasmodium* waged a biological skirmish in complete ignorance of each other. This created an opening for a New England author eager to observe, describe, and profit from the spectacle of Americans remade by western nature. Flint interpreted malaria as a symptom of conquest and settlement. His illness was a metaphor for territorial possession. Overcome by his environment, he lost his mind and his memory. A spirit seized his tongue; he spoke languages he didn't understand. The rains, miasmas, emulsions, dews, and tides of the Mississippi Valley surrounded him like embryonic fluid. The West reduced the forty-five-year-old man to a babbling infant. Flint and *Plasmodium* emerged from the sweats and chills having accomplished a similar goal: both had pioneered new homes.[14]

Seasoning, wrote Flint, "is the summit of the gradual process of acclimation." Illness turned immigrants into natives, which raised a problem for Flint. He didn't approve of most western natives. Indians frightened him. He believed them numb to their environment and human morality. They "did not so easily or readily sympathize with external nature," and they stood by as white traders had sex with their wives and daughters. "The body of the savage," he wrote, "seems to have little more sensibility than the hoof of horses." Indians felt so at ease in the wilderness that they felt nothing at all. Flint treated the Native Americans' white doubles—the backwoodsmen—more generously. He defended them against eastern critics. They looked "rough," but they weren't, as some reported, "the scum of the Atlantic states." No, he asserted, "I have found the backwoodsmen to be . . . hardy, adventurous, hospitable, rough, but sincere and upright race of people." At the very least, the backwoodsmen were better than the French who shaved their chins and dressed more fashionably but couldn't stay away from Indian women.[15]

In Flint's view, labor in the western forests had created a new race of Americans—whites at home in the wilderness. Backwoodsmen deserved town-dwelling gentlemen's praise rather than their "contempt and horror." Cultural loyalty prevented the backwoodsmen from devolving into savagery. They may have been a race apart from easterners, but they were not race mixers. Flint dramatized the birth of white natives with a fireside chat. Travelers on the frontier, he reported, often gathered around the campfire at night and recounted the "exploits of the old race of men, the heroes of the past days, who wore hunting shirts, and settled the country." The founders worked ceaselessly in the "boundless forest full of panthers and bears, and more dreadful Indians." They chopped from sunrise to dusk, and the blows of their axes rang throughout the forest. The sound drew Indians. Instead of killing the intruders, however, the Natives welcomed the powerful warriors into their tribe. To survive, the backwoodsmen agreed, and they "feign[ed] contentment" to win their captors' trust. Then, on a dark night, the heroes rose and killed their adoptive families. Afterward, they escaped into the strange woods, eating berries and roots until they returned to their own clearing. Picking up their axes, they resumed their attack on the forest.[16]

Labor and murder, rather than sex or intermarriage, naturalized the backwoodsmen. They took ownership of the West by chopping trees, hunting beasts, and slitting throats. Their skills mirrored those of Native Americans. Yet, while they looked and lived like Indians, something in the backwoodsmen's character stopped them from joining the savages. What prevented them committing race treason when all the physical evidence pointed toward their cultural disloyalty? That would be the imagination of Timothy Flint. The laboring men he interviewed during his travels contradicted his portrayal of backwoodsmen's racial chastity. Flint tried to write around inconvenient evidence, but his desire to cast western workers as heroes of the "old race" exposed him to biracial couplings and relationships he didn't want to see. His fetish for backwoodsmen made Flint ripe for manipulation, and his informants—those children of work in nature—often teased, misled, and outwitted him.[17]

The needling commenced outside Philadelphia. The teamsters driving the wagon train to Pittsburgh cursed, caroused, and offended so spectacularly that Flint ranked their crudeness above "sailors, boatmen, or hunters." Bursting the shackles of humanity, these flamboyant jerks were "a new species." Soon, other man-creatures met the train. Pennsylvania hunters and farmers from the other side of the Alleghenies greeted the wagons and answered the immigrants' questions about the road and the region ahead. They rattled the neophytes, telling them horror stories "not calculated to sooth our feelings, or to throw pleasing associations over our contemplated residence beyond [the mountains]." The forest dwellers called their baggage "plunder," a turn of phrase that tickled Flint. Along with the wolf, bear, and bald eagle emblems adorning the signs on the taverns where the immigrants stopped at night, "plunder" announced the end of civilization. Only men on the edges of polite society would joke about the legality of their possessions with strangers.[18]

Later, outside Ste. Genevieve on the Mississippi River, Flint eavesdropped on a shouting match between a group of poor American farmers and the crew and the passengers on his boat. Men and women often gathered on the Mississippi shore, begging the boatmen to stop and rescue them from their hardscrabble plantations. Some did escape, but most were looking for a brief respite from their labors and the boats supplied an audience. Teasing passengers and crews was a rural entertainment, a nineteenth-century version of tipping cows.

Flint watched the crowd of men on the bank. They appeared jaundiced and exhausted; ague and fever raked their bodies. Still, they puffed up for the boat, declaring themselves "the genuine and original breed, compounded of the horse, alligator, and snapping turtle." Their bona fides confirmed, they lectured the audience on the niceties of rural combat. Gentlemen fought duels with pistols or swords, while the original breed of westerners plucked their opponents' eyes out. Flint spotted more than one one-eyed farmer on the bank. But even gouging had rules. The men reserved the technique for "black-guards," assuring the boat that "no 'gentleman' ever got gouged."[19]

Flint placed scare quotes around the word "gentleman" to underscore the absurdity of these guys knowing a respectable person from a black bear. They perverted the social hierarchy, ranking men by their ability to inflict damage rather than their character, their birth, their wealth, or their piety. The "best man" in the settlement looked the roughest to Flint. He was "tall, profane, barbarous, and ruffian-like." He had secured his position by "whipping" all the others. The hayseeds conducted politics like animals. The strongest ruled; the meek patched one eye and did as they were told.[20]

At night, when the crew landed the boat, Flint overheard another working-class performance. After dinner, the boatmen rested around the campfire and talked about their "adventures" in the West. Some had been up the Missouri; others the Arkansas and Red rivers. There, they traded for skins and hunted beaver as well as manned keelboats. The West, according to Flint, demanded "hardihood and endurance." The men "patiently pursue their trapping, and contract a dexterity, a capacity to avail themselves of circumstances to circumvent the Indians and the game, an unshrinking spirit to suffer, almost beyond humanity." Flint associated western adventure with pain, but the boatmen remembered pleasure. They fondly recalled their "dusky loves." Flint cruised past the specter of interracial sex as fast as his pen would carry him. He mentioned the love affairs, snickered at the boatmen's notions of amour, and left it to other authors to "dress" their wild stories in "modern description" and sell them to the public as "tolerable romances."[21]

The purest western transplants, the ones Flint championed, rejected cultural amalgamation. They founded western homes and came to physical terms with novel environments through work. They acclimatized through chopping and shooting and declined Indian offers of adoption. The actual laborers Flint met, however, transgressed racial and cultural divisions. Instead of reassuring their white countrymen, the Pennsylvania hunters scared them. The malarial farmers performed a satire of masculinity and confused species boundaries. The boatmen spiced up their evenings with recollections of cross-cultural dalliances.

All of these visions of transplanted easterners were artful. Flint whitewashed national expansion with his creation—the pure frontiersman. The small planters, hunters, and boatmen told stories about men altered by nature for different reasons. Unlike Flint and his middle-class readers, the workers couldn't distance themselves from actual toil. Their labor immersed them in the region's soils, rivers, swamps, and forests, and since landscapes flowed into people, their bodies would tell observers if the West intended harm or promised rejuvenation. Whether they achieved equilibrium or sank in the mire, the boatmen, farmers, and backwoodsmen would go first. People watched them like coal miners observed canaries, and the workers repaid all this attention to their humors with humor. They played and teased and confirmed worst fears.

Yet, while their laughter poked fun at the upper crust, working-class jokes often hid misery and cloaked weakness. While they spun tales of romance at twilight, the boatmen waged a losing physical battle during the day. "In no employment," wrote Flint, "do the hands so wear out." The freedom of river work impressed farm boys stuck on the shore, yet "with all these seductions for the eye and imagination, no life is so slavish." Loading cargo, fighting currents and snags, polling, paddling, and cordelling dissipated and eventually broke the mightiest specimen. The price of labor, not its transformative magic, informed the boatmen's western stories. After a long day on the river, stories of sex and hunting in faraway places lulled them to sleep.[22]

Authorities could wield humor as a bludgeon as well. The editors of the St. Louis *Missouri Gazette and Public Advocate* and its successor, the *Missouri Republican,* used humor to mock runaways and randy young men. In 1824, Edward Charless—son of Joseph Charless, founder of the *Gazette*—offered a one-cent reward for the apprehension of his "indolent and careless" printing apprentice. Years earlier, he published a help-wanted notice requesting "a few spruce young gentlemen to stand at the church door . . . for the devout purpose of staring at the ladies out of coincidence." No qualifications were required other than a "good share of impudence." In September 1821, in the *Gazette*, Joseph Charless ran an ad for an alligator visiting St. Louis from New Orleans. The notice lampooned the manners of the upper class, portraying the reptile as a "gentleman" touring St. Louis to escape the "sickly season" farther south. Under the protection of one Mr. O'Riley, the gentleman invited the town's virtuous citizens to come gaze at him at the steamboat landing. He hoped to raise money for the "benevolent fund," and to improve relations between himself, representing denizens of swampy Crescent City, and the community. He asked curious gentlemen to pay "twelve and a half cents" for an introduction, while ladies and children could make his acquaintance for free.[23]

The gator's owner mocked the manners of polite riverborne society. Like their runaway servants, elites moved up and down the Mississippi watershed, and their mobility threatened to change their identities.

With all this shuffling about, how would gentlemen and women recognize one another? Ritualized introductions—letters of reference, calling cards, and published announcements—eased the transfer of status for some, but the alligator underscored the riskiness of a hierarchy founded on manners: anyone could adopt the trappings of privilege.

Still, Joseph Charless and his readers seemed to have confidence in the security of the upper end of their class system. Mr. O'Riley bought the advertisement to lure well-bred St. Louisans to the wharf, not to offend them. He expected ladies and gentlemen to laugh at his pretentious reptile. The sturdiness of the top tier of their social hierarchy dulled the jest's barb. Members of the upper class could smile at animals raising money for faux nonprofit organizations even as they grimaced at their eye-gouging alligator-horse neighbors. They assumed they could spot and stop gentleman impostors; they were less sure they could keep their rough working-class and rural countrymen from devolving into new, hazardous species.

The Charlesses' newspapers recorded serious working-class affronts to polite society in the 1820s. In 1822, "vagabonds" descended on St. Louis at night and raised hell. People couldn't sleep, women felt unsafe, and "even the very Negroes follow their example." It's hard to say who belonged to the editor's "they." They seemed to be white, drunk, loud, and fond of irking respectable citizens. They paraded the streets at night, swore at homeowners at their doors, and hurled invective at ladies. "It is hoped," wrote the editor, "that the police of the town will interpose their authority to put a stop to such shameful excesses." In 1824, a group of St. Louisans placed a notice asking the region's masters who sent their slaves into the city to work for wages to tighten their oversight. The hirelings, the notice declared, had joined with "free Negroes" to "seduce & corrupt our servants, by their idle dissolute and thievish habits." The citizens threatened to seize the "disorderly Negroes" and sell them if their owners didn't take them home or find them employers with fiercer discipline. In 1825, Edward Charless inserted a brief paragraph with a query: "what has become of the City Patrole of late?" For several nights, drunk and "riotous" Negroes had been spotted in the streets, and "two houses have been broken open and things stolen from them."[24]

Every so often in St. Louis in the 1820s, crowds of multiracial, drunken men formed at night to attack the city's gentlemen and women. In 1825, eight "ruffians" broke away from the larger population of "midnight marauders who go about from dram shop to dram shop, and disgrace our streets by their nocturnal shoutings and brawls" and molested a group of well-to-do revelers on their way home from a party. Sons and daughters of respected and wealthy St. Louisans, the ladies rode in a carriage, while the men followed behind on foot. The ruffians threw a rock at the carriage and broke a small window. The gentlemen rushed to the scene, but decided to forgo "combat" when they saw what they were up against. The ruffians followed, taunting them with "abusive language." They called them "dandies." Finally, the groups converged. Duncan Pell tripped; Edward Ferguson received a punch to the eye; David Lambert lay dead in the street. The coroner announced that multiple blows had killed the young gentleman. A grand jury indicted the attackers, and Charless published their names. The ruffians were "all of them young men, and most of them apprentices to, or work at some mechanical business."[25]

Edward Charless was a bit of a prig. He loathed disorder, and he blamed the city's working class for keeping him up at night. Yet, while he laid out his vision of reality boldly in ink every couple weeks in his paper, he never had the final word. Ruffians, vagabonds, and disorderly Negroes answered him back. They spoke loud vulgarities. They cheered and laughed into the wee hours of the morning. They abused gentlemen and made ladies blush. Language—not violence—played the leading role in almost all the social-chaos horror stories published in the newspaper. In 1824, an anonymous citizen wrote in, complaining about the "most improper and vulgar words" being "loudly and publicly used with impunity" at the town's market. The ruffian incident stood out as an anomaly, an instance where words led to violence and tragedy. Most class struggles ended with less blood and more drama. Apprentices and mechanics mocked polite society, and the upper class fired back in the newspapers, recasting their servants, employees, and slaves as marauders, vagabonds, blackguards, and wretches. Print culture vied with street theater across class lines in 1820s St. Louis. Hugh Glass arrived a year too late to participate in the vagabond uprising, but it would have been hard for him to miss the verbal warriors who crowded into the dram shops and sinks of degradation he frequented.[26]

The retired mountain man George Yount belonged to a tradition of working and westering dramatists. He crafted Hugh Glass's early traumas during storytelling sessions in his commodious Napa Valley ranch house. He built the log structure in 1836, and twelve years later, the Gold Rush supplied him with ears to bend. He cemented his reputation as a storyteller with tales of Indian fights and bear deaths, but the centerpiece of his oeuvre was his "story of Glass, the hunter." Richard Henry Dana, the celebrated author of *Two Years Before the Mast*, heard Yount tell the tale in 1859 and published a description of the performance in his *Journal*. Dana wrote it down in a shorthand of bodily harm. He noted the mauling, "shoulder torn, neck open, wind pipe open," and the thwarted revenge, " 'If God forgive them, I will.' " Then he wired the rest of the story together with a series of brutal "next times."

> Next time Glass wounded by arrow, companion cuts out stone by razor. Got Well. Next time, betrayed into Indian village, guns taken, Glass and six others run for it—pursued 5 killed . . . Next time, [Glass] last seen making for thicket pursued by Indians. Gets in nearly starved. Last of Glass, is that leaves fort, to camp in open air, and is found on rock, killed by Indians.

In Dana's eyes, Yount seemed "a man of unimpeachable integrity, and moderate and reasonable in his views, and does not exaggerate." But it took a lot of homemade wine (of which the Napa pioneer had plenty) to make his listeners swallow this line. Facts didn't pester George Yount much.[27]

But something else did. Evidence, reason, and conscience weigh down truthful people. Liars hover above such concerns: they can pick from a universe of details, plot twists, rationales, and character traits. Yount could have fabricated a heroic, funny, or tragic "Glass, the hunter." Instead, he served up a human piñata. Yount left out (or Dana failed to note) Glass's pirate career when he performed the saga for the famous author, but the omission altered the story little. The Lafitte and Pawnee episodes cut Glass off from his maritime past, recast him as a hunter, and moved him to St. Louis, but the adventures offer few insights into the demons (or angels) that may have driven him. Taken captive, he witnessed terrible crimes and horrendous torture. He wandered lost for thousands of miles and wound up a member of a Plains Indian tribe. A shell of a man, he endured repeated imprisonments, desperate escapes, and ghastly physical injuries. Yount didn't capitalize on this mayhem. It's as if his Glass suffered from a pretraumatic stress disorder. Long before he met the grizzly, he walked numbly from disaster to catastrophe. Offered the freedom to indulge in the biographical contrivance of foreshadowing, to give his hero a psychological kink that would act as a narrative mainspring, Yount declined. Why was his hero so blank?

Perhaps Yount wasn't as unencumbered as he seems. He shared Glass with other storytellers, and together they forged a legend that reflected their concerns. Yount learned the tale from fellow trappers. He claimed that Glass himself told him about the pirate episode. Later, in the narrative recorded by Orange Clark, Yount cited a man named "Dutton" as the source for one of Glass's run-ins with the Arikaras. Many people were telling Hugh Glass stories in the years after the bear attack, including Glass himself. James Hall introduced the story of the mauled hunter to a national audience in 1825, but even after the publication of the legend, amateur authors, many of them illiterate, continued working on the tale. They talked life back into a laboring body. Then they abused that body again and again. His fellow hunters wished Glass no harm; they didn't starve, impale, freeze, rend, or concuss their versions of him out of spite. They punished him to comprehend themselves. Hugh Glass helped them make sense of the physical transformations they endured while laboring in the West. Like Herman Melville, Judge Hall, and Timothy Flint, the working-class verbalizers snatched the body of an environmental American to understand the spectacle of men remade by western nature. Unlike the semiprofessionals, however, these authors struggled to maintain a distance between their physiques and the place. The West was not far from them. They carried remembrances on their skin and in their bones. The West and work had marked them.

During storytelling sessions, they deciphered the inscriptions and read them aloud to a dubious public.

Suspicion lay behind and ahead of the mountain men. Prior to journeying up the Missouri and becoming minor celebrities, they attracted oversight as laborers in the Mississippi Valley. Authorities and authors noted their behavior, deportment, clothing, and especially their physical oddities. Runaways and backwoodsmen shared an audience—Americans enthralled and horrified by the fluidity of landscapes, markets, and identities. Herman Melville pitted his raccoon-capped hunter against servant boys, but the two groups sprang from common sources: flowing rivers and human bondage. Melville targeted the Mississippi because pretenders and changelings from every class of society infested its waters. Duplicitous and flight-prone workers helped inspire his novel of lying, false appearances, and forged identities.

Melville's fallen West, however, shouldn't be mistaken for a real place, and neither should the contrary version offered by one of his favorite punching bags, Henry David Thoreau. In his 1862 essay "Walking," Thoreau linked westward movement, nature, and American freedom. He split a series of oppositions with an East/West cleaver. To the east lay civilization, the past, Europe, farms, and human "improvements." West led to nature, wildness, and the future. While optimistic about finding liberation in nature to the west, Thoreau was not as dippy as Melville made him out to be. The territorial expansion of the United States and the specter of slavery spreading with it (as well as the prospect of thousands of farmers applying their labor to the wilderness, transforming a restorative Eden into a cow pasture) worried him. He wanted to save the West from a slave-owning agrarian civilization.[28]

Hugh Glass stepped in a direction unfamiliar to both Thoreau and Melville. At the same time grim and liberating, his West was more uncertain, unsettled, and upsetting than either writer imagined. Glass and his fellow trappers shared some of the hopefulness of Thoreau's "Walking" mantra: "Eastward, I go by force; but westward I go free." The quip, however, would have suited them better if Thoreau had swapped his cheerful period for a Melvillean question mark. The hunters sensed that more independence lay to their west, but they also knew the doggedness of eastern force. They had long experience with employers, owners,

masters, fathers, captains, and jailers. Many had bridled against or severed the bonds that commanded their labor; many had run away before. Instead of breaking with the eastern labor system, the journey west extended the practice of workers using mobility to keep more of the wealth their muscle, skill, and daring could win them.[29]

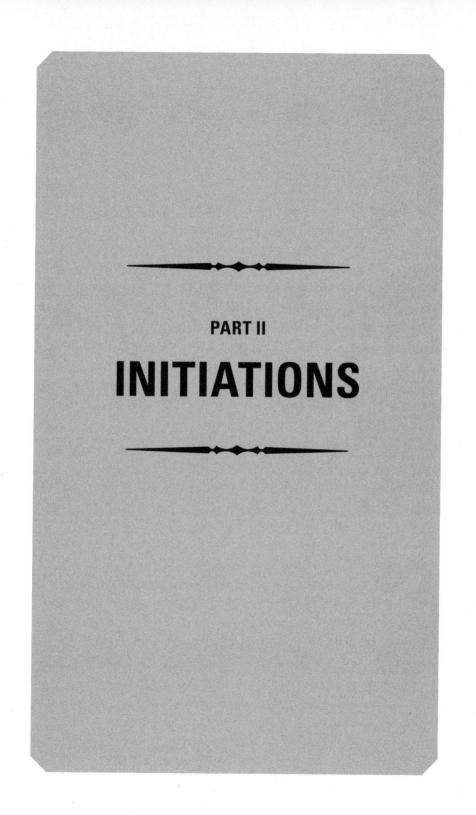

PART II

INITIATIONS

THREE

THE NAKED AND THE DEAD

On the morning of June 2, 1823, the Arikaras shot John S. Gardner. As he bled out, he pleaded with Glass to write his folks and tell them of his "sad fate." The bullet wound in Glass's own leg ached, but informing the kin hurt worse. He seems to have liked Gardner; he certainly hated his killers. They had ambushed Ashley's men after pretending friendship. Their treason warranted retribution; he promised the family that Indian bodies would follow their son's into the void.

> Dr Sir
>
> My painfull duty it is to tell you of the deth of yr son who befell at the hands of the Indians 2d June in the early morning. He lived a little while after he was shot and asked me to inform you of his sad fate. We brought him to the ship when he soon died. Mr. Smith a young man of our company made a powerful prayr wh moved us all greatly and I am persuaded John died in peace. His body we buried with others Near this camp and marked the grave with a log. His things we send to you. The savages are greatly treacherous. We traded with them as friends but after a great storm of rain and thunder they came at us before light and many were hurt. I myself was shot in the leg. Master Ashley is bound to stay in these parts till the traitors are rightly punished.
>
> Yr Obt Svt
> Hugh Glass[1]

The man peering out of the condolence letter bears little resemblance to the grouchy insubordinate many observers saw. Glass comforted Gardner's parents by reassuring them that he, their son, and even their son's commander observed and obeyed higher powers. Jedediah Smith, he wrote, invoked God at the burial, speaking a "powerful prayr" over the grave that "moved [the men] greatly." "I am persuaded," he wrote, that "John died in peace." Glass introduced his employer as "Master Ashley," an odd epithet considering that most of the letters generated by the Arikara affair (the fight and U.S. military's controversial response to it spawned dozens) acknowledged Ashley's militia rank: he was "the General." Why didn't Glass flaunt Ashley's combat experience?

Perhaps he imagined the Arikaras disciplined like riotous servants rather than military foes. A master, not a general, was what the circumstances called for. He may also have wanted to signal, by using the more ubiquitous master title, that Ashley, while impressive, reported to even grander authorities. Glass concluded the letter with a sentence driven by a mysterious passive-voice verb: "Master Ashley is bound to stay in these parts till the traitors are rightly punished." What "bound" Ashley? The familiar script? The debacle at the Arikara villages certainly fit the western story line. Ambushes and casualties preceded American assertions of power. A stumble was the first step in possessing the West. Families lost members; investors lost fortunes; armies lost battles. People dropped through the floor of civilization into the basement of hell. To rise, they fought, drawing blood and making homes. A nation's fantasies of righteous vengeance demanded that Ashley stay and whip the Arikaras.

Hugh Glass donated ten sentences to posterity; it's hard to glean intentions from such slim pickings. Still, whether he intended to summon the metaphysics of Indian hating with the passive-voice verb or simply tell the Gardners what he thought his master might do next, he left the distinct impression with his friend's loved ones that someone or something American—God, Ashley, racial destiny—was in charge in the West.

He lied to make them feel better.

Glass had signed on to a venture that exceeded American authority. The United States government issued Ashley a license to trade in the

Dr Sir

My prayer... moved us all greatly and I am persuaded Seth died in peace. His body was buried with others near this camp and marked the grave with a log. This change we will send to you. The savages are greatly treacherous. We marched over them as friends but after a great storm of rain and thunder they came on us below...

upper Missouri country, but paperwork mattered little above Fort Atkinson, near Council Bluff, Missouri, the westernmost American settlement along the river. Traders who journeyed beyond that point entered a realm they neither controlled nor fully understood. The U.S. military's response to the Arikaras' "outrage" underscored the feeble state of American influence. To punish the Arikaras, agents of the U.S. government asked the Sioux, the rising power on the western Great Plains, for help. The six hundred Indian recruits outnumbered the "three hundred effective white men" in the combined mountain-man and regular army force. At the villages, the Sioux initiated the attack. They raced ahead of the whites and caught the Arikaras outside their pickets. Several Arikara warriors died in the skirmish, and the leader of the Sioux directed his wives to beat and dismember the corpses. The Americans interpreted the mutilations as a sign of the Sioux's essential, ungovernable barbarity. But this was wishful thinking; Native politics were never that simple. The Sioux participated in the campaign to remind the Arikaras of their tributary status. The nomads considered the village dwellers their dependents, to be treated as trade partners or as raid victims depending on the mood. After making their point (and stealing seven of Ashley's horses), the Sioux departed, leaving the bug-eyed Americans and smarting Arikaras to work things out for themselves.[2]

The assault on Ashley's party stoked the Americans' racial ire, but when they tried to act out their prejudices, they fumbled their lines and lost their sense of direction. Instead of a nineteenth-century revenge melodrama with obvious white heroes exacting their revenge on hordes of dusky savages, the Americans barged into a drama more Samuel Beckett than John Wayne. They and the Arikaras played subordinate parts, while the Sioux seized the commanding role. The Americans' enforcer, Colonel Henry Leavenworth, eventually sided with the Arikaras and chastised the unruly fur traders for disturbing the peace. Hungry and abused hunters strayed from their expeditions and the revenge plot line. They invented new Westerns based on their near-death experiences in nature. The Arikara battle opened the curtains on a theater of the absurd rather than a manly celebration of destiny.[3]

The Americans floundered in the West at the peak of the beaver trade between 1820 and 1840. Haughty ideologies inflated their self-regard, but they didn't have the men, or the guns, or the economic leverage to force the region and its residents to swallow American notions of civilization, racial superiority, and national exceptionalism. The people in charge of fur-trade expeditions couldn't even command their own workers. Following the Arikara fight, forty-three of the one hundred hunters and boatmen in Ashley's expedition refused to join the counterattack. Glass fought to revenge Gardner, but he disobeyed orders at other times, and his spotty record of compliance epitomized the threat of mutiny that hung over the fur-trading parties like swarms of mosquitoes. When aggravations bit too often or too deep, hirelings bucked. Sometimes they verbally and physically assaulted coworkers and superiors, but mostly they ran from the sources of their irritation.

Western fur laborers communicated their displeasure with their employers, their natural surroundings, and their Native hosts through insubordination and flight. But running away in the West led workers into a wilderness of their bosses' making. Ashley had transported his workers into an economic and political climate that was the inverse of their home environment. Unlike in the Mississippi watershed, the economy of Missouri country flowed through Native channels. Europeans and Native Americans had been trading animal skins along the Missouri and in the Rocky Mountains for decades, and Indian custom governed these exchanges. Europeans crafted alliances with Native suppliers through gifts and marriage. They erected trading posts and waited for their partners to bring them furs. Ashley thought he could outfox this system by hauling his own labor to the prime beaver streams and having his workers trap the animals. The United States government outlawed this practice because it disrupted older arrangements and invited attacks. Indian Agent William Clark and Secretary of State John C. Calhoun sanctioned Ashley's venture with a license, knowing full well that he intended to hunt as well as trade. They winked at his indiscretion to counter the British Hudson's Bay Company push into the Missouri River trade. They broke their own laws in order to secure the Louisiana Purchase. When some of Ashley's men discovered the precariousness of being pawns in other men's stratagems, they fled. But instead of moving into an integrated river economy that might land them a safer job, when they abandoned their master, they exited the market entirely.

The workers described the experience of leaving in terms of persecution, nakedness, and endurance. Running away hurt, and the hunters venerated their pain by displaying their scars. These marks signaled the men's toughness as well as their vulnerability. They doubled as evidence of adventure and misadventure, of both manly fortitude and emasculation. The scars spoke to the predicament of laboring in other people's homelands for masters who couldn't protect you but demanded your obedience nonetheless. Seeking to manage their workers, bosses naturalized the metaphysics of race, nation, and manhood. They told workers that they needed to follow orders, especially when commanded to place themselves in harm's way. Embracing the privilege of suffering for the bosses' property, good workers showed themselves to be white, American, and manly. The bad ones looked rascally; they were ruffians, cowards, brigands, and foreigners. They were dark.

Unsurprisingly, workers didn't like being shackled to ideologies that battered them and enriched their employers. They deployed American environmentalism, linking race, nation, and manhood to the trials they endured instead of the commands they followed. The West wrecked their bodies, altering and perhaps damaging the source of their privileged identities. The men worked to safeguard their whiteness, their nationality, and their manhood by making their scars the wellspring for their exceptionalism. And they used the experience of being remade by western nature to counter their bosses' authority. From their perspective, environmental Americanism gave them the right to tell their employers to go to hell and the power to decide for themselves what their race, nationality, and gender meant.

The struggle over employers' authority and employees' dignity reached back decades in the upper Missouri fur trade. Ashley and his men inherited their risky business strategy as well as their rickety labor practices from Manuel Lisa, the St. Louis entrepreneur who staged the first end run around a centuries-old trading-post arrangement. Until 1800, French fur traders established government-licensed "factories," trading posts, in Native territories. The Indians hunted and processed the furs in exchange for European goods. The system minimized violence by creating multicultural ties and limiting the intruders' geographic excursions. The collision of hunting parties, which became the hallmark of American fur-trade violence, rarely happened when Indians harvested the hides and Europeans sat in their blockhouses. Lisa dreamed of his own trading post high above the ones on the lower Missouri controlled by the elite St. Louis fur companies. There he would not only trade with Indian hunters; he would also send out his own employees to kill and collect the luxurious pelts generated by the cold winters at higher elevations and northern latitudes. Lisa's business plan coupled hostility and profit. The more pelts he acquired, the more people he angered—both his Native hosts and his coworkers.[4]

In 1809, Antoine Dubreuil and Benito Vasquez sued Manuel Lisa in the St. Louis Circuit Court. Lisa had contracted Dubreuil and Vasquez to work as beaver hunters for three years. He promised to supply them with transportation, provisions, guns, ammunition, and "sixteen beaver traps." He also promised to let them eat at his table "consistently." In return, Dubreuil and Vasquez swore to give Lisa two-thirds of their proceeds and their obedience. They were "to take care and have care taken of the effects of said Manuel, to obey him in case of attack by Indians: to aid him in all which he thinks the common safety, and work with said Manuel at all the labor he should employ himself about." To cement the deal, the three men "bound themselves to each other" for the sum of one thousand dollars.[5]

Now back home, Dubreuil and Vasquez wanted the grand. Once upriver, they reported, Lisa deceived, abused, and insulted them. He never produced "one good Rifle, Fusse, Gun, or Carabine." Worse, he refused to work with them and barred them from his table. He treated his bond-mates like slaves. His haughtiness proved especially galling, because Lisa denied Dubreuil and Vasquez the pleasure of bossing others on the trip. Along with the food, firearms, and transport, Lisa had promised underlings—two servants, Pierre Cruzat and Caleb Montardy. Dubreuil and Vasquez resented Lisa for treating them as they wished to treat others.[6]

Were Dubreuil and Vasquez disgruntled servants or disgruntled masters? The confusion over their status arose from the riskiness of their enterprise. To safeguard property and lives, fur-trade leaders commandeered emergency powers. Duress turned commercial expeditions into military camps with the chief investor (or his representative) acting as general. Danger converted employees into soldiers, which, ironically, imperiled their bodies even more. Military discipline rested on the threat of corporal punishment; generals protected the chain of command by inflicting pain and, in the worst cases of insubordination, taking lives. No one involved in the fur trade knew the limits of the employee-as-soldier metaphor. Could bosses stretch the comparison to cover the execution of mutinous servants?

"*Sí*," answered Lisa. During the same 1807 expedition that so infuriated Dubreuil and Vasquez, an *engagé* named Antoine Bissonette ran away. Lisa directed his expert guide, George Drouillard, to track him down and bring him back "dead or alive." Drouillard found the runaway, shot him, and returned him injured but breathing. Bissonette then died from the bullet wound. At the time, Lisa congratulated Drouillard ("that's well done, that's a rascal who got what he deserved"), but when the boss and his manhunter returned to St. Louis fifteen months later, Drouillard was charged with murder and both he and Lisa were thrown in jail.[7]

Manuel Lisa had the personality of an ingrown hair. Angry partners and employees dragged him into court repeatedly, and he initiated a raft of suits (twenty in 1806–7 alone) in return. Many of the lawsuits involved runaways. Even after he displayed his willingness to hunt down and perhaps kill deserters, Lisa lost men. To secure hunters and boatmen, he had to pay part of their salary up front. The workers often consumed their advance in the St. Louis bars prior to departing on a multiyear errand that might end their lives. Once upriver, they fled when hardship or hard treatment endangered their safety or insulted their dignity. That Dubreuil and Vasquez decided to settle their gripe with Lisa in court indicated their status. Benito Vasquez ranked second in command to Lisa. A major entrepreneur in the fur trade, it made sense for him to sue his boss to protect his honor and collect a thousand dollars. Though less well known than Vasquez, Dubreuil served as the chief plaintiff in the case. He presented himself as the other men's equal. Most workers didn't have this luxury. They couldn't trust that the authorities in St. Louis would side with them, and even if judges and juries rallied to their cause, the aid would come too late. Workers bolted from fur-trade parties out of desperation. They left to find food, to avoid battle, and to escape bullying. Their reasons for flight had to be gripping, for in the West there was plenty to run from, and very little to run to.[8]

The loss of property, health, and identity distinguished running away in the upper Missouri country and the Rocky Mountains from self-stealing in the Mississippi watershed. The advertisements that proved the latter were often filled with lists of clothing. Escapees accumulated wardrobes in order to alter their appearance and rework their identities. Reinventing themselves was the key to bettering their circumstances through movement and the market. The fur-trade employees, however, cut ties with the market when they deserted their bosses and their bosses' goods, and when they mused about leaving, they told stories of stripping rather than swapping. Along the Mississippi, runaways changed their clothes; up the Missouri, runners lost them, symbolically and often literally. Naked Americans weren't an uncommon sight on the high plains in the early nineteenth century.

The godfather of all western streakers was John Colter. In 1808, "five to six hundred" Blackfoot warriors captured him on the Three Forks of the Missouri River. After killing his partner, they ordered him to disrobe, and while he stood naked, they debated the entertainment value of several capital-punishment scenarios. Some wanted to stand him at a distance and fire arrows into him, but the leader of the war party had a more creative idea. "How fast are you?" he asked with a grin. The chief gave him a quarter-mile head start and loosed his hunters. Colter ran so quickly he shocked himself. He chugged for miles, kicking up prairie dust even as the thorns of cacti tore into his bare feet. Panic and exertion burst the vessels in his nose; blood poured down his chest and torso. A mile from the Jefferson River, an especially swift pursuer closed the gap to a spear throw, but the sight of Colter dripping gore startled him and his lance missed its target and broke. Colter grabbed

the tip and killed the man. Upon reaching the river, Colter jumped in
and swam to "a raft of drift timber." He dived under the tangled branches
and found a hiding place. He shivered in the stream as the Indians
clambered over the raft in search of their lost quarry. At nightfall, they
gave up, and Colter floated away. He emerged from the water a natural
and national icon.

> He was completely naked, under the burning sun: the soles of
> his feet were entirely filled with the thorns of the prickly pear;
> he was hungry, and had no means of killing game, although he
> saw abundance around him, and was at least seven days journey
> from Lisa's Fort, on the Bighorn branch of the Roche Juane
> river. These were circumstances under which most any man
> but an American hunter would have despaired. He arrived at
> the fort after seven days, having subsisted on a root most es-
> teemed by the Indians of the Missouri, now known by natural-
> ists as *Psoralea escolenta*.[9]

Colter's miraculous escape stripped him to the essence of his being: he
was a man, a hunter, an American. The Blackfeet relieved him of his
gear (his clothes and his weapons) and turned him into prey. Huddled
in his driftwood lodge, Colter resembled the beavers he killed for a living. Yet the crossover into the realm of helplessness empowered the
trapper. How? How did an epic tale of humiliation and physical torment
earn Colter virile national glory? How did western nature, in the same
instance, strip and arm him?

To answer these questions, we need to account for the story's root—
the Latinized one in the final sentence. The *Psoralea escolenta* announced the presence of a coauthor. This partner translated Colter's
oral performance into print; he held tremendous sway over the staging
and interpretation of the adventure; and he backed up Colter's survival-
artist credentials—which requires an explanation, for John Bradbury was
an unlikely champion of American exceptionalism. A British naturalist,
Bradbury published Colter's tale in *Travels into the Interior of America*, a
journal of his wilderness trek up the Missouri River from 1810 to 1812.
Bradbury hoped to discover rare plants and animals and cart their re-

mains back to Liverpool, England, his hometown. He didn't want to conquer nature or merge with the wild, just to collect a few specimens and boost his standing with the transatlantic community of enlightened gentlemen. Bradbury displayed his class credentials early in the opening pages of his book. He mentioned his sojourn with Thomas Jefferson at Monticello before traveling west, and he dedicated the book to De-Witt Clinton, the governor of New York and president of New York City's Literary and Philosophical Society. Bradbury wrote to be taken seriously by the upper crust on both sides of the Atlantic. The last thing he needed was a blowhard alligator-horse chomping holes in his credibility.

Colter's story ripped and roared. It was a curiosity like the frontier roots and pelts Bradbury collected, and the scientist included the escape as a specimen of exotic Americana. Furthermore, Colter was colorful and credentialed. Only a couple degrees of association separated the hunter and Thomas Jefferson. Colter had served famously on the Lewis and Clark expedition. The scientific reputations of his former bosses and their august commander in chief rubbed off on him. Bradbury repeated the story and even seconded the tale's environmental Americanism, but he still took care to inoculate his main narrative. The naturalist resorted to the academic equivalent of eating his cake and having it too: he presented the story in a footnote.

Bradbury had visited with Colter twice in 1810, once in St. Louis as he prepared for the expedition up the Missouri and again near the village of La Charette in the company of his fur-trade escorts. Colter told him the story of his escape in St. Louis; Bradbury jammed the episode into his journal as an extended footnote attached to a description of their later meeting. The story didn't belong in the main text because Bradbury refused to bend time. When he met Colter in St. Louis, he hadn't begun his scientific journey west or his official account of it. His insistence on chronology reflected his mission. Bradbury kept and published his journal to verify his specimen collection. He had hitched a ride with the North West Company up the Missouri River. While the *engagés* towed the boats and the hunters pillaged the wildlife, he picked leaves and flowers and gunned down bears, skunks, and passenger pigeons. He pressed the flora in the pages of a giant book; he dressed the skins and feathers and packed them in bundles. His journal noted the location and dates of his finds. The book grew even more critical to his mission when transportation glitches, an extended illness in St. Louis, and the War of 1812 cost Bradbury major chunks of his collection. Then, to add plagiarism to misfortune, a rival naturalist "by the name of Pursh" inspected the remnants of Bradbury's specimens without his permission and announced the discovery of the most curious ones in the appendix to his *Flora Americae Septentrionalis*.[10]

All this left Bradbury with a problem. He wanted credit for his work, but his evidence was shaky or published under another's name. His collection's shortcomings threatened his reputation as a scientist and a gentleman. To guard against character assassins, Bradbury tamped down expectations. He wrote a preface worthy of Eeyore: "whoever undertakes a mission of the nature which I did, where the duty is to be performed in a wilderness, ought to give account how he performed it; even in his own defense; as it often happens that men are found, who, from interested or malignant motives, will vilify his character. . . . To many," he moaned, his journal "will be of no value." If his lackluster writing style were to meet with criticism, "I shall neither be surprised nor disappointed." Neither artful nor grandiose, the book was just the truth.[11]

Bradbury wanted his enlightened comrades to take note of his scientific contributions, but at the same time he wanted to dull the critics among them. This made his inclusion of Colter's story all the more surprising. A blood-soaked nude man sprinting through fields of prickly pear to avoid a killing squad of five to six hundred savages hardly qualified as humdrum subject matter. Even with the protection of the footnote, why did he chance a larger-than-life adventure when he was trying his best to put his readers to sleep?

Unlike the semiprofessional American regionalists who searched the West for stories of the wilderness refashioning Americans, Bradbury had no interest in naturalizing the United States through Colter's naked physique. Yet he did. He pronounced to the world that John Colter endured "circumstances" that would have caused most men to "despair." His pain tolerance, survival instincts, and violent tendencies marked him as an "American hunter," a national predator tougher than the French in St. Louis or the Canadians in the North West Company.

Perhaps he repeated Colter's story to please his American benefactors, Jefferson and Clinton, or maybe he did it to bump up his book sales. Whatever the rationale, Bradbury's gift to American history—and to the biography of Hugh Glass—was his predicament. Caught between enlightened reason and American frontier hokum, he went with the hokum. He published a wild account despite having good reasons to leave it alone. He placed his confidence in Colter, and he opened the way for the hunter to tell his version of environmental Americanism.[12]

Through Bradbury, John Colter spun a tale of exposure and suffering at odds with the semiprofessional regionalists' vicious national origin myths. Whereas Timothy Flint's "frontiersman" and James Hall's Moredock slaughtered Indians in the wilderness to advance American civilization, John Colter merely endured. He survived injury and privation, and his agony won him a fantastic story that he deployed to assert his American manliness. He did indeed kill an Indian, but the Blackfeet played a supportive rather than a generative role in Colter's epic. In Flint's and Hall's racial blood feuds, Indians kicked history into motion by kidnapping and murdering white people. They summoned the West into being through violence. The Blackfeet neither confirmed the purity of Colter's whiteness nor provided him an excuse to sate his rage. The essential chore they performed was separating him from his clothes. They exposed his skin to nature, and Colter's superiority as a man, an American, and a hunter arose from his unmediated contact with prickly pear thorns, icy rivers, and esteemed roots. With the Blackfeet's help, he met and ate the West uncooked, and he survived. Fur-trade workers like Colter told many versions of the same story of vulnerability and woe, and they expected their listeners to respect and admire their wrecked bodies as well as their unbowed spirits.

James Pearson Beckwourth raised the stakes on the workingman's Western. Following Colter's lead, he brewed a white-hunter persona out of equal parts gall and suffering. Beckwourth's literary and physical refashioning, however, was far more audacious. No gentlemen with social and scientific bona fides like John Bradbury, Thomas Jefferson, or Lewis and Clark vouched for him. The son of a white master and a black slave,

Beckwourth (spelled Beckwith until his coauthor, Thomas D. Bonner, changed the surname in the memoir the two concocted in 1856) traveled to St. Louis from Virginia with his father in 1806. Manumitted as a teenager, he apprenticed with a blacksmith until he fell in love and began wooing his girlfriend late into the night and fighting with his master during the day. After an argument concluded with the two throwing hammers at each other, Beckwourth ran away. He joined a treaty expedition to open the lead mines in Missouri to the Americans, jumped a steamboat to New Orleans, and returned to St. Louis after surviving a bout of yellow fever. In 1825, he signed on with William Ashley, who was in town to gather yet more men for the Rocky Mountains.

In his memoir, Beckwourth listed his job title as "hunter." This was a stretch. Ashley hired the young blacksmith apprentice as his personal valet and horse groom. Over time, Beckwourth rose to hunter, but he had to prove himself first. He achieved status and won respect (became a man, an American, a hunter, at least in his own eyes) through stories of bodily prowess and personal orneriness. Like Colter, Beckwourth survived an interlude of exposure in western nature. Unlike Colter, he kept his pants on, sacrificing pounds of flesh instead.

A resupply mission for Ashley's hunters in the field, the twenty-nine-man expedition departed St. Louis on October 11 and reached the Kansas River without meeting a story-worthy event. They halted, and Ashley asked for two volunteers to jog three hundred miles to the "Republican [river] Pawnees" and purchase horses for the Plains traverse. Moses Harris raised his hand, which caused the other hunters to quickly pocket theirs. Harris, according to Beckwourth, was a hard case. An experienced mountain man, he knew the country and its Native inhabitants. He had "long legs," meaning he could outmarch most men and endure "extreme privation and fatigues." All these traits recommended Harris, but his habit of leaving colleagues to die alone in the wilderness when they couldn't match his bone-rattling pace scared away potential travel mates. When no one else stepped forward, Ashley ordered his valet/groom to accompany Harris. Beckwourth, it seems, was the one member of the expedition that Ashley could compel to walk hundreds of miles on the Plains at the cusp of winter with a speedy, pitiless jerk.[13]

Beckwourth's participation in the horse-buying venture signaled his low position, but he turned the forced march to his advantage in his remembrance of the journey. First, he stood up to Harris and promised him bodily harm "if I should give out on the road, and you offer to leave me to perish, . . . if I have strength to raise and cock my rifle, I shall bring you to a halt." Harris demurred. He would select their path; Beckwourth could take the lead and control the pace. Then "it will be your own fault, if you tire out."[14]

The two ate lustily ambling to the Pawnees. Harris shot four turkeys, and they dined on the "choicest portions," tossing the guts and gristle to the wolves. When they reached their destination, however, the site turned their stomachs. The Pawnees were gone. They had relocated to their winter quarters, a dire turn for the Americans. The Indians, they assumed, would feed them while they dickered over horses. Nostalgic for the entrails they had thrown away earlier, they trudged back toward the Missouri without provision. Days passed; no edible beasts crossed their paths or their lips. Harris weakened and "seemed almost disheartened." Beckwourth cheered him by killing an emaciated elk and building fires to warm them. Nearly a week after their last taste of meat, Harris broke. He could no longer walk, and he begged his companion not to forsake him. Beckwourth told him to stay put and jogged for help. He found a troop of Indians on the path to a fur-trading post. They backtracked to Harris, who was sprawled on the dirt groaning, "Ho Jim! come back! come back! don't leave me!" Thus, Ashley's valet saved the long-legged Harris. By outgutting the flinty endurance specialist, Beckwourth stepped away from his servant past and entered his freer, manlier, and whiter future.[15]

His body registered his social transformation. "Hallo, Jim!" his friends greeted him at the trading post. "What is the matter with you? Is it yourselves, or only your ghosts?" The plural "yourselves" and "ghosts" suited Beckwourth. He switched identities like Mississippi runaways swapped outfits. Eventually, he jumped from slave to apprentice to manservant to beaver hunter to Crow Indian to California innkeeper and toll-road operator to Denver entrepreneur to militia scout. During his six-year residence with the Crows after leaving Ashley's employ, he changed his name repeatedly to mark his ascent from adoptee to warrior to chief. A serial personality, Beckwourth spurred mistrust. Many Jims spoke from the autobiography, and critics dismissed each of them as a "gaudy liar." Yet, while Beckwourth was no slave, especially to the truth, he picked his fibs with care. He built his western persona through acts of daring and sacrifice. Following his victory over Harris, Beckwourth took on his boss. He and Ashley fought a running battle that pitted the general's military and capitalist authority against Beckwourth's remade body. Beckwourth won in the end; Ashley declared him "a singular being" and rewarded his loyalty and hazardous toil with an apology: he regretted speaking to the survival artist like a common servant.[16]

A small, brutal incident triggered Beckwourth's revolt. After nearly starving with Harris, Beckwourth swore off the West and returned to St. Louis, only to find Ashley lying in wait. In town to muss his newly made wedding bed and to recruit a few hunters from the saloons along the wharf, Ashley convinced Beckwourth to try for the mountains once more. The expedition left in early May 1826 and spent the summer buying horses, collecting employees (a rejuvenated Harris reupped), and raiding lower Missouri farms for laughs and sustenance. By late fall, however, the amusement had dimmed. The men were hungry and dispirited: "No jokes, no fire-side stories, no fun; each man rose in the morning with the gloom of the preceding night filling his mind; we built our fires and partook of our scanty repast without saying a word." Beckwourth brightened the mood for a while by killing a flock of ducks, but as the camp moved west, the food gave out again and aggravation spoiled into mutiny.[17]

At the apex of the crabbiness, Beckwourth decided to beat Ashley's horse. He was angry; the animal kept withdrawing its hoof in the middle of a shoeing. Ashley watched his groom assault his mount and gave the failed blacksmith apprentice a severe tongue-lashing. "Feeling hurt," Beckwourth turned on his master. How dare Ashley "curse and rage" at him, a prime hunter "successful in killing game when his men were in a state of starvation"? Beckwourth reminded Ashley that he had risked his life for him and had treated him "like [his] own brother." He threw down the hammer and huffed: "There is one more nail to drive, general, . . . which you may drive for yourself, or let go undrivin, for I will see you dead before I will lift another to serve you." The next morning, Ashley commanded his underling to pack two pigs of lead "and sundry items" on the back of a gravely malnourished horse. Beckwourth complained but obeyed.[18]

The nag and his escort fell behind the group. The horse stumbled and dropped to the snow. Beckwourth unpacked him, propped him up, and loaded him again. The animal collapsed. Beckwourth unpacked and reloaded. The beast toppled once more. Beckwourth grabbed his hammer and bashed in its skull. "There," he said, "take that! I only wish you were General Ashley." At this juncture, the storyteller Beckwourth and the scribe T. D. Bonner exited reality stage left. The master-versus-servant drama required further boiling, and the coauthors ramped up the tension by positioning Ashley behind a bush near Beckwourth and the horse. He saw and heard everything. And he answered Beckwourth's murder-fantasy monologue with a theatrical "You do, do you?" The two drew their guns. Beckwourth threatened to kill the general if he did not apologize for speaking rudely to him; Ashley promised to make Beck-wourth suffer for his insolence. Fingers on the triggers, the master and servant seemed to have reached the tipping point where language swings into action. Yet this was Beckwourth's story, and he could imagine one more line, a nonviolent retort that would leave him unscathed and victorious. With his boss in his crosshairs, Beckwourth gave him notice of his intention to run away.[19]

By now Ashley had stiffened into Beckwourth's ventriloquist dummy, and the servant filled his boss's mouth with the words he wanted to hear: "Tell him I want him to stay"; "Anything you say Jim, I will follow"; "I am under great obligations to you"; "I wish you to forgive me, and desire to part in friendship." All fibs. The real Ashley kept a journal during this expedition, and he never mentioned the "singular individual" James P. Beckwourth. Why would he? The strangeness of the West and the problems it created for his fur profits worried him more than his valet's injured pride. Ashley recorded place-names and river crossings, meetings with Native hunting parties and the locations of bison herds. When people appeared in his journal, they usually carried titles: general, captain, major, or lieutenant. Neither Beckwourth nor his rank-and-file chums warranted inclusion. Ashley wrote more about his horses than his men.[20]

Scholars have shot holes in Beckwourth's account of his relationship with Ashley. They point to the climax—his rescue of Ashley from
the Green River "suck"—as the ultimate example of a supporting actor
distorting the historical record to play the hero. Beckwourth never dived
into a swirling vortex of doom to save his master, and Ashley never
thanked him for preserving his life, nor invited him into his St. Louis
home to meet his wife, nor declared him a superb hunter, nor warned
him, out of fatherly kindness, to limit his risk taking. A fabulist, Beckwourth manufactured a past to ease his transition from a black servant
into a white hunter. Readers inherited his wishful thinking.

He exaggerated and mixed up dates and details. His ethnographic
perceptiveness rivaled his sympathy for animals. He disfigured the
Crows' culture much like he mangled the scrawny horse's head. The
Indians come off as bloodthirsty, self-mutilating dupes, incapable of re-
sisting the leadership of the only "white man" among them. And T. D.
Bonner didn't help Beckwourth's credibility. A Gold Rush opportunist,
he indulged and endorsed the fibs, adding a few strange touches of his
own. Bonner was a temperance advocate as well as a heavy drinker, and
he inserted several odes to sobriety that jarred with Beckwourth's enthu-
siastic liquor trading and guzzling.

Historians look at James Beckwourth and see what he refused to
give them: a clear window onto the early American West. Bonner and
Beckwourth clouded their narrative with so many falsehoods, it's hard
to look past their snow job. But, if you consider their fibs from another
angle, they can illuminate as well as obscure. Social and labor historians pore over wills, court records, employment slips, church documents,
tax receipts, and newspaper ads for glimpses of the underdocumented
masses. Early-nineteenth-century slaves, ex-slaves, and working-class
men and women simply don't jump out of the scarce and fragmented
sources as fully formed, recognizable people, and few clues have survived to reconstruct their interior lives—their thoughts, their anxieties,
and their dreams. Ergo, the magnitude of Beckwourth's literary achieve-
ment: he recorded his fantasies. He wished a world into print and filled
it with bosses that acknowledged the "severe toil, privation, suffering,
peril, and, in some cases, loss of life" underneath the "immense piles"

of animal skins that constituted their fortunes. Beckwourth dreamed of a West dominated by a species of men with long legs, sharp eyes, and stratospheric pain thresholds. The masters depended on these exceptional and singular white American men to collect furs for them, to save them from Indians and starvation, and to pluck them from sucks. In return, they showered them with presents and respect. They loved them like sons. Or, at least, they treated them better than horses.[21]

Meanwhile, outside Beckwourth's head, in a less-than-fantastic West, General Ashley forbade his human servant from exercising power over his equine property. The animals were too valuable. Their muscles carried men and goods to the mountains and back. After the Arikaras closed down the Missouri to the Americans, animal traction insured fur-trade profits. Ashley communicated the significance of horseflesh when he saddled Beckwourth with a scrawny nag as punishment for abusing a fit animal. The starving beast negated the vigor of Beckwourth's western body. Stuck behind with the nag, he fell off the pace and languished in the snow, losing the ground he gained by outdistancing Moses Harris.

The drop in status must have stung the aspiring white hunter. Masters had a long history of justifying slavery by reducing African Americans to the level of brute animals. In the St. Louis newspapers, only the bodies of horses received more notice than the bodies of runaway slaves, apprentices, and servants. Indeed, the ads for the two forms of chattel property often ran side by side. On March 22, 1820, the *Missouri Gazette and Public Advertiser* published a hundred-dollar reward for Dick, the runaway slave of John Foster from Shawneetown, Illinois. Dick was "5 feet 8 inches high, stoutly made . . . very black and ugly." He carried knife scars on his forehead and left breast. His feet were "singularly shaped, being very narrow at the heel and broad at the toes—his eyes are generally red." Across the page from ugly Dick, Adam Steel offered a twenty-dollar reward for a stolen sorrel mare. The five-year-old horse measured fifteen hands and a half high. A natural trotter, the animal had "scars on the inside of her thighs" and a "small scar on each jaw." The owners of wandering horses and slaves described their property in similar terms. They noted skin and hair color, scars, gaits, ages, heights,

genders, and dispositions. An emancipated slave and runaway apprentice, Beckwourth knew masters tended to conflate servants and livestock, and his cruelty toward the nag suggested how much he disliked
being ranked with animals. He had proven his worth as a man, an
American, and a hunter after defeating Harris. His altered western body
made him exceptional. Horses reminded him that in an unfree labor
system cuts, brands, hair, and hide color stigmatized rather than elevated the bodies of servants and livestock. Distinguishing marks imprisoned them, eased their capture, and signaled their shared status as
owned, subservient beings.[22]

Beckwourth labored in his autobiography to reclaim his body and
reinterpret its markings. Most spectacularly, he portrayed himself as
white. The West supplied him with new reference points for his racial
self-description. He considered the Indians nonwhite savages, and when
he sojourned with the Crows, he pretended to be one of them. (He assumed the identity of a warrior killed by the Cheyenne years before.)
With reality in his possession, he reset the coordinates of his passage
between races. Instead of a black or a mulatto starting point, he picked
a white masculine one. He was a white man, an American hunter, passing himself off as a Crow. When he left the Indians, he reverted to his
old, true race. Thus, the Crows finished the job Moses Harris began.
Beckwourth entered the West a mixed-race runaway apprentice; he
emerged a white hunter who looked black or "Mexican" and sometimes
played Indian.[23]

Historians continue to puzzle over Beckwourth's race, but his contemporaries knew what to call him. He was a liar. The prominent Boston writer Francis Parkman biologized this mistrust. Informants out
West told him that James Beckwourth was a "mongrel," a "compound of
white and black blood, though he represents otherwise." Parkman
alerted the rest of the nation in his book *The Oregon Trail*. Beckwourth's
blood prevented him from consummating his journey from slavery to
literary self-mastery. The stew of hemoglobin that coursed through his
veins chained him to the truth. By feigning otherwise, Beckwourth revealed himself a "ruffian" rather than a white man.[24]

Yet, when placed alongside John Colter or Hugh Glass, Beckwourth
appeared more conventional. He belonged to the corps of environmen-

tal Americans. The West laid these men bare, stripped off their clothes as well as the outer layers of their identities. The experience terrified and emboldened them. Schooled in the theater of slavery, they understood that people scrutinized their bodies for the imprints of work, nature, and corporal punishment. According to the newspapers, their scars and skin color provided all the information onlookers would need to pick them out in a crowd. Their bodies were their identities. Frances Parkman heard "mulatto" and ejected Beckwourth from the national conversation about America and the West. The fur hunters, however, countered such expulsions. If the wilderness, or the backcountry, or the frontier bred exceptional Americans, then their near-death misadventures up the Missouri River qualified them for an additional cultural dispensation. Shriveled from starvation, punctured by cacti, and blown to mush by projectiles, their wrecked bodies were their stories, and they owned them outright because Indians and western nature injured and inspired *them*—not their bosses. James Beckwourth tried to explain how the Indians turned him white, how they helped him write his own body and his own story. Boston readers may not have believed him, but his authorship sprang from the same environmental Americanism that rooted their exemplary nation in the West. Through his transformations, Beckwourth promoted American futurity.

Still, what practical benefits derived from literary emancipation by way of national founding myths? Even after Colter and Beckwourth told their stories to their coauthors and established their credentials as magnificent American hunters, they had to wake up the next morning and shoot a possum for breakfast. Neither achieved success nor accumulated power in any real sense. Colter farmed in Missouri and fought in the War of 1812 before dying from jaundice in 1813. Beckwourth lived longer and continued to reinvent himself. He entertained travelers in California and Denver, ran businesses, trapped and hunted, and acted as a negotiator with Indian tribes. He assisted the Colorado militia during the massacre at Sand Creek in 1864, though his exact role in the slaughter has never been determined. Beckwourth surfaced in so many guises at so many epochal western moments he qualified as the region's Zelig. Yet, for all his shape-shifting moxie, observers continued to belittle him, reducing his complex persona to "nigger Jim."[25]

Neither Colter nor Beckwourth converted their stories of punishment and endurance into social or economic power, but their dramas revealed the cultural democracy that flourished in the chaos in the early years of Americans' expansion into the West. In 1823, the Arikaras punished the nation's most aggressive fur-trade entrepreneurs. The defeat bewildered the Americans. The Arikaras upset plans, profits, and ideologies. The white American hunters expected the Indians to respect and dread rather than ambush them. Once exposed, the newcomers scrambled to regain their composure. A throng of bosses—among them Ashley, Major General Benjamin O'Fallon, Colonel Henry Leavenworth, and the Indian agent and acting member of the Missouri Fur Company Joshua Pilcher—hustled to the scene. They rallied the troops for a counterattack with stories of racial and national destiny. They instructed the men to rouse themselves like good employees, to behave like respectable Missourians, white men, and Americans. Wronged and bloodied, the hunters were free to indulge their violent fantasies. Their bosses urged them to combat savagery with savagery. But, given the opportunity to act out their revenge, almost half of Ashley's men refused to budge, and instead of leveling the villages, Leavenworth, much to the displeasure of the other bosses, decided to negotiate a treaty with the Arikaras. Both Leavenworth's passivity and the mutineers' resistance contradicted the metaphysics of Indian hating and revealed how chaos and bewilderment created an opportunity for countervailing narratives. Alongside retribution, some Americans found room for stories of exposure, weakness, doubt, and mercy.

This plurality of Westerns grew out of nationalists' desire for physical evidence of American exceptionalism. The trauma of working-class hunters planted the nation in the West and generated a "new race of man" uniquely qualified for continental dominance. The Arikara battle proved, however, that hunters produced culture as well as they absorbed punishment. They could author Westerns, too.

The hunters itched for sunrise. Beached on a sandbar outside the Arikaras' village in a thunderstorm, they needed the day to break so that they could grab the horses and flee. The hunter Aaron Stephens was dead. He had sneaked into the village earlier that evening with Edward Rose, the mulatto interpreter. Rose came back, but Stephens offended somebody and his forehead met a scalping knife. Rose said Grey Eyes, the village headman, had declared war. Morning seeped through the upright logs that picketed the village. The rain calmed. The Arikaras fired into the huddled hunters. William Ashley lost a dozen employees in fifteen minutes. He watched them die from the keelboat anchored in the middle of the Missouri River. He ordered his boatmen to rescue the survivors, but they refused. The Arikaras exposed the limits of the general's authority.[26]

While Ashley's vessel floated out of range, some men on the expedition's second keelboat, the *Yellow Stone Packet*, launched a rescue attempt with two skiffs large enough to carry thirty passengers. The Arikaras assassinated the oarsmen as they neared the sandbar. The skiffs drifted away, five men in one, none in the other. Seeing the mess, James Clyman skittered from behind his cover—"a dead hors"—and dived into the river. He misjudged the current and sailed past the boats. Drowning, he stripped off his rifle and pistol belts, his ball pouch, and his buckskin hunting shirt. Reed Gibson saved him. Gibson had swum after the empty skiff and regained control of it. He noticed Clyman's trouble and paddled after him. After hauling the exhausted hunter aboard, Gibson screamed, "Oh, God, I'm shot," and collapsed. Clyman steered the boat to the opposite shore. He saw three Arikaras emerge from the water on his side of the river. He hid the badly injured Gibson in the bushes, promised to write his folks in Virginia and tell them what had become of him, and ran into the open prairie. One Arikara followed. Clyman had weathered a damp, sleepless night on a clump of sand; he had breakfasted on adrenaline in a firefight and nearly sunk in the Missouri River; now he raced for his life for "about an hour" until heart palpitations stopped him. He dived into a stand of weeds; his pursuer jogged by. Clyman spotted the keelboats retreating downriver. He rejoined the company and learned that Gibson had been saved. Gibson, who lay in the boat's cabin, his bowels perforated with lead, died within the hour.[27]

The Americans holed up twenty-five miles below the villages to bind their wounds and whet their quills. Ashley notified the public and the authorities of the Arikaras' "outrage." He wrote to newspapers in St. Louis and Franklin, Missouri, and to Major General Benjamin O'Fallon, the United States government's upper Missouri Indian agent. He opened the letters with a gust of egotism: "On the morning of the second instant I was attacked by the Ricaree Indians, which terminated with great loss on my part." Ashley commended the best part of the hunters stuck on the bar—"never did men in my opinion act with more coolness and bravery than the most of the men on the sand beach"—but his self-nomination as the primary target of the Arikaras' attack measured his team's spirit more accurately. In a crisis, the Americans had splintered into the naked, the dead, the heroic, the cowardly, and General Ashley.[28]

Although the group was united by vocation, gender, labor contracts, and a common perception of being far from home, the expedition fell apart with remarkable ease. The collapse of Ashley's command shocked and angered O'Fallon. He had recommended Ashley to John C. Calhoun, the U.S. Secretary of War, and William Clark, the U.S. Superintendent of Indian Affairs. Traders, trappers, and hunters worried Calhoun. He didn't want a green squad of gun-toting expectant capitalists wrecking the peace on the lower Missouri by trespassing on Indian lands. O'Fallon and Clark reassured the secretary that Ashley was no ordinary businessman. A general and a lieutenant governor, Ashley would not only resist the urge to "alarm and disturb the harmony" among the Indians and the Americans near Council Bluff, he would "cultivate the friendship of the more distant Tribes by a regular & conciliatory course, which . . . most probably strengthen the confidence those Tribes may have in our Government." A gentleman and a master, Ashley would perform government service while gathering his fortune.[29]

The Arikaras exploded this fantasy, but their aggression opened the way for the fulfillment of another. For years O'Fallon had wanted to send an army detachment up the Missouri for a summer tour. Every spring he lobbied Calhoun and Clark for funds and men. Warriors, guns, and horses, he argued, were the political language of the upper Missouri. An extended parade would intimidate the Indians, ensure their good behavior, and secure fur-trade profits. It would also serve as a warning to the British Hudson's Bay Company that the United States was ready to defend the Louisiana Purchase and compete for the Oregon Territory. The Arikara incident gave O'Fallon the excuse to demonstrate American power. Calhoun ordered the U.S. Army's Sixth Infantry under Colonel Henry Leavenworth to move on the villages. O'Fallon traveled ahead of the troops to deputize the fur companies and the Sioux. With all these guns trained on the Arikaras, the upper Missouri tribes, especially the troublesome Blackfeet, Assinoboines, and Gros Ventres, would see how the Americans smote their enemies.[30]

Yet before the curtain could rise on the revenge drama, O'Fallon had to mend Ashley's broken party. The general had tried to rally his men for a counterattack the day after the initial slaughter, but the majority of hunters and nearly all of the boatmen balked. "[T]o my great mortification and surprise," Ashley wrote, "I was informed, after the men had been acquainted with my intentions, that they positively refused to make another attempt to pass the towns, without considerable reinforcement." Ashley pleaded for daring and acquiescence; they threatened him with a group "resolution to desert." He sent the mutineers farther downriver to Fort Atkinson, and set up camp with thirty stalwarts, including Hugh Glass, to wait for reinforcements. Weeks passed; Ashley wrote and waited. Rations grew short, but he refused to permit hunters to scour the area for game. Instead of bagging a goose or an elk, he imagined them ferreting out the nearest path and running away from him. One wrote home: "Out of the hundred men, the number [Ashley] left St. Louis with, I question whether he will arrive at the Yellow Stone with more than ten." He intended to be one of the ten. The Arikaras had killed two of his friends, and he promised to stay with Ashley "until I assist in shedding the blood of some of the Ricarees." He stayed to revenge his comrades, not Ashley.[31]

O'Fallon arrived at Fort Atkinson on June 19 to confront those who had chosen differently. He posted a letter intended to prompt the deserters to rejoin the expedition. O'Fallon addressed the forty-three boatmen and hunters as "fellow citizens." He reminded them of their allegiances to the United States and to Missouri. He brought up Ashley: "he is my friend, he is your friend, he is the peoples friend—The most enterprising—the most energetic, and amongst the greatest military chieftains of the State of Missouri." He scolded them: You abandoned "him in the savage wilderness, far from home." And what of your friends? You left them, too, and the Arikaras "mangl[ed] the bodies and decorated themselves with the reeking sculps." You can't go home after that. What would you tell your wives and children, your friends and acquaintances? Help us. Volunteer your lives, your guns. Let's give "the most barbarous and vilanous nation of human beings that ever disgraced humanity . . . the most favorable impression of our strength and military skill." Join the show, "terrify, punish" the villains, and redeem "your Character." Sixteen men accepted O'Fallon's offer; the rest chose shame, or indifference, or self-preservation.[32]

O'Fallon sought to bring Ashley's men—and through them the upper Missouri country—to order. He hammered away at their consciences with ideas that organized and obliged people in the United States: national and state loyalties, profit, honor, deference, gender, military rank, justice, race, and civilization. In his world, men dueled to the death for such ideas. Yet, while he possessed the ingredients for a superb motivational letter, O'Fallon's notice stirred fewer than half of the deserters. On June 19, 1823, at Fort Atkinson, some of the most deeply held and pervasive American values crashed against sterner stuff. What kind of citizen turned his back on his country, his state, his race, his employer, his general, his capitalist enterprise, his comrades, and his civilization during a crisis? In the West in 1823, survival artists did.

None of the deserters wrote down his reasons for leaving; they turned their backs on history as well as their countrymen. No matter. Their actions betrayed the limits of American authority in the West. When expeditions blew apart, workers chose the men and the orders they wished to follow. Some stuck; some fled. Either decision assumed that in chaotic circumstances hunters and boatmen had the freedom to choose their poison. Staying risked further mismanagement, catastrophe, and pain. Exiting often meant prolonged exposure to a hostile environment and perturbed Natives. Whichever gauntlet they picked, if they lived, they strengthened their environmental Americanism. Their transformed selves, not their obedience to their masters, defined their singularity.

The men countered the argument that they owed their employer complete obedience by insisting that their remade bodies gave them the right to choose their ordeals. O'Fallon presented the masters' under-standing of the chain of command in his letter to the deserters. Instead of fleeing, he told them, you should have defended "yourselves, your Employer, his property, and at the same time sustaining the dignity and reputation of your country." When you signed your contracts in St. Louis, he argued, you promised to fight for your nation, your boss, and your boss's possessions. American power—defined here as the freedom to take beaver hides out of the upper Missouri country without Native interference—rested on the strength of the bonds in this sequence. The hunters and boatmen abandoned their dignity, their character, and their manhood when they reneged. In O'Fallon's estimation, the employees couldn't walk away from Ashley and remain honorable Americans.[33]

O'Fallon missed, or couldn't bring himself to see, the men's dis-comfort with chains. Many didn't want to embellish Ashley's power; they wanted to check it. Ashley had the goods on them. He was their supplier. All their traps, ammunition, trade items, and much of their food came through him. The money they hoped to gain hunting furs would come from him. In an emergency, he asserted military command over them. His choices might end their lives. To blunt this power, the men insisted that whatever the conditions of their employment, they could reclaim their physical beings and leave.

Perhaps this explains all the nude scenes in the workingmen's Westerns. The episodes translated abject humiliation into narratives of strength and regeneration. The nudists wandered free of the chain of command and discovered new sources of authority: their injured bod-ies. The West plucked their last fig leaf, but unlike Adam, Eve, General Ashley, and Major General O'Fallon, the hunters weren't easily morti-fied. O'Fallon ordered them to be ashamed for not staying with Ashley or not participating in the humiliation of the Arikaras. The entire Amer-ican colonial project, he argued, depended on subordinates accepting and administering shame. But this was a tough argument to make in the Missouri country in the 1820s. Fur-trade employees drifted off of expeditions like dust off the backs of comets. They escaped into their own wildernesses, the chaotic spaces opened by their employers' blunders and their nation's fecklessness. The lucky returned, adding survival artist to their white-American-hunter résumés. A subset of these encountered coauthors eager to sell books and write down the stories of men remade by nature.

Jack Larrison stumbled into Ashley's camp two, three, or four days after the Arikara ambush. James Clyman forgot the exact date, but he remembered Larrison's appearance. He was "naked as when he was born and the skin peeling off of him from the effects of the sun." A musket ball had excavated a tunnel through one thigh and lodged in the meat of the other. Larrison had suffered the injury early in the fight. Shocked and bloodied, he squirmed between two dead horses to escape further damage. The corpses hid him from his enemies as well as from his comrades, who abandoned him in his hidey-hole. Larrison peeked out in the quiet that followed the Americans' retreat and discovered his solitude. He decided to swim for it. He stripped and jumped into the Missouri. The Arikaras fired at his bobbing head, but he reached the other bank unscathed. With the Indians behind him, he trudged into his wilderness— alone, lost, and naked as a newborn babe.[34]

Did Jack Larrison interpret his ordeal as a rebirth? Did he, like Colter and Beckwourth, tell a tale of manly endurance, personal transformation, and status enhancement? It's hard to know. Clyman described the incident, and he ground down his rhetoric while others let theirs fly into fantasy. He described his own nude interlude in the river in the same matter-of-fact monotone. He didn't conjure up five hundred or six hundred Indian warriors, blood-gushing footraces, or melodramatic showdowns with rivals and bosses. The rushing water ripped the clothes off his back; he ran from the Arikaras wild with fear. The experience colored his interpretation of Larrison's misadventure. Larrison stumbled into a paragraph Clyman opened with a confession of weakness rather than a rush of braggadocio. Before the Arikaras' attack, he wrote, "few men had Stronger Ideas of their bravery and disregard of fear than me." But the morning on the sandbar "cooled my courage." The death of Gibson sent a shiver as well. His friend perished saving him. Such acts came with responsibilities. Clyman had promised Gibson that he would write his friends and family and tell them how he died. He broke this

promise. He couldn't remember the address, and he didn't want to revisit the memory anyway.[35]

Larrison appeared in the next sentence. Clyman introduced him at a moment of loss, doubt, and shattered confidence. Larrison symbolized Clyman's despair. Instead of pumping up their American hunter credentials, the Missouri country stripped these men to the bone. Larrison's peeling skin captured the sensation best. He was a walking nightmare, the embodiment of dying alone in a land far from home, a fear that lurked below the surface of the wilderness survival stories.

James Clyman perished in California in 1879, but the story of his naked flight didn't gain wide exposure until 1925. He first gave his account of the Arikara fight to a local newspaper in 1871. Years later, the California Historical Society serialized this account along with large portions of his later diaries. In 1928, the society compiled the material into a book. They recommended the fur hunter to their members as "the offspring of Daniel Boone and the Fenimore Cooper Leatherstockings, [who] has only lately become associated with the cowboy and the wild, two-gun Westerner of fiction and melodrama." Connoisseurs of backwoodsmen and outlaws would find him palatable, if not delicious. The editor disinterred Clyman from his historical environment and placed him in a line of iconic western males that stretched from Kentucky to Hollywood. Clyman, however, never claimed membership in the guild of frontier heroes. The trauma of the West tempered his appraisal of his past. He understood all too well the tremendous price some men paid for their American bodies.[36]

FOUR

BEARS IN BLACK AND WHITE

In an 1824 letter to a Pennsylvania friend Daniel Potts accidentally scored a literary first: he wrote down the Hugh Glass legend. One of Andrew Henry's hunters, Potts had remained at the company's fort on the Yellowstone River while his boss and a crew of volunteers reinforced Ashley for the Arikara showdown. After Leavenworth quashed their revenge, Henry herded his men back to the fort, and Potts soaked up their adventures. The Mandans and "Groonvants" attacked them along the way, killing two and wounding two, then "one man was also tore nearly all to peases by a White Bear and was left by the way without any gun who afterwards recovered." Glass's trek into American arts and letters began as a coda to an injury report. Potts didn't celebrate him; he didn't even mention his name. The bear displayed more personality. Her aggression earned her capital letters and an adjective: she was a White Bear. Next to the animal, the participants who most impressed Potts left Glass and took his gun. Only then, as he lay alone, isolated and hidden from view, did Glass perform an act worth mentioning: he recovered.[1]

Potts established the basic structure of the Glass legend—trauma, betrayal, and recovery—but who cares? He voided the human at the center of the drama, rubbing away the quirks and passions that made him recognizable and sympathetic. In his letter, Potts could only muster the descriptive energy to call him "one man." The first author of the Hugh Glass legend dumped Hugh Glass.

Potts captured the paradox of Glass's fame. The mangled hunter surfaced in American culture at the moment he disappeared into western nature. Glass's companions assumed that the bear had extinguished the spark of personhood in the corpselike mess gurgling at their feet. He was a goner, prompting a question upon his return: Where did he go? The nude runaways before him met a hostile environment stripped of costume and artifice. Freed from their duds, they experienced nature intimately; they felt the barbs sink into their flesh. Glass went further. He crossed into an existential wilderness. He crawled to the frontiers of civilization, humanity, and being. His journey to the edge of nothingness and back sickened and titillated observers. He redefined for his audiences what it meant to be alone and adrift. The very conditions that hid Glass from history ushered him into the limelight. He reached celebrity through obscurity.

Glass vanished into nature, and upon his return, he talked a lot and wrote very little, thereby clouding the historical record. The literary authorship of his story passed to others, and the first one to write it down left a hole where a hero should have been. Instead of expounding on the details of the man dismantled by a wild beast, abandoned for dead, and miraculously recovered, Potts lingered with the bear. He makes you want to scream: Excuse me, could we *please* stay with the casualty on the verge of national stardom? This desire for a human close-up, however, reflects my compulsions, not his. Potts stared at the bear, and his fixation, while seeming misplaced to me, summoned a truly historic tableau: when nineteenth-century spectators gazed at hunters like Hugh Glass, animals often jumped out at them.

In this chapter, I follow Glass into his animal environment. The trail leads into the thickets where the she-bear mauled him but also into southwestern humorist literature, electoral-campaign propaganda, grizzly bear ecology and social organization, and the written reports of fur hunters. To pursue Hugh Glass, I argue, is to lose him. But instead of grumbling about his disappearance, I want to contemplate the animals caught in the search's headlights. American market hunters like Glass often slid into animal environments and guises. Professional nimrods amassed natural capital, trading skinned and butchered animals for cash and sundries. Hides served as their lifeline to the international economy. To acquire their commodities, these entrepreneurs spent months, even years, in animal environments. They grew hairy, exchanged their textiles for mammal skins, and immersed their intellects in the habits, tastes, and vulnerabilities of their prey.

These predators belonged in haunts that nourished wolves, panthers, turkeys, raccoons, possums, beavers, bison, deer, feral pigs, and black, brown, and grizzly bears. Through lengthy exposure, they adjusted to terrains that killed untutored easterners. In the deep woods or on the high plains, the men ventured beyond civilization. Upon their return, some of their fellow citizens questioned whether they still belonged. And here's the twist: the seasoned men represented the United States best when they resembled humans least. In their transmuted form, they epitomized the new race rising in distant western lands whose labor forged American genius. Their beastliness underpinned their nation's exceptionalism even as it undermined their membership in the white race, the male gender, the American polity, and the species *Homo sapiens*.

Heroic and horrifying, these transformed men inspired prophylactic measures. Writers and audiences isolated them and questioned their veracity. They stationed them at the edge of a far West or pushed them back in time to irretrievable frontiers. They called them gaudy liars. And they smiled, snickered, and guffawed. Humor kept the hunters away from civilized America. Laughter excused them from serious consideration and uncomfortable questions: Were they humans, men, whites, Americans? If so, what did these categories mean? Audiences desired the men's bodies and consumed their stories of dismemberment. The witnesses, however, could do without the stench of blood, panic, and oblivion that wafted from the men's actual injuries and corpses. Environmental Americanism was best accomplished at a distance.

In the early nineteenth century, cool winds, heat waves, noxious clouds, and swampy gases entered and exited humans and animals alike; permeability defined their bodies' relationship with the material world. Furry behemoths, bears were obviously inhuman, but sinuous environments entered and exited them as well. They may have lacked language and dexterous thumbs, displayed little talent for constructing tools or wielding them, and operated according to instinct rather than reason or compassion, yet bears' vigor—like humans' vim—depended on the proper balance of humoral fluids. If bears ran too far too fast, for instance, their fluids could overheat and cause their systems to boil over.[2]

Bears and Americans suffered porous boundaries. Hide and bone encased their bile, phlegm, blood, and organs. Environments passed through both, and their common susceptibility to nature encouraged imaginative forays across the species line. Bears and Americans moved, ate, slept, hunted, and reproduced. She-bears suckled their cubs and took the time to educate them. As opposed to fish, horses, or iguanas, bears' eyes faced forward in their skulls. Bears and people could stare at one another. Both species rose up on two legs and stood on the soles of their paws/feet. Bears could tuck their tails and sit on their haunches like humans, and both mammals could rotate their forelimbs freely in their shoulder sockets. Bears and humans ingested almost anything—from blueberries and pine nuts to marrow and intestines, and their common diet generated piles of similar-looking excrement. Hunters marveled at the eerie resemblance between a small skinned bear and a dead human being.[3]

In nineteenth-century jokes, folktales, and regional satires, hunters exchanged places with their quarry. Malarial farmers adopted alligator–horse–snapping turtle stereotypes to shock travelers and middle-class prudes. Humorists celebrated backwoodsmen who growled and harrumphed, wore animal skins, and behaved like brutes. Along the Mississippi, whole populations crossed the species line and either amalgamated with or reverted to beasts. Their transmutations entertained onlookers. Americans purchased books, magazines, and theater tickets to enjoy the spectacle of marginal people devolving into wildlife.

Hugh Glass and his many coauthors seized upon the appeal of humans swapping places with animals when they built his bear tale. That Glass seemed the least eager among them should come as no surprise. The crossover into the beastly realm exacted a price. Americans observed a common ground with bears, but they ringed this space with razor wire. They demolished bears, chopped them up and processed them, selling their skin, flesh, and fat for profit. They also killed them to protect crops and livestock. When bears stumbled into barnyards and farm fields, they devoured marketable vegetables and protein. Their trespasses won them vermin status, and Americans slaughtered them as pests.

Nineteenth-century Americans thought all animals beneath them, and they persecuted animals that violated private property in agricultural landscapes with vicious enthusiasm. To be likened to an animal put a human at risk. Black slaves and Indians suffered terribly from their proximity to domesticated livestock and woodland creatures. Labeled unfeeling and unthinking, they dropped from the ranks of humanity, and their inferiority sanctioned brutal discipline and violent reprisals. White working-class hunters on the geographic fringes of the nation stood close to beasts as well. Steeped in nature, they took on the characteristics of the prey they slew for a living. Their work—the accumulation of pelts and skins for sale in urban markets—cast them outside, away from civil society.[4]

Two nineteenth-century black-bear hunters from the Mississippi watershed exemplified the risks and rewards of species confusion. Like Glass, Jim Doggett and David Crockett had uneven connections with reality. A complete fiction, Doggett sprang from the imagination of the southern humorist Thomas Bangs Thorpe, while Crockett was a half-truth cooked up by himself and the Kentuckian Thomas Chilton, a friend and fellow congressman. Both hunters killed black bears for profit, subsistence, and rural pacification. In the process, both slipped into bear territory and animal guises. Their intimacy with varmints embarrassed the men. They appeared stupid and feckless at times. Still, even as bears reduced them to punch lines, the animals empowered them as storytellers. They became regional spokespersons, natural tale spinners who inflicted humor as well as bore it.

Scholars of folklore and Americana have declared Doggett and Crockett stellar representatives of a national type: the comical backwoods blowhard. With guns in their hands and twinkles in their eyes, they epitomized the rambunctiousness of a young democracy where men from obscure backgrounds exploited their commonness (rather than hiding it) to achieve national prominence. Both Crockett and Doggett grew tall through encounters with large mammals in remote locales, but they conspired with American black bears, not grizzlies, and the subspecies' differences contributed to the men's stories and personas.

Black bears were subservient and ridiculous. The humans they resembled most were black slaves. When Hugh Glass entered the brush along the Yellowstone River and met his she-bear, the color of the long guard hairs on her back signaled his journey from one animal environment to another. When sunshine hit them right, the follicles of some bears looked white. To understand the difference the tint made, we need to first delve into Americans' relationships with the white bears' black cousins. Crockett and Doggett will act as our guides.[5]

David Crockett served three terms in Congress, died a national martyr at the Alamo, and provoked hundreds of almanacs, biographies, novels, children's books, movies, and pop tunes (not to mention raccoon-cap fads). For all his renown, however, he properly belonged to the human flotsam that labored along the Mississippi and its feeder streams. Born poor, he ran away from home and then from a string of masters. He married, moved west, and raised corn, pigs, and children. While many politicians sympathized with hardscrabble farmers, penniless squatters, and hungry settlers, Crockett lived their struggles. He was the most famous loser in Jacksonian America.

The corpses of black bears announced Crockett's economic and social marginality. Poverty compelled his hunting. The meat sustained his family; the hides bought luxury items (sugar, coffee) as well as supplies for more hunts (lead, gunpowder, and curing salt). Crockett launched his predator career in 1809, soon after the births of his eldest sons and his realization that he "was better at increasing [his] family than [his] fortune." While he hunted for profit the rest of his adult life, Crockett blossomed into an alpha nimrod very late in the autobiography he and Chilton crafted in 1834. They filled most of the text with reminiscences of his childhood and service in the Creek Indian War as well as accounts of his loves and losses (Polly, Crockett's first wife, died in 1816; he married his second, Elizabeth Patton, the following year). Bear hunting seized the narrative when Crockett approached middle age and national celebrity. In 1822, he turned thirty-six and drifted west, first to Shoal Creek in Lawrence County, Tennessee, and then to the cane-brakes along the Obion River near the Alabama border. His constituents elected him to the state legislature twice, in 1821 and 1823, setting the stage for his attempts at federal office in 1825 (a loss) and 1827 (a win), but his success as a getter of votes took a backseat in the narrative to his prowess as a gatherer of pelts and meat.[6]

The Obion was a weird place. A landscape of sloughs, marshes, rivers, and immense thickets of *Arundinaria,* a native species of bamboo, the region grew even more exotic in American eyes after a hurricane and several earthquakes knocked down a swath of forest and opened fissures in the ground in the 1810s. The "harricane," as Crockett called the wreckage, teemed with black bears. They foraged, hid, and hibernated in the broken timber and rotten logs. It was their ideal habitat, and their enthusiasm for the Obion abetted Crockett's and Chilton's political ambitions. The pair wrote the autobiography to distance Crockett from the nation's leading westerner, Andrew Jackson. Crockett began his career a Jackson man, but he disobeyed the general on several occasions, and by 1834 his recalcitrance had made him unwelcome in Jackson's Democratic Party. After winning the presidential election in 1828, Jackson, Chilton and Crockett argued, succumbed to his new environment. Washington overwhelmed the frontiersman, turning a defender of squatters and debtors into a champion of wealth and privilege. Years away from home had changed "Old Hickory" into "the Government."

Bear hunting launched Crockett in the opposite direction. In his pursuit of game, he sank into western Tennessee. In the winter of 1822, Crockett ran out of gunpowder and his family ran out of meat. Against Elizabeth's wishes, he hiked over five miles through snow and slush to retrieve a powder keg from his brother-in-law. He waded in sloughs until his "flesh had no feeling in it." Crockett's flirtation with hypothermia would have terrified his nineteenth-century readers. He not only tempted frostbite but physical devastation. By submerging his body in ice water, he flooded and cooled his dry and hot humors. The journey to his brother-in-law's and back might have ruined his body forever, catapulting him into off-kilter derangement. Instead, he survived the trip and killed more than a hundred bears that season. His passion for shedding animal blood counteracted the frigid liquid.

Near the end of his trek, when the extreme cold almost doused his inner flame, a path opened through the thin ice that coated the slough. He imagined its creator: a black bear had ventured out on the frozen water and crashed through; panicked, the beast scrambled to shore, leaving the aisle behind. The fantasy warmed Crockett: he "was determined to make war on him." He ran after his imagined bear only to discover his home. Elizabeth had sent out Crockett's "young man"—his slave—to hack through the ice and bring back what she assumed would be her husband's corpse. The boy ventured out as far as he could until the intense cold turned him back. He was the "bear."[7]

Black bears and black people rolled around together in Crockett's and Chilton's brains. Weeks after the slough episode, Crockett awoke one morning and told his hunting companions that he "had dreamed the night before of having a hard fight with a big black nigger, and I knowed it was a sign that I was to have a battle with a bear; for in bear country, I never know'd such a dream to fail." A vision of racial fisticuffs predicted a scrap with a big black animal, and Crockett did indeed find and kill his dream beast that day. His hounds treed a six-hundred-pound bear, "the biggest ever was seen in America." Two shots dropped the animal from his perch. The giant smashed a dog, but Crockett reloaded quickly and dispatched the bear with a third bullet to the head.[8]

Neither Crockett nor Chilton romanticized black bears—even enormous, predicted ones. The animals were subservient beings akin to black humans, and killing them, like fighting black people, earned whites no manly honor. In both cases, white combatants fought to establish their mastery over inferiors rather than defeat respected foes. Black bears struggled and died without intelligence or nobility. They responded to hunters and their packs of dogs with fear and evasion. When threatened, they scaled trees, swam rivers, and hid in logs and crevices. Their cowardice defanged them. Crockett professed a reluctance to have one "hug me altogether too close for comfort," but he displayed an astonishing lack of concern for his personal safety around bears. During one hunt in the "harricane," Crockett and his hounds treed a black bear at sunset. The darkness prevented him from shooting the animal from a safe distance, so he kindled a fire to burn down the tree. The smoke flushed the bear. The animal jumped down, and the hounds pushed him into a deep earthquake crack. Crockett shoved his gun in until he felt the bear and fired. The animal jumped out, fought the dogs for a while, and then retreated back into the crack. Crockett lost his gun in the ruckus. Unconcerned, he grabbed a stick and "concluded I would punch him awhile with that." Since the bear didn't respond to the pokes, he decided to jump into the crack. With the dogs keeping the bear occupied by barking at his head, Crockett reached out in the gloom, touched the bear's rump, and then his shoulder. He lunged with his "long knife" and "stuck him right through the heart." The animal died in his arms.[9]

The Obion country, with its fissures and tree falls, created moments of violent intimacy. Hunters crawled into caves, logs, and hollows to attack hibernating bears. Bears and men startled one another in canebrakes and brambles, triggering bouts of hand-to-paw combat. Following their encounters, humans stripped the bears of skin and flesh, wearing the first and ingesting the second. People and animals came together in a worrisome fashion. When Crockett emerged from this landscape to run for Congress, he declared his environmental Americanism: he was "the bear hunter; the man from the cane." Yet the sojourn in the wilds that turned him into a natural nationalist also compromised his racial identity. He "crept out of the cane, to see what discoveries I could make among the white folks." In the forest hunting animals, Crockett labored beyond white society. He had chased after black bears and dreamed of black men for so long that he no longer felt at ease among white people.[10]

Chilton and Crockett flirted with the boundaries of class, race, and humanity to foist their creation—the backwoods political celebrity—on the voting and book-buying public. They planted Crockett firmly on the margins of America, setting him against the men at the center, the Democrats who "hunted [him] down like a wild varmint" in the press. Crockett served "the people" rather than the party. He swore he would never wear a collar with a tag that read "My Dog" followed by "Andrew Jackson." Crockett belonged to common folks, and his prodigious talent for hunting as well as his utter ineptitude for business proved it. The last adventure recounted in the narrative involved barrel staves, not black bears. Crockett and some associates loaded two boats with thirty thousand staves cut from the trees along the Obion River. They intended to ship them to New Orleans and sell them for a hefty profit. The Mississippi River, however, sank the boats and nearly killed Crockett. He was in the cabin of one of the vessels during the wreck. The collision blocked the exit, and the boatmen saved him by hauling his body out a small window. The sides of the hole stripped the clothes from his back and scratched the length of his body. He "was literally skinned like a rabbit." Capitalism and the river had downgraded the mighty bear hunter to a shivering bunny.[11]

Ambitious men, Chilton and Crockett trusted the spectacle of western impoverishment. They wrote the autobiography in part to test the waters for Crockett's run as the presidential nominee of the Whig Party. But the Whigs never seriously considered Crockett. How could they? The more fame he acquired, the goofier he became. Playwrights, almanac publishers, and unauthorized biographers treed the politician and turned him into a Bunyanesque joke. When they got through with him, he ripped the tales off comets, rode lightning bolts, and wrestled monsters. He also attacked the powerless. A rank bigot, "Davy" Crockett demeaned and hated African Americans. The real Crockett escaped to Texas in 1836 to resurrect his political career and restore some gravitas to his image.[12]

Black bears helped construct Crockett's predicament. Animal familiars, they roamed the space between humans and nature, a frontier they shared with black people. This proximity explained why Crockett interpreted a "fight with a nigger" as a sign for a successful bear hunt: black humans and black bears inhabited the same niche in the American social order. Where you found one, you found the other. Crockett the hunter chased after them both. Chilton and Crockett signaled the commonness of their political creation with animal metaphors. At different moments "the man from the cane" transmogrified into a "beaver," "a wild varmint," and a "rabbit." The only animal identity he refused was Jackson's dog. The metaphors signaled Crockett's closeness to nature. An uneducated backwoodsman, he lived near the species divide, and he could slip to the other side. Laughter softened the implications of this passage. Chilton and Crockett winked at their readers when they wrote "varmint," but they misjudged the effectiveness of their humor. Tipping readers off when they associated with animals and slaves that they were only joking nevertheless raised alarms in a nation worried about confidence men who preyed on victims' trust and sincerity.[13]

Crockett addressed these anxieties with more jokes. On the stump, he famously compared his smile to a rival's. Crockett admitted he had a mighty grin. Raccoons leapt from trees when he hit them with it. During one of his first political campaigns, though, he had to admit that his opponent had an even stronger smile. "Therefore," he told audiences at his stump speeches, "be wide awake—look sharp—don't let him grin you out of your votes." Crockett, the anecdote implied, was too good-natured to use his charm on human beings. Hunting, his political biography suggested, expressed and confined Crockett's robust appetite for violence and lies. He tricked and killed animals instead of men. He shot enormous black bears while he dreamed of punching black people. The charity he showed the members of his species, however, rested on opposing ideas that Chilton and Crockett never could quite balance. They tried to convince voters that Crockett was smart enough to deflate haughty Democrats while at the same time too dumb to trick the public.[14]

Jim Doggett took Crockett's predatory charm to its logical extreme. The southern humorist Robert Bangs Thorpe invented Doggett in 1841 and sold him to highbrow readers on the East Coast. Doggett appeared in William T. Porter's *Spirit of the Times*, a literary and sporting magazine that also published frontier tales. Doggett resembled Crockett. He hunted on the margins of nature, and long exposure to wild animals made him stupid, innocent, and charismatic. Like Crockett, he was an environmental American who excelled at tale telling.

Doggett related a series of wild adventures in Thorpe's short story "The Big Bear of Arkansas." In Arkansas, Thorpe reported, nature outgrew logic. The trees were gigantic, the rivers miles wide, and the mosquitoes wielded swordlike snouts that drained "Yankees" dry. But no animal reached grander proportions than the black bear Doggett hunted down in the story's finale. Doggett was the best hunter in the region. When "varmints grew over-cunning by being fooled with by greenhorn hunters, and by this means got troublesome," the abused community sent for him. The bear was equally credentialed. He stood eight inches taller than any black bear along the Mississippi River. An accomplished robber, he infiltrated corncribs and devoured wandering pigs.[15]

Buzzards circling hog corpses helped Doggett locate the bear, and when he found him, he chased after "the big critter" on horseback with his hounds in the lead. The bear, however, enjoyed long runs, and after several pursuits and an especially taxing eighteen-mile sprint, the dogs and horse broke down. These failures wore on Doggett. "Missing the bear so often took hold of [his] vitals," and he "wasted away." He became obsessed, seeing the bruin "in every thing [he] did." His world flipped upside down; instead of tracking the bear, the bear stalked him.[16]

Doggett relates several near misses and his growing frustration. He treed the bear with the aid of a greenhorn companion. The greenhorn, not knowing better, shot the animal in the head. The bullet glanced off the bear's skull, enraging rather than disabling the target. The bear leapt over the ring of hounds surrounding the tree, rumbled to a nearby lake, and swam to an island near its center. The canines and the hunters paddled after him. The dogs cornered the bear in a thicket, and when it dashed for the water once more, the men fired and managed to kill it. Bowie knife drawn, the master hunter approached his nemesis. But this bear was too small, and female. It was not "THAT Bar." Doggett went home and informed his neighbors that he would go after "the devil" one last time. If he failed, they could divide up his settlement. He, echoing Crockett, was moving to Texas.[17]

The night before the hunt, the man cleaned his rifle and placed "caps" in every one of his pockets to insure quick and easy access to dry gunpowder. He woke early and stumbled out of his cabin to relieve himself in the woods, taking his gun and his favorite hound with him as was his habit. The bear approached him as he squatted in the morning dew. Doggett rose, fired, and fell to the ground, his "inexpressibles" wrapped around his ankles. The bear died this time, but the triumph felt empty. "I never liked the way I hunted him . . . I never could understand, and I never was satisfied at his giving in *so easy at last*." Finally, he concluded that the bear was "a creation bar," "*an unhuntable bar, and died when his time come*" (emphasis in original).[18]

A creation bear. This sounds like a biblical reference, but the term could apply as easily to the effects the bear adventure had on the hunter. Doggett's tussle with a mythological animal turned him into a legendary creature. He, not the unhuntable beast, was "the Big Bar of Arkansas." A fabulous storyteller, the human Big Bar rumbled into the saloon on a

Mississippi river steamboat. Thorpe's narrator, a passenger and onlooker, described the tableau—another nineteenth-century version of the bar scene lampooned in Melville's *Confidence-Man*. A peddler from New England jostled against a southern planter. A gambler sat next to a bishop. The boat contained "men from every State of the Union, and from every portion of the globe." The Big Bar of Arkansas represented the regional subspecies, the "half-horse and half-alligator" men from the "old Mississippi." His animal pedigree showed on his face. His eyes twinkled, betraying his "good natured" simplicity. The man-bear was loud, profane, funny, and irresistible.[19]

He was also less than a person. He was a caricature. The Big Bar roamed the southern backcountry with violent, uneducated, flamboyant, and semifictionalized colleagues like Crockett, Mike Fink, Simon Suggs, and Sut Lovingood.[20] But Doggett's black bear opponent was different. Huge, smart, and fearless, THAT Bar broke free of the engrained behaviors that defined his subspecies as inferior vermin. Larger than any other black bear, larger than life itself, the death of the "creation bar" deepened the Big Bar, bringing a cartoon to the cusp of revelation. Struggling to comprehend the meaning of the animal's surrender, the hunter confronted a "mystery" that "made a strong impression on his mind." The affair prompted "superstitious awe." A common reaction among backcountry folk, Thorpe reports, when faced with "anything out of their daily experience." By killing the mythical bear, the Big Bar of Arkansas became aware of something beyond his world. And since this was a fantasy world created by Thorpe, the animal's death jars the Big Bar out of character. He ends the story a self-reflective regional stereotype, a postmodern half horse and half alligator that knows some mysterious author exists behind the scenes of his humorous existence.[21]

THAT Bar created the Big Bar, but Doggett created THAT Bar just as Thorpe created Doggett. A daisy chain of generative lies, "The Big Bear of Arkansas" poked fun at the half-serious attempts of writers like Chilton and Crockett to convert western bear hunters into respectable national heroes. A superb dispatcher of animal souls, Doggett was an even better assailant of the truth. He didn't even hide his dissimulation. He dropped hints throughout the story to alert his listeners to his game. He told them the bear was a creation, and as the literary scholar John

Bryant has noted, "Jim's 'character development' is the setup of a hoax; all that he really bears is his bottom." It was all crap, Crockett included. Thorpe took a potshot at the famous Tennessean with the Big Bar's human name. By replacing "Crock" with "Dogg," the humorist achieved the species transference Crockett and Chilton said they'd never accept. He turned the man from the cane into a canine.[22]

Thorpe's "Big Bar" anticipated Melville's Pitch. Both absorbed the environmental lessons of the Mississippi Valley. They knew its nature, and they reported their findings to eastern audiences that didn't want to accept their wisdom. Travelers, greenhorns, and immigrants hoped that Doggett and Pitch would reveal the metaphysics of western nature. They wanted the hunters to tell them that America, faith, love, philanthropy, or sublimity could be found in the trees, stones, creeks, and animals on their nation's fringes. A consummate grouch, Pitch knocked down these allegorical fantasies quickly by pointing out that cholera was as natural as the "yarbs" doctors prescribed to cure it. The Big Bar toyed with his audience longer. He reeled them into his confidence with tall tales of forty-pound turkeys, boulder-sized turnips, and corn plants that grew so vigorously they caused pigs to die from concussions when their stalks burst from the fertile soil. He built up to his hunting story by emphasizing his good-natured simplicity. He was too dumb and humorous to perpetrate a fraud; therefore, his audience could trust the education THAT Bar gave him. Through its Christlike sacrifice, the unhuntable animal reached the metaphoric stature that some nineteenth-century Americans were seeking in western nature. But, alas, twisted long johns deserved more credit for flooring the Big Bar than celestial inspiration. That was the joke: black bruins couldn't stand in for God or truth or salvation. They were lowly creatures, too puny and too cowardly to bear the weight of the universe.

Farther out West, however, other hunters encountered other bears with more metaphysical potential. Grizzly bears' massive size and social behavior (their tendency to bully smaller subordinates, including humans) fascinated the Americans who lurched into the region in the early nineteenth century. Unlike their smaller cousins, grizzlies sometimes

attacked people, and their ferocity astonished onlookers more accus-
tomed to laughing at bears than fearing them. Grizzly bear teeth and
claws inscribed flesh, and their victims puzzled over the marks. What
was the character of these creatures? Were they funny, inferior animals
or soul-crunching monsters? What did their size and aggressiveness say
about the nature of the Missouri River Valley and the Rocky Mountains? Did the scars they doled out weaken or fortify the humans who
bore them? Could these injuries help marginal men lay claim to the
West and the nation through environmental Americanism? Or did they
symbolize loss—the disappearance and dissipation of the very things
the humans wanted to secure and enhance: their property, their nation,
their whiteness, their manhood, and their humanity?

Instead of running from the dangerous omnivores, American hunters encircled them, seeking answers. Their investigations centered on
the bears' bodies, and their appraisals followed a procedure. First, they
looked for difference. How were these bears distinct from the bears they
knew? Second, they considered sameness. They may have been extraor-
dinarily large, angry, and grizzled animals, but they were still animals.
Finally, they attempted to plug grizzly bears and the environmental
Americans they created into the story of natural nationalism. The animals and the men reached celebrity together, and they both endured
rendering and processing to get there: neither arrived on the American
main stage whole.

The Americans could hardly miss the bears' most distinctive trait—
their size. Girth organized grizzly society. Males could weigh from 800
to 1,000 pounds, while females averaged 350 to 400 pounds. The animals' huge bodies suited their lifestyle. Grizzly bears were magnificent
scroungers, building enormous bodies on tubers, leaves, berries, rodents, and carrion. In the spring and summer, they wallowed in landscapes brimming with calories and digested the energy other organisms
invested in fruit, roots, and muscle.[23]

Grizzly bears grew large for two reasons: they needed a store of fat
to survive their winter hibernation, and they needed to be big to survive
each other. Large males continually jostled for dominance, brutalizing
one another in the process. The biggest and toughest won their choice
of food resources, territories, and mating partners. The bears' hierarchy

rewarded bigness across generations as large bears spread more genes than their smaller rivals. Thus, grizzly society seems classically Darwinian: the strong flourish, cementing their genetic legacies through tooth-and-claw competition.[24]

But there were twists in the bears' social system. The same dominance hierarchy that rewarded burly males threatened their immature offspring. In a society organized around size, diminutive cubs were in constant peril from aggressive adults. Young bears needed time to put on weight, and it was their mothers that bought them this time. While half the size of the slightest boars, grizzly mothers ascended the ranks of the bear hierarchy to reach a level just below the alpha male, and they established their dominion through chilling displays of ferocity. In 1963, a grizzly sow in Yellowstone National Park attacked a pickup truck that had inadvertently driven between her and her cubs. She slammed into the vehicle's front fender with enough force to shatter her own spine. Growing cubs huddled under this maternal determination for two years until they were big enough to fend for themselves. Grizzly mothers submitted to alpha males, but the rest of beardom deferred to cub-rearing sows.[25]

Long before Hugh Glass discovered the wrath of a she-bear protecting her cubs, grizzlies' size and ferocity were impressing American onlookers. They described the bears' nature in a language of difference that felt natural to them: they assigned the mammals a color. The 1803–6 Lewis and Clark expedition, echoing earlier reports, publicized the animals' size and ferocity but also their whiteness. The color signaled the grizzlies' anatomical and behavioral difference from black bears—huge versus small, bellicose versus docile—and the term indicated the Americans' willingness to equate size and aggression with eminence. (Massive North American bears actually came in many colors—black, brown, white, and mottled or grizzled combinations. Today, experts lump polar, grizzly, and brown bears into the same species: *Ursus arctos*. Hair tint isn't a meaningful indicator of genetic or ecological variation; whiteness meant more to the Americans than to the bears.) If black bears resembled slaves and servants, then white bears took after masters, sometimes literally. Grizzly bears' lethal and unpredictable nature corresponded with their social stature. They weren't lowly, cowering creatures but massive spectacles of western-ness. American authors knew that readers would want to get near them, and they relied on mountain men to bring them in close. The hunters introduced the grizzlies to the nation through their stories, and since many of them were as mottled as the bears, the encounters broached a question. If western nature could turn eastern Americans into a new race, could white bears alter the racial composition of their human adversaries? Could they turn a mulatto hunter into a white one?

James Beckwourth thought so. In the summer of 1825, Beckwourth killed a charging grizzly with a single shot. Earlier, the "enormous" bear had attacked Baptiste, an Ashley employee. The animal knocked him off his horse, flayed his head "completely," and inflicted "several dangerous wounds in various parts of his body." After the bear ran off, Beckwourth found the man and helped carry him back to camp. As soon as he sat him down, he heard a "great rush of horses" and saw "a party of our half-breeds" stampeding the bear toward him. Beckwourth froze, "so terrified that I hardly know whether I was standing on the ground or was in a tree." The bear closed in, sniffed the gush of blood coming from Baptiste, and paused. Beckwourth seized his gun and dropped the creature with a bullet through the heart.[26]

Beckwourth's encounter had all the ingredients for a grizzly reckoning. In 1834, the trapper Osborne Russell also destroyed a mammoth white bear with a shot to the heart. Instead of feeling triumphant, however, Russell "trembled as if I had an ague fit for half an hour." He and his "mulatto" companion butchered the animal into fat, meat, and skin. The trophies left Russell feeling even more empty and scared. Russell pursued the bear to become "acquainted with the nature of these animals," and he came away with the "lisson" many hunters gleaned after violent episodes: you trifled with grizzly bears at your peril. He vowed "never to molest another wounded grizzly bear in a marsh or a thicket."[27]

Beckwourth's ursine wisdom, though, veered in the opposite direction. Following Baptiste's mauling and his own escape from the charging boar, he trifled with the next bear he met. He belittled a captive grizzly bear, proclaiming his eminence through dominating a white animal. Unlike Crockett, who grew less white through his association with black bears, Beckwourth whitened himself by blackening a grizzly. He seized the role of master by making a bear his slave.

In the fall of 1825, on their way back to St. Louis, Ashley's company met up with a U.S. Army expedition commanded by General Henry Atkinson and Indian Agent Benjamin O'Fallon. Also headed east, they had just finished a summer tour of the tribes along the Missouri River. Atkinson and O'Fallon negotiated treaties while their troops paraded American muscle. Eager to protect the year's harvest in beaver pelts, traders flocked to the protection of the federal guns. Joshua Pilcher, head of the Missouri Fur Company, and his hunters had already joined the party; now Ashley added himself and his employees. Beckwourth recalled the soldiers fondly. During the day, he and the other mountain men hunted buffalo and deer for them. At night, "the soldiers listened with astonishment to [their] wild adventures" and fed them whiskey. At Fort Kiowa, Pilcher introduced another source of amusement. He gave Ashley a "large grizzly bear for a plaything." Chained to the cargo box of one of the keelboats, the bear "seemed to think himself captain; he was more imperious in his orders than a commodore on a foreign station." The men teased him but stayed off his deck.[28]

When the expedition reached St. Louis, the job of escorting the animal off the boat fell to Beckwourth. As usual, he attributed snagging this assignment to his superior strength and valor. Ashley begged his master hunter to remove the monster blocking the access to his bales of pelts. Beckwourth grabbed a stick, unchained the bear, and spoke "sharply to him." Cowed, the animal "looked" him "in the eyes for a moment, and, giving a low whine, drooped his head." The pair walked through town and stopped at Major Thomas Biddle's house. Beckwourth fastened the grizzly to an apple tree in the yard. Biddle came out, spotted Ashley's attempt at a humorous regift, and quaked with fear. His new "pet" swatted a pig that wandered in too close and the swine flew into the street, "not a whole bone [left] in his body." The major invited Beckwourth in for a drink, and the men toasted their health while the bear fumed.[29]

The grizzly pet slipped into Beckwourth's narrative as comic relief. The joke capped an arduous year in the mountains as well as the seventh chapter of his life story. A humanized animal clown, the grizzly bear amused Beckwourth and his readers with his pretensions. Though captured, chained, and exchanged as an item, he continued to resist. He raged like a free man—a master, a captain, or a commodore—at his imprisonment. He was a lowly animal at war with his place in the chain of being. The grizzly made powerful men quiver. He brought them down, for a short while. People could smile because they knew the bear's destiny. In time, Biddle or one of his underlings would shoot him, ending the "monarch's" reign.

The bear fit into an American tradition of humor that highlighted the subordination of slaves and animals by endowing them with a comical superiority. Americans named dogs and slaves Caesar, Venus, Prince, or Duchess. They told stories of black bears unmanning rural patriarchs and slaves outwitting naïve masters. The humor depended on the shared assumption of white storytellers and their audiences that they knew the true nature of animals and African Americans. They enjoyed the creatures' attempts to beat and fool them, confident in the permanence of their own nature—their skin color, their gender, their humanity. Americans biologized their social rankings along with their nation, which gave working-class hunters like James Beckwourth some leverage. Their transformed bodies signaled the rise of a uniquely American nation in the West. Beckwourth displayed his natural prowess when he subdued the grizzly bear. Had he stayed a blacksmith's apprentice, he would have been on the wharf trembling with the rest of St. Louis. Instead, he mastered the animal, delivering him to Biddle in chains like a slave. The grizzly bowed to Beckwourth's new western body—his new nature—and so did his white superiors. The bear terrified Ashley and Biddle. By manhandling the animal, Beckwourth bettered them and stepped into their rank. He and Biddle toasted the soundness of their equal bodies.[30]

Well, maybe they did. It's hard to know what Biddle thought. The humor in the anecdote muddied its meaning. Beckwourth (and Bonner) wanted his audience to laugh at white men trembling before a chained animal, but their laughter could just as easily have been directed at him. Beckwourth played the master to the bear's slave, yet the hunter and the beast also resembled each other. The West emboldened

Beckwourth. After he established his physical toughness, he refused to bow to bosses who mistook him for a groom or a mulatto. Like the bear chained to the cargo box, Beckwourth snarled at his natural superiors. Neither the bear nor the man accepted the eastern paradigm of racial or species dominance. Their spectacular bodies—big, strong, and lethal—whitened them. Still, while their physiques drew crowds, the man and the animal attracted ridicule as well. Both faced the same problem: the larger they grew, the more ridiculous they appeared. Audiences enjoyed watching them climb the social and racial hierarchy. They knew the structure's durability: it would bear the weight of a hunter and a grizzly scrambling to the top. They laughed in anticipation of their fall.

Audiences could hoist Beckwourth on his own petard because they shared his estimation of grizzly bears' animal status. Big and aggressive, the white bears were magnificent, but they were inferior nonhumans nonetheless. The dual nature of grizzly bears—the simultaneity of their physical power and their animal subordination—puzzled Americans and confused their depictions of them. Were they funny inferiors like black bears, or serious foes, more likely to crack your skull and slurp your brain than offer you comic relief? Should men treat them with respect or mess with them? The mountain men split their opinions and divided their reactions. They joked and they trembled.

The ferocity of grizzly bears sometimes darkened western hunting stories to the point where existential terror replaced hearty backslaps and underwear-induced pratfalls. The bears could strip away grins and force the Americans to confront the possibility of being consumed by the nature they sought to convert into trade items. In 1823, the same season Glass met his bear, Jedediah Smith tangled with his own. Ashley put Smith in charge of the group that split with Andrew Henry's contingent following the Arikara debacle. James Clyman accompanied the expedition, and he wrote about the attack. The men were in the bushes, walking their packhorses single file in the "brushy bottom" of the Powder River. The "Grissly" charged the middle of the column, then turned and ran up the line. In the lead, Smith emerged from a thicket, pivoted toward the ruckus, and came "face to face" with a monster. The bear rose and clamped its jaws around his head. The animal shook him and tossed him to the ground. Aiming for the torso, he bit Smith's shot pouch and butcher knife instead, snapping the belt attaching them to his body.[31]

Clyman's narrative leaves the grizzly here. Presumably, the hunters killed the bear. Clyman mentions that "he" broke the knife and "ball pouch" and in the process cracked several of "his" ribs, "cutting his head badly." The confusion of third-person pronouns inadvertently collapses the identities of the bear and the man, underwriting the confusion and horror of the attack—or, rather, the memory of it. Clyman recalled the event forty-eight years later, from his farm in Napa Valley, California. Time, however, had not softened his recollection of what happened next. Together, Clyman and Smith performed one of the more hard-core acts of first aid in American history. As Smith lay bleeding, his scalp lacerated horribly, his men dithered. None of them had any "surgical Knowledge," and none wanted to touch the captain. Smith ordered two men to fetch some water and asked Clyman if he had a needle and thread. He did; scissors, too. The trapper cut the hair away from the wounds and saw for the first time that Smith's right ear was no longer attached to his head. It flapped on the "outer rim" of a "white" furrow the bear's incisor had carved in his scalp. Clyman sewed the cut, but when he reached the mutilated ear, he told his patient that there was nothing he could do; might he trim the crumple off? "O," cried Smith, "you must try to stich [it] up some way or another." Holding the bits of flesh together with one hand, Clyman passed the needle "through and through and over and over" until a nub appeared.[32]

Why was Jedediah Smith so attached to his ear? His willingness to undergo wilderness reconstructive surgery without painkillers has repeatedly bowled over historians, biographers, and enthusiasts of all things mountain manly. The bear made him an American badass, a symbol of national grit, masculinity, and power. "Jedediah," wrote one historian, "bore the marks of the encounter to the end of his life . . . these were honorable scars." Clyman, however, didn't interpret the wounds this way. In fact, he didn't ponder them at all in print. He ended the episode ruminating on the bear's interior makeup rather than his captain's state of mind. Smith's mauling "gave us a lisson on the charcter of the grissly Baare which we did not forget." Like Daniel Potts, he abandoned his hero and concentrated on the animal instead.[33]

As a reporter, Clyman rarely indulged in melodrama. He also eschewed punctuation; his sentences tend to plunge into one another, creating a drone that flattens the difference between mundane events and violent catastrophes. Smith's "O," therefore, popped out, like a spew of emotion. It commanded attention. Smith, Clyman, and their fellow hunters read scars as indicators of power. They knew masters and bosses memorized distinctive physical features and identified servants and slaves through the marks on their bodies. They also knew scars elevated their place in stories of western endurance and survival. Blemishes could enslave their hosts or single them out for national glory. The grizzly that attacked Smith raised a quandary: Were the furrows, flaps, and gashes he carved into his victim signs of American genius or symptoms of degradation? Smith answered with his "O." He would endure the searing pain of amateur needlework to repair his damaged head. For him—and for many mountain men—losing parts of their faces to an animal was the end of their environmental Americanism.[34]

Humans and bears shared expressive faces. Bears signaled their moods with their ears (pinned back forecasted aggression). Humans registered anger through cues and gestures as well, but they attributed far more portent to their faces. They mixed culture into the genetic arrangement of lips, eyes, noses, chins, foreheads, hair, brows, and cheeks to make their faces the physical embodiment of their selves. Though highly evolved body linguists, bears would never sprout goatees, apply makeup, or don wigs. Only humans affixed ideas like beauty, individuality, and worthiness to their surface features. Still, bears could perform tricks with their faces that people couldn't—like snap femurs with them. Large grizzly bears could generate twelve hundred pounds of pressure per square inch with their massive jaw muscles. Their bite force rivaled gorillas' mashing power but fell short of the grabbing and shearing talents of wolves and large cats. Bears rooted and scavenged more than these strict carnivores, and they rarely had to bring down prey larger than themselves. Yet, while weaker than some, grizzly bears' jaws were bigger than almost all their rivals'. A wolf skull—or a human head—fits comfortably in their maws. Their giant muzzles transformed their faces into devastating weapons as well as signaling devices, and bears attacked each other's heads during fights to disable the brutal snouts. When startled bears rushed human adversaries, they zeroed in on their heads and jaws as well. Bears rearranged human faces, turning the seat of identity into a battleground. Grizzly bears' tendency to attack the epicenter of human reason, individuality, and personhood highlighted the animals' remarkable ferocity and thus their distinctiveness. They embodied the far West, and their bites left regional impressions. But victims and onlookers couldn't embrace these carvings of exceptionalism without reservations. The scars that turned Jedediah Smith and Hugh Glass into singular Americans made them and their coworkers queasy.[35]

On November 13, 1821, Lewis Dawson probed the inside of a grizzly bear's mouth with his head. A hunter, Dawson supplied meat to the U.S.-government-sponsored "voyage of adventure and discovery" up the Arkansas River to the Rocky Mountains. Colonel Hugh Glenn and Major Jacob Fowler commanded the expedition; Fowler served as the group's journalist. Camped in brush along the Purgatory River shortly after spotting the "Spanish peaks" of the Sangre de Cristo Mountains in the distance, the men scattered to hunt and pick grapes. Fowler heard a gunshot followed by "the Cry of a White Bare." Colonel Glenn grabbed his gun and organized the pursuit of the wounded beast. Glenn, Dawson, and three others charged into the thicket to flush their quarry. The bear hid until the humans drew close, then leapt from the undergrowth and snagged Dawson. The bear ravaged his body while Glenn fiddled with his gun. The baying of a dog joined the "dredfull Screams." The dog rushed into the fray and drew the bear's attention. Dawson rose, staggered threes steps, and the bear tackled him again. Obsessed, the animal seemed "intent upon his destruction." The dog harassed the bear a second time, giving Glenn and the resilient Dawson time to scramble up a tree. Glenn went up first, followed by Dawson, followed by the bear. The animal grabbed one leg while the Colonel hooked the other. The two played tug until Glenn managed to swing his gun down and fire it. The bear fell, and other hunters rushed to the scene and killed the beast.[36]

Fowler examined Dawson's injuries. The bear had clenched the man's head in its mouth twice without delivering a killing bite. When "the monster give the Crush that was to mash the man's head," the skull would slip out, gouging deep valleys in the scalp. When the hunters examined the animal's teeth, they discovered just one intact incisor; the others had rotted away. The missing teeth saved Dawson—for a while. The men sewed up his wounds. Deep cuts grooved his head. For a while, Fowler thought he might recover. Dawson "Retained His under Standing" during the surgery and talked "cheerfully"—though he kept saying that he heard his skull break in the bear's jaws. Given the boar's dental health, Fowler thought this unlikely. The next day, however, Dawson became "Restless and Some What Delirious." Fowler took a closer look at his head and found a "hole in the upper part of His Wright temple" where his brains were leaking out. The caregivers "then So-posed that he did Heare His Skull Break." Dawson perished the third night after the attack. The others buried him under a pile of logs to keep wolves and bears from eating the corpse.[37]

Dawson's attack resembled Glass's. None of those who witnessed Glass's incident wrote about it, but details spread by word of mouth. James Clyman heard the story and reported his version to a California newspaper years later. As with Dawson's episode, a bullet launched a rampage. The sow charged Glass after he shot her. He tried to climb a tree, but she "caught him and hauled [him] to the ground tearing and lacerating his body in fearful rate." Glass and the bear became so en-tangled that the rescuers who sprinted to noise of the fight held their fire: they couldn't see where the man ended and the bear began. After a while, the animal calmed and turned away from the body. Two or three hunters squeezed off rounds. The sting from this new torment she took out on Glass, giving him a "second mutilation." The bear settled again, and more balls punctured her skin. She pawed at Glass one final time, then collapsed dead on top him.[38]

Clyman ends the story here, but Fowler's account predicts the next part. Following attacks, onlookers pored over the bodies of men and bears for answers. They comforted victims, staunched their bleeding, and sutured their cuts. They noted signs of delirium or cheerfulness. They wondered if the injured men would return to their jobs or enter the ground. Bears effectively dragged their victims away from human society. The injured began to resemble their adversaries more than their comrades; laid side by side, bear and human casualties bled together. The spectacle mesmerized witnesses, and they searched the bodies for conceptual handholds. What did the trauma mean? One thing was sure: the bears were to blame. Their aggression and orneriness, not the Americans' inability to stay out of the bushes or their itchy trigger fingers, caused violent misadventures. Thus, witnesses paid special attention to the animals' corpses in the aftermath of such encounters. That's why the bears often subsumed their human victims in the reports. The animals held the answers; plus, the men were hard to look at. Even if they survived, they would be more western and American but also less human.

The Americans quizzed grizzly bodies. They hypothesized that an essential ferocity drove white bears to ambush them, and they located that ferocity in the animals' flesh, especially in their fat. Size differentiated "grizzled" bears from black ones, and the Americans measured size in both body weight and height, which they tended to exaggerate, and in pounds of marketable grease. The grizzlies' fat was doubly intriguing because the gelatinous tissue collected rifle balls. At the end of a skirmish, when butchers dressed the corpses, five, nine, or sometimes a dozen lead spheres collected in the bottoms of their fat rendering pots. After they pulled the hide off Lewis Dawson's killer, for instance, they skinned the bear and investigated the insides. Fowler declared "him a large fat animal." The meat, however, was funky. The tissue smelled of "Pole cat so Strong" the men refused to eat it. Did this internal corruption explain the assault? The hunters tossed the muscle aside after melting the fat and packing the "grease" into deerskin pouches. The bear's pelt and the animal's stored winter calories accompanied the expedition into the mountains, while Dawson's body rotted beside the mound of skunky bear flesh. Later, when the men considered Dawson's fate, they could pull out the bear skin and recall that terrible encounter.[39]

Bear parts and products defined grizzly bears' split nature—their western eminence and their animal subordination. James Clyman used body parts as a yardstick to measure the stature of a California grizzly he saw killed and processed in the 1840s. The animal absorbed nine rifle balls before he succumbed. The bullets had "taken good effect but owing to the greate thickness of the fat on his sides only one had passed in to his lungs." The bear, Clyman reported, was "a noble animal," yielding "more than three Hundred pounds of oil." The amount of oil he gave and number of projectiles he withstood defined the bear's greatness. American hunters discovered and harvested grizzly nobility by isolating and ganging up on the creatures. They surrounded individuals and took turns "one firing at a time in slow succession." Stung and confused, the bear "kept continually fighting the ball holes . . . so that he has no time to attact the hunters until it is to late." Hunting in packs, humans would drive grizzly bears toward extinction in the next century.[40]

The circle hunts and the bear parts and products they yielded solved the Americans' white-bear conundrum. What was the nature of grizzly bears? They were growling ambiguities—frightful commodities, magnificent vermin. They were awesome and disposable, noble creatures and grease bags. This solution had negative implications for the men remade by bears. Clyman hinted at the danger in his comments about the California grizzly. For him and many citizens of the United States, the West was a staging ground for economic and cultural transmutations. Hunters entered the region and converted beavers, bears, wolves, cats, and bison into commodities. Authors preyed on the hunters and merchandised the lucky few nature reworked into environmental Americans. Both bears and men traveled distances. A bear born and reared on the Yellowstone River might visit St. Louis or London as a rug. A grungy hunter might show up at a literary salon in downtown Philadelphia as a topic of conversation. Severe pain accompanied the bears' and hunters' passage between forms. Rifle balls and lacerations measured their greatness. Their bodies were their tickets into global markets. While keenly interested in physical transformations, Americans didn't want to reside near jaws that bit or mouths that talked back; they sought to own the distilled versions of western beings. The Americans possessed metaphysical aspirations for their West. They aimed to take the land and its people, animals, forests, rocks, and streams, and turn them into something else—grease, farms, Christians, laborers, hides, boards, minerals, reservoirs, and literary analogies.

Still, the metaphysics of bear hunting didn't appeal to everyone. Charles Wilkins Webber satirized the notion of finding transcendence chasing grizzlies in his 1845 short story set in the San Saba hills, and several celebrity mountain men balked at the revisionist impulse of U.S. imperialism. These hunter/storytellers hoped to exploit their environmental Americanism in print, but they declined the route to natural nationalism offered by Crockett and Thorpe. The last things they wanted to become were far western "Big Bars." Instead of embracing their social proximity to bears, they distanced their identities from the animals, using race and humor to create space. Some hunters, like James Beckwourth, blackened white bears; others ridiculed grizzlies and poked fun at men who feared them. Each tried to push back from the species divide and protect their humanity, their manhood, and their whiteness.

In May 1805, Meriwether Lewis reported that his men were "keen for action with the bear" and that he hoped "these gentlemen [his nickname for grizzlies] will give us some amusement shortly." Later that summer, after tangling with several huge white bears that absorbed musket balls like flea bites and nearly killed several hunters, Lewis could still describe a bear hunt as a "frolick." Mountain men and their coauthors portrayed pack-hunting grizzly bears as a sport and an entertainment. Joe Meek, for example, had a lot of fun around grizzlies. He laughed off attacks; he teased companions for looking silly while running from bears; and, in one instance, he guffawed from a treetop as a giant bear rummaged through his campsite and snuffled at a colleague pretending to sleep under a blanket.[41]

The humor surrounding grizzlies reflected the duality of Americans' understanding of them. They were white animals. Lewis's "gentlemen" nickname indicated the twin pathways down which American sentiments could run. A straightforward reading of the quip reflected the bears' distinctive size and audacious behavior. Set next to cowering black bears, grizzlies exuded lordliness. But insert a wink and a nudge, and "gentleman" took on sinister overtones. American gentlemen did not bite off each other's faces or fire dozens of rifle balls into one another. They engaged in respectful mayhem. They dueled according to the rules of honor. Lewis and his men didn't honor grizzly bears. They pummeled them like social inferiors—tweaked their noses, in effect— and laughed at their cruelty.

The record of grizzly bear encounters overflowed with sick humor.

The mountain man Isaac Rose displayed a special flair for bear atrocities. Rose, a hunter and trapper employed by the Boston merchant Nathaniel Wyeth, and "some of the boys" attacked a grizzly along the Bear River in 1834 with bows and arrows borrowed from a Ute hunting party. The trappers possessed guns, but the Indians' weapons seemed more amusing. Seizing "this good opportunity to have some sport," the men fired fifty arrows, "not one of them . . . deep enough to be mortal." The bear chased after the sources of his pain, but every time he neared a mounted hunter, another on the opposite side would plunk an arrow into him. Finally, a Ute hunter rode up and put "an end to the animal and the sport at the same time."[42]

As the Americans learned to hunt in packs for safety, humor and brutality displaced apprehension and horror. They started toying with their "monsters" before destroying them. Soon after the arrow episode, Rose's party met another grizzly in the bushes. The bear charged a trapper named Caleb Wilkins. Wilkins was riding a mule. The animal couldn't outrun the grizzly, so he trotted along and defended his rear with his hooves. The mule kicked the bear, "nearly dislocating his jaw." While the animals bucked and roared, the humans chuckled. "All this time the trappers were laughing and shouting: 'Look out, Caleb!' 'Go it, Caleb!'" Then, when it looked like the bear might bring down the mule and the man, a hunter galloped up and shot the grizzly. The animal turned and ran after his attacker, "and for some time he was kept busy wheeling and facing each new enemy, till at last a ball from one of the rifles struck him in a vital part, and he fell over and died." They named the bear Caleb, and they called the grizzlies they butchered Caleb "from that time forward."[43]

When Hugh Glass's companions abandoned him, they left him somewhere between James Beckwourth and Caleb Wilkins. Beckwourth enlisted grizzly bears in his quest to stand above other men. He wanted his adventures in the West to carry him away from his former life as a slave and an apprentice. Coming home, leading a white bear on a chain, he announced his dominance. Environmental Americanism lifted him out of the ranks of the enslaved and humiliated. Western nature made him a singular individual. Bear comedy also cut in the opposite direction, however, expressing Americans' terror at the possibility of wild beasts dragging them out of human society and into animal territory. Glass traveled farther than most into this social dead zone, and he came back pissed. He emerged from his solo in western nature a homicidal maniac, an avenger bent on killing the former pack mates who left him to die next to the corpse of the bear.

Glass's hobble back from oblivion will fill the next chapter. But before leaving the bear, it's important to note that, at least in Daniel Potts's estimation, Glass never returned. The hunter that existed before the attack disappeared when the she-bear grunted her last, then fell and engulfed him. The bear and the man entered an afterlife bound in obscurity and celebrity, a skin and a story.

JUST ANOTHER WORD
FOR NOTHING LEFT TO CHEW

Doctor Willard listened, but he didn't believe, until the old man lifted his kilt. In the glow of the campfire, Hugh Glass stripped, and the sight of his body set his audience abuzz. What a heap! The crumbling physique drew gasps even before its owner disrobed. Glass looked much older than his "middle aged" hunting companions. "Probably 75," Willard guessed. Wearing highland garb to signal his nativity, the mountain man told the doctor that he immigrated to the United States from Scotland as a youth and drifted west to seek his fortune. Glass may have earned a substantial income from beaver pelts, but he amassed nothing. The old man, the doctor reported, bobbed along on a current of alcohol. Booze lured him to the settlements, sucked him dry, and flushed him back into the mountains so that he could accumulate more hides and start the cycle anew.[1]

Willard bumped into the hunter on the Santa Fe Trail in 1825. Glass and his partners, Stone, Andrews, and March, had lost two of their three mules and a majority of their traps in a river on their way to the headwaters of the Rio del Norte (the upper Rio Grande). The remaining mule wobbled under the entire crew's baggage while the hunters ambled to Taos to reequip. Willard's commercial outfit presented the four men a quick money-making opportunity. They were hired on to kill bison and antelope for the greenhorns.

Glass fed Willard's mess and the two struck up a friendship. In time, the old man told the doctor about the bear. Up north, along the upper Missouri, he and a trio of hunters (the same three he traveled with still) broke off from a larger American expedition to try their luck on a side stream. One morning, while his partners checked their traps, a female grizzly bear jumped him while he prepared breakfast for the crew. The animal burst out of the underbrush and bit him. She threw him down and "began her work of destruction." The commotion alerted Stone, who was wading in a nearby creek. He ran to the camp, saw his cook pinned, "the monster mounted upon him," and leveled his gun. He killed the bear with one shot. She fell and smothered Glass.[2]

The bear's death cued the storyteller to hop out of his clothes. He ditched his tartan and let the doctor "examine" him. Willard traced the scars with his eyes and his fingers. He noted "the large chasms upon the right arm and shoulder blade the crest of which was wanting, also the upper portion of the right thigh." The folds and ridges attested to the veracity of the story, though Willard supplemented this "ocular proof" with testimony from Stone. Glass, the doctor felt certain, had nearly been destroyed by a white bear.[3]

The strip-down boosted Willard's confidence, and the doctor lapped up the rest of the tale:

> It sounds from what he told me, that about the time the young men left, his wounds began to supperate [sic] as the inflammation gave way, followed by healing action. The weather was warm, and their provisions being meat only, soon spoiled, hence starvation seemed to stare the old man in the face, but fortunately he was left near a spring of water, to which he could crawl upon his hands and knees, and in a few days move. [He] came to the conclusion to work his way up the trail of the company, and gleaning as he went such roots as he could masticate for food, and I think he had not gone far, before he could bear his weight upon his legs and finally succeeded in overtaking the company which had commenced trapping again.[4]

Many American hunters tussled with white bears, but only one scrambled back from the dead, traveling alone over such a vast distance. His incredible journey elevated his story out of the realm of entertaining mishap and into the rarefied air of national origin myth. The crawl turned Glass into an epic environmental American.

In 1825, Rowland Willard watched a mountain man named Glass perform a campfire story about a bear attack and a miraculous recovery. Glass took off his clothes and let the doctor inspect the residue of his trauma. Willard wrote down his observations, and his family collected them for posterity. Eventually, Yale University's Beinecke Library acquired the documents. The memoir, unknown to earlier Glass biographers, qualified as a coup for me: A doctor had examined Hugh Glass's wounds and written about them. A literate, trained medical professional had ogled and poked him. I needed a pinch myself; it felt too good to be true.

And it was.

Willard accompanied a caravan of Missouri traders headed to Santa Fe. Mexican officials had recently opened the trail, and the country's northern frontier intrigued Americans in search of commercial opportunities and close encounters with Spanish exotica. Willard sensed this curiosity and kept a daily journal to fortify his memory for later publications. Once in Mexico, he wrote articles for the St. Louis newspapers and reported for Timothy Flint, who included the doctor's observations in his *Western Monthly Review* and at the tail end of his edited volume of James O. Pattie's mountain-man narrative. The story of Glass stripping down and enacting the white bear story appeared in none of Willard's contemporary accounts (though the doctor did scribble Glass's name multiple times in the journal). Willard wrote about the bear and the crawl years later in a handwritten memoir he composed for his family.[5]

The nearness of Glass, therefore, was an illusion. Willard zoomed in on the old man from the distance of his own advanced age. (He composed the autobiography in his seventies and eighties.) He could reach out and touch Glass because he actually stood far away from him. To the memoir's further discredit, Willard fumbled verified elements of Glass's biography. Instead of moving north to their winter fort, Willard thought Henry's expedition traveled back to St. Louis after abandoning Glass. He claimed that Southwest Indians clubbed the old man to death along the Colorado River a couple of years after they met. (The Arikaras killed Glass near the Missouri River in 1833.) He abbreviated Glass's first name with a poorly executed *W* or a sloppy *M* rather than an *H*. Time, memory lapses, and fabrications crippled the doctor's account.[6]

Distance both tarnished the doctor's report and made it possible. Had the doctor's report emerged from the past lucid and impeccable, it might never have mentioned the crawl. A more authentic and trustworthy account, one closer to Hugh Glass in space and time, would have cut to the white bear in an effort to comprehend the nature of the attack. In the 1820s, white bears, not their mutilated victims, held the meaning of the wilderness. The imperfections in Willard's vision opened a sight line into the blindest alley in the Glass saga.

After his companions left him for dead, Glass disappeared into a total eclipse of information. He vanished from culture like the "Indian-hater *par excellence.*" The frontier and nature swallowed him; his crawl existed on the far side of news, biography, and history. No one but Glass could speak about it. He reported his own death struggle, which should have set off alarm bells; Glass wasn't a reputable guy.

Willard acknowledged as much. He connected Glass's wasted body to his wasteful habits. The cycle of debauchery and dissipation that drove Glass back and forth from towns to beaver streams made him a prize storyteller and a social pariah. His cultural authority—the power to attract, to command, and to buffalo an audience—grew from his decaying form. The environment starved, scarred, and aged him; the trade added to his disintegration by facilitating cycles of epic bingeing and purging. Glass consumed Falstaffian proportions of liquor, food, and conviviality during summer rendezvous and settlement sojourns. Back in the hills, he abstained like a monk. The mountain men swelled and shrank with the wild swings in their access to food, markets, and luxuries. The radical changes in their appearance underwrote their environmental Americanism. Through bingeing and purging, nature and markets reworked them into new species and races.

Yet, as Willard noted, these cycles of excessive celebration and extreme privation violated middle-class ideals of frugality and moderation. The men's ethics seemed as unsound and repulsive as their bodies. Written decades after their encounter, the memoir gave Willard the space he needed to perform a contortionist's maneuver: it allowed him to embrace and reject Hugh Glass simultaneously. Willard could admire Glass's capacity for withstanding nature's torments while denouncing the old hunter's self-abuse. His ruined body proved that an epic confrontation between man and nature did indeed occur; his wasteful habits proved that he wasn't fit for civilization. Both dissipations worked in favor of environmental Americanism.

The story of the crawl secured Glass's legend even as it strained belief. Who could buy the proposition that a horribly injured man not only survived for weeks alone in a hostile environment but also dragged his mangled limbs hundreds of miles to the nearest outpost? Who could trust the words of a ne'er-do-well hunter with a drinking problem? Glass's body nourished confidence and cynicism. Something dreadful happened to him; the scars proved that much. But what? The doctor who probed his injuries and listened to his tale offered several reasons for his destruction. His work, his habits, and his immorality wrecked him. Others suggested that the bear, the West, or the wilderness ravaged him. Nationalists thought America got him. Whatever the cause, Glass's body demanded a narrative that explained its impoverished state. Glass furnished a story that fit his experiences as a fur hunter. He oriented his survival tale around food, markets, and freedom. The crawl signaled Glass's final initiation into his western environment, a matriculation process that began with the Arikara attack and continued with the bear mauling. The survival tale detailed the economic whipsaw that flung the mountain men between abundance and famine. The bear and his friends sent Glass to the outer limits of privation. He came back to fill his belly, declare his free agency, and show off the damage he earned at the far reaches of capitalism.

Twenty-one years after Glass fed Rowland Willard, Lewis Garrard underwent his own gastronomic seasoning on the road to Santa Fe. For the most part, dining in the West thrilled Garrard. Eating meant hunting, and the seventeen-year-old greenhorn from Cincinnati relished gunning down wildlife along the trail. The Pawnees, however, had tired of travelers from the United States poaching their game, and they harassed nimrods who traveled too far from the wagon ruts. Until they reached the territory of their trading allies, the Cheyenne, the leader of the train, Cerain St. Vrain, kept his hunters close in. This policy kept everyone hungry. The men fell into a cycle of feast and famine. They rode for days without food and then gobbled up the few animals they met on the trail. Garrard let his stomach do his grumbling for him, while others voiced their complaints. A man named Bransford especially disliked the routine: "'Darn this way of living, anyhow; a feller starves a whole day like a mean 'coyote,' and when he *does* eat, he stuffs himself like a snake that's swallowed a frog.'" Garrard sympathized. His "ravenous appetites scarcely knew bounds" after extended bouts of abstemiousness.[7]

For the greenhorn, acclimating to the West required dietary experimentation. Garrard put unthinkable items in his mouth—bison innards filled with half-digested cud, puppy meat, and mule flesh—and he endured lengthy periods of tasting nothing but his own spit. Hunger pushed him into new cuisines, while starvation unshackled him from the recommended allowances of health and propriety. "One remarkable peculiarity," he wrote, "about buffalo meat—one can eat beyond plentitude without experiencing any ill effects." The West turned the Americans "greasy hungry," and they accommodated their new environment by violating the strictures of race, class, and humanity. They starved like curs and gorged like reptiles.[8]

The radical fluctuations in their girth underscored their environmental Americanism, and overindulgence helped endear mountain men to a national audience. Travel writers knew this. Garrard kept his on-the-road-to-Taos epic well within the ruts of the genre. The audience for mountain-man narratives inhabited cultural and biological environments that promoted moderation. Eating or drinking too much or too little could throw the human body out of balance. Stuffing your gullet with rich food and stiff drink was an excellent way to get sick, especially in unfamiliar climates. The respectable elements in society encoded these health beliefs with moral judgments. Gluttony was a character flaw, a sin. The lurid tales of mountain men starving in blizzards and pigging out at summer rendezvous underscored the separation of East and West, the middle and working classes, not to mention civilization and savagery.

The travelers like Garrard who marketed their western adventures to eastern audiences built in safeguards to protect their bodies from over-contamination. Western foods, they theorized, were digested differently than eastern dishes. Thus Garrard could scarf down fistfuls of bison meat without feeling "ill effects." Narrators toured the West for only short periods, and they reacquainted their bodies with eastern nourishment as soon as they reached the settlements. They tasted the region, but they didn't imbibe too deeply. How did they know when to resurface in order to escape the environmental bends? They peered at the "old men" of the fur trade to see the consequences of overexposure. When you started to look, behave, talk, and smell like Hugh Glass, it was time to go home.

After the bear attack and the crawl, Glass was so fully acclimated as an American that he was frightening. He was so seasoned that he had gone to seed. He sunk roots in shifting sands that rewarded unsteady habits. He had grown used to starving and gorging, and the story of his crawl as well as his reputation for boozing reinforced his claim to having been remade by western nature. He exhibited the symptoms of cultural biogeographical isolation. He lost touch with his home population like a small mammal who had hitched a ride on a raft of palm fronds to a strange island and evolved over generations to take advantage of his host environment. With enough time and separation, the small mammal might sprout into a new species incapable of interbreeding with representatives from his natal community. Glass's isolation was far less complete, but he had adapted to the West to such an extent that his return to civil society no longer seemed possible or desirable.

The crawl shipwrecked Glass. Laid flat in the wilderness, he wriggled away from promises that bound him to other humans. After his solitary interlude in nature, Glass left the supervision of Henry and Ashley. He hunted where and when he pleased and bargained on his own with the fur companies. Unchained from the quasi-military expeditions, he moved closer to the freedom Henry David Thoreau anticipated in the West. He nullified old arrangements, shrugging off contracts, military orders, corporal discipline, and group responsibilities. He also severed his supply line, canceled his income, and ditched his backup. Thoreau walked into the freedom of the West; Glass crawled there. He achieved personal independence on all fours, which hinted at the drag his environment placed on his liberation. He might sneer at his former bosses, but he would never escape the need to eat.

Since the West satisfied appetites at erratic intervals, the place cultivated unsteady habits. Free hunters earned a reputation for stuffing their stomachs, abusing their livers, and placating their carnal desires whenever they reentered capitalist markets. They famously overconsumed in the settlements and at summer rendezvous. Their bacchanals wasted their profits and indebted them to their suppliers, driving them back into the field to acquire more pelts. Thus environmental upheaval abetted market servitude. Free hunters found a measure of self-determination at the economic, geographic, and cultural margins, but the realities of subsistence and the market continued to frame their choices.

Food, markets, and freedom: these topics infiltrated Glass's crawl like fat marbled into muscle. They formed the story's historical subtext, the muffled conversation that can be picked up with an adjustment in focus. To find the discussion below the din of environmental Americanism, it's critical to remember that before the crawl reached a wide audience, the story traveled in hunters' circles, a workplace drama stuffed with workplace references.

Before he wrote about the white bear tearing an unidentified man nearly to pieces, Daniel Potts described his own gnawing adventures. One of the original "enterprising young men," he signed up with Ashley and Henry as a hunter in 1822. His letters offered a dark portrait of the expedition's opening months. One of the unlucky employees stuck rowing and cordelling a keelboat, Potts suffered horribly. By July (the expedition had left St. Louis in April), he and his mates had been "reduced to the sad necessity of eating any thing we could catch as our provision where exhausted and no game to be had." They ate their dogs' flesh, then singed the hair off the canines' hides, roasted the dermis, and choked down the "hearty" skins. Meals like this so discouraged Potts that he decided to run away with eight other men. They headed back toward "the fronteers" of Missouri. Potts got separated from the others and wandered the country alone without ammunition for his gun or "cloths to [his] back." He stepped into the western emptiness, the null zone between races and markets. He asked one correspondent, a friend from his hometown in Pennsylvania, to imagine his predicament: "being four hundred miles from any white people or even knowing where to find Indians; now my dear friend how much must I have felt, young Birds, frogs, and snakes were exceptable food with me and not means of fire." The crunch of hatchling bones and slime of reptilian guts hung in the back of his throat. The wilderness made him gag.[9]

Potts eventually ran into some Indians who "treated [him] with great humanity." He rested with them for four days; on his departure, they gave him three-quarters of a pound of bison suet and directions to the nearest fur post, two hundred miles away. When he finally reached the fort, he stumbled into William Ashley. The general had taken command of the keelboat filled with replacement supplies for the lost *Enterprize*. He was on his way to meet up with Henry. Ashley collected Potts and delivered him back to the outfit the young man had risked his life to escape.[10]

Potts kept to himself his reasons for recasting his lot with Ashley. In an 1826 letter to his brother, he explained: "I met with Gen. Ashley, on a second expedition with whom I entered the second time." Why did he agree to follow a boss no more likely to feed and protect him than he had the first time around? To rebuild his reputation? Cover up the shame of running away? Or did something happen to him in the wilderness that stiffened his resolve and boosted his confidence? Had James Beckwourth narrated Potts's desertion, the greenhorn would have emerged from his ordeal a formidable mountain man. His endurance tested and his fortitude confirmed, he could preen and brag like a seasoned vet. Perhaps Potts rejoined Ashley out of newfound boldness rather than humiliation. Perhaps he perceived himself an equal deserving of respect and fair treatment rather than a pathetic novice worthy of scorn and abuse. It's possible. Yet, unlike Beckwourth, Potts never trumpeted his physical strength. Quite the opposite; he played up his frailty.

His constitution was shaky before he traveled west. He left Philadelphia in 1821, and on his arrival in Illinois "was taken with a severe spell of rheumatism which continued with me for about two months." His close brush with starvation endangered him further. Abstinence unbalanced his humors. Safe at the trading post, he spent six days of "eating too much," and his good fortune triggered "a severe spell of sickness which all but took my life." Later, when he reached the mountains and began hunting beaver, Potts wandered away from his company and lost his bearings in a snowstorm. A group of Indians (Potts didn't know who they were, only that they weren't Crows, his trading allies) guided him over a mountain pass through waist-deep drifts. Potts froze his "feet severely so that I lost two toes e[n]tire and two others in part." He recuperated with his rescuers until spring. Potts paused in his letters home to thank them: "I am obliged to remark on the humanity of the natives towards me, who conducted me to their village, into the lodge of their Chief, who regularly twice a day divested himself of all his clothing except his breech clout, and dressed my wounds til I left them." The Indians' kindness, coupled with the "astonishing" scenery, natural wonders, and prodigious vegetation and animal herds, split Potts's opinion about the region. He proclaimed the West beyond dangerous: "a man in this Countrey is not safe neither day nor night, and [I] hardley ever expect to get back." But in the next breath, he declared, "this Countrey is the moste healthey in the world I believe." The West abused Daniel Potts's gastrointestinal tract and nabbed his toes, yet the place still topped his list of salubrious locales.[11]

The secret to his geomedical schizophrenia lay in the crosscurrents of food, markets, and freedom in the 1820s western fur trade. Potts saw the potential for wealth, pleasure, and nurturance all around him. He touted the "grass and herbage" in the valleys of the Wind River Range, and measured the gallons of "pure oil" gurgling from the soil near present-day Lander, Wyoming. In the future, ranchers and oilmen would profit from this bounty. Potts could envision a different age for his occupation as well. He imagined the enjoyment his hometown chums would have chasing down "White Bear, Buffalo, Elk, Deer, Antelope, and Mountain Sheep." Instead of killing animals as labor, these future men would experience "glory in the sport" of the hunt. Potts interpreted the hot springs he encountered in a similar vein. The volcanic marvels altered the climate of high country valleys, providing a refuge from the brutal winters. The "hot springs, boiling Sulphur, and Oil springs, also salts, salt Peter, and Volcanoes" symbolized the well-being, revenue, and amusement smoldering beneath the region's harsh rind.[12]

The West bit and clawed, robbed and bewildered. It bloodied flux, stoked fevers, gnarled joints, and turned stomachs. Still, despite all its invasive power, the country inspired wonder as well as dread. Like all places, this location could swing for or against you. The wilderness emerged from the radical swings in the arcs of fortune. Nature vacillated between sickness and health, poverty and riches, famine and feast.

Potts saw multiple possibilities in his environment, but his choices depended on his associations with groups with more power than he alone could muster. Humans with superior knowledge, numbers, firepower, boats, mules, or sundries arbitrated his enjoyment of nature's bounty. To reach the valleys with the hot springs, he needed Indian guides and caregivers. To reap dollars from furs, he needed hunting partners and Ashley's supply line. Without connections, the West was empty and impossible. That's the lesson he took from his solitary walk following his desertion. To escape the void, he had to find and solicit "humanity." People skills mattered more to him than survival expertise. Veteran fur hunters cultivated the art of making friends and severing relationships. Their profits—and often their survival—hinged on the timing and persuasiveness of their sociability. Rejoining Ashley wasn't a defeat but a temporary alliance against the wilderness.

Human affairs and environmental relations crisscrossed in the West. Food exemplified the tangle. Calories brought people together and drove them apart. Hunger was a social as much as a physical condition. Native and Euro-American traders adapted the word "starve" differently, reflecting their mutually incomprehensible ideas about material possessions and social obligations. White traders often portrayed their Native partners as beggars, and many Indians did indeed approach market transactions from a position of weakness. They presented themselves as miserable and poor. This was actually an aggressive (or at least an assertive) stance. From their perspective, trading partners relieved each other's wants. If a friend had surpluses of guns, corn, or hatchets and you had none, the friend owed you the items you most needed. The redistribution of surpluses generated reciprocity, and reciprocity undergirded all alliances. Rather than barring one side from the exchange, poverty fueled transactions.

A refusal based on the one side's inability to pay on delivery endangered the friendship. Empty bellies played a leading role in communicating neediness. Starving people demanded immediate attention. To remedy their suffering, they required emergency access to markets. Hence, hunger spurred credit. Natives expressed these complex ideas to European traders through the imperfect word "starve," and over time both cultures mashed together three or four meanings into that shared term. "White" hunters soon could starve like Indians.

By the 1820s, the verb had become so imprecise and complex that a British fur entrepreneur could author a through-the-looking-glass statement such as "[He] brings us the lamentable news that Many of the Indians are starving and have eaten their Furs, and that it is firmly believed that one family have actually starved of Starvation." The anthropologist Mary Black-Rogers discovered this quip in her research on the semantics of "starving" in the fur trade. She unearthed multiple instances of Natives and Euro-Americans using the term to underscore market, rather than caloric, deprivation. Even fat Indians and whites starved when the demands of immediate survival distracted them from gathering furs. When the work of caring for their bodies overtook the labor of acquiring commodities, hunters "ate their furs" and had nothing to offer traders in exchange for items they may (or may not) have needed just as desperately as food. Like all metaphors, starvation could stretch to encompass many situations: lethal malnutrition, social reciprocity, economic scarcity, and comic overstatement. The term's multiplicity of meanings exasperated trading partners. Fit-looking allies might be in real trouble, or they might be massaging the truth, aiming to fleece. Friendships built on exchange turned on the interpretation of the word.[13]

Starvation in all its senses awaited the Americans in the 1820s as they pushed up the Missouri River and into the Rocky Mountains. Their bodies registered their up-and-down diets, and they inherited a trade language to describe the relationships of authority that structured their access to calories. Hunters reclaimed fur-trade notions of social obligation to galvanize their fights against despotic employers, chaotic supply lines, and inferior bargaining positions. Hunger became the primary excuse for running away, and deserters manipulated the starvation metaphor to justify their rebellions.

As we know, American expeditions hemorrhaged workers. Men disappeared as quickly as Ashley could recruit them. The premature departure of miffed employees threatened the experiment of using "white" men to hunt furs. Expedition leaders, government officials, and St. Louis entrepreneurs assumed that outfits needed military discipline to reach and mine the rich beaver habitats of the Rocky Mountains. The Americans had to band together to protect one another and secure their supply line against entrenched Native and British competitors. Ashley and Henry relied on wages and long-term contracts to bind men together. To get their money, hunters had to stick with the company for a year. The contract laborers helped transport and defend their masters' trade goods. They promised to pole and cordell keelboats; they agreed to feed and care for pack animals. They devoted countless hours to moving and babysitting their boss's stuff. Theoretically, all this toil benefited them as well. Ashley and Henry had to get supplies into the mountains and pelts out to meet their payroll. The capitalist magic of turning tree-biting rodents into cash depended on fur-trade workers knowing their roles and shouldering their loads. Everyone's profits (and personal safety) rested on the willingness of individuals to submit to the discipline of the group.

Given the benefits of unit cohesion, why did so many workers flee the herd at the first opportunity? They left because they were starving. Nothing ruined morale like a few bowls of jellified dog skin. But the language of the fur trade armed deserters with a range of motivations that originated in physical discomfort and radiated out to financial calculations, masculine honor, and racial embarrassment. Their employers starved them of windfalls, pride, and whiteness as well as victuals. The labor they devoted to hauling and defending the company's goods prevented them from harvesting beaver. Hunters walked free, upright, and proud in the wilderness. They matched wits with varmints and traded skins for cash; they didn't carry loads like mules and masticate pelts in desperate attempts to stay alive. References to "eating fur" registered the disappointment of expectant capitalists who traveled west to advance their bottom lines and achieve heroic reputations and instead found a cornucopia of disagreeable tasks.

The St. Louis newspapers printed the high expectations that often crashed in the expeditions' first months. In the papers, Ashley and his employees oozed youth, dash, and moxie. They were brave, enterprising, and "completely" equipped. They came from good stock—"respectable

employments and circles of society." Their age, manliness, and upbringing prepared them for the "arduous but truly meritorious undertaking"
in front of them. Their character insured their success, and they anticipated spectacular returns.[14]

In 1838, the editor for the *Missouri Saturday News* remembered
Ashley's 1822 conquistadores. The general, he enthused, hired only "select" woodsmen. Far from being the dregs, his men represented the
cream of humanity. They were civilized gents ready to test their mettle in
"desperate encounters with the red men, or his genial spirit the grizzle
bear." They seemed like "a crew of a man of war about to cruise against
an enemy's squadron," and because they expected a long and taxing
journey, they "indulged deeply" in the charms of the city. With few opportunities to enjoy pleasurable commodities, they would be forced to
abstain in the West. But those who survived and returned "laden with
the fruits of their toil and privation" could "taste again the luxuries of
civilized life." Hunters delayed gratification to acquire the financial
wherewithal to consume spectacularly when they came home.[15]

The papers hinted at the calculus of starvation that led to mutinies.
Fur hunters signed up for pain. They expected arduous journeys and
linked the endurance of hardships to personal character. The fortitude
to go without luxuries defined their masculinity and their whiteness.
Yet, while they braced for punishment, they anticipated splendid pay-
offs. They suffered to enjoy the fruits of their labor—to see furs turned
into gold. But the contracts Ashley extended to hunters muddied this
dream. He asked employees to bear misery for the welfare of the company. He ordered them to cordell keelboats loaded with his trade goods;
he sent them on long-distance treks in search of horses to pack with his
supplies; and he required them to guard his inventory with their lives.
After a while, the pain of fur hunting lost its original meaning. Instead
of facilitating the accumulation of capital, Ashley's chain of command
kept hunters away from pelts. Instead of gathering furs to enjoy commodities back home, the men labored and died in the wilderness to secure Ashley's goods. The general starved them to enrich himself, and
runaways sought their freedom to restore the proper relationship between their labor and the market. Their work should bring them closer
to luxuries, not strand them in the backcountry gnawing dogs.

Deserters found true independence terrifying, however. Daniel Potts left Ashley and wandered into the void between market connections. Reduced to eating snakes and frogs, he confronted actual rather than metaphoric starvation. His survival depended on grabbing hold of another supply line, and the Indians finally tossed him one. Without their aid, knowledge, and sundries, he would have passed through the stages of confusion, panic, and delirium that accompany severe malnutrition. After burning away his fat, Potts's metabolism would raid his muscle tissue, and the breakdown of proteins would leave him smelling like ammonia. With his muscle gone, his body would feed on his liver, kidneys, and heart. His brain would go last. In a frantic effort to save itself, the organ would scroll through visions of friends, family, and lovers; emotional attachments might inspire hours of desperate clinging. Starvation altered minds, inducing mystical episodes of cosmic visions and introspection. Hauled back from the precipice, survivors often had wild and entertaining stories to tell.[16]

The metaphors of starvation escaped the fur trade and invaded the nationalist rhetoric of environmental Americanism through mountain-man narratives. Survival artists like Colter and Beckwourth dramatized privation. Abstinence, endurance, and violence confirmed their superiority to other men. Beckwourth sold his persona in the form of memoir, but his body building and race switching took place outside the market. He proved his toughness in a venue devoid of class distinctions. He could battle Ashley because the general's money counted for nothing in a competition that turned on physical prowess. A former slave, Beckwourth had ample incentive to avoid scenarios where buying and selling determined a person's worth. But other narrators saw capitalism as an ally rather than an obstacle. They sold eastern audiences their knowledge about the West's exploitable resources. And in the process, they reinterpreted the meaning of starvation yet again. In the fur trade, hunters starved when the need to seek food diverted their labor away from the market. Ashley's work of transporting trade goods starved mountain men in this fashion. Fed up with the torments of organized expeditions, many ran and starved. Adrift and bewildered, they withered and dreamed. They suffered visions, hallucinating encounters with distant friends and loved ones. They also saw huge swaths of the country, and some, like

Potts, glimpsed a future where profits seeped from hot springs and oil puddles. In their narrative delirium, some provided telling market indicators.

Story lines of economic progress helped reorient some mountain men, enabling them to recover their bearings after they lost their minds. Instead of malcontents who broke contracts, abandoned colleagues, and disobeyed masters, some runaways recast themselves as scouts and explorers. They blazed trails for businessmen to follow. The bony edge of capitalist expansion, skeletal wanderers surveyed real estate and identified resources. Their desperation enhanced their credibility. Incapacitated by hunger, they couldn't exploit the sweet grasses of high mountain valleys or mine the wealth hidden in the soil. But the Americans coming after them would bring livestock and shovels. They would enjoy the rewards of the frontiersmen's suffering. Looking back from the prosperous future, the mountain men's personal disasters appeared formative economic episodes.

In 1870, Colonel Robert Campbell dictated a sketch of his life to William Fayel, the secretary to Commissioner of Indian Affairs Felix Brunot. The old fur trader accompanied Fayel and his boss to negotiate a treaty with the Sioux leader Red Cloud at Fort Laramie. Nightly gatherings around the campfire put the colonel in "the reminiscent mood," and Fayel scribbled furiously during Campbell's "recitals." A citizen of repute, the Scots-Irish immigrant had scrambled to the top of the St. Louis fur business through courage, intelligence, and fortitude. Campbell was a role model, an exemplary frontiersman. Little was known about his early years in the mountains, and his campfire orations supplied a unique and authoritative history of his and the country's youth.[17]

Campbell joined Ashley's company in 1825 at the age of twenty-one, the same year James Beckwourth signed up. The expedition set out for the Rocky Mountains in November. Jedediah Smith, Ashley's partner, led the hunters to their winter quarters along the Republican River while the general stayed behind in St. Louis to wrangle with suppliers. Campbell remembered the company's anguish. To survive, they robbed the Pawnees' cached corn (the Indians were on the plains hunting bison) and killed a smattering of buffalo and wild turkeys. When the weather broke, they crossed the Republican and journeyed to the Platte

River. The Americans continued to go hungry until provisions reached them. Ashley lifted the famine, but as soon as the march resumed "a good many of the men—about twenty-five or thirty—had deserted." Campbell witnessed Americans with access to store-bought provisions disobey their employer and commanding officer because he continued to "starve" them.[18]

Campbell's tale of want and sedition sounded familiar. The organizers of fur-hunting expeditions had watched hundreds of contracted workers mutiny by 1825. Ashley and Smith knew the routine. Why hadn't they changed their tactics to minimize insubordination? Actually, they had. Campbell's narrative demonstrated that the bosses hadn't remained stationary while their underlings fled. Jedediah Smith's ascendancy to ownership (he partnered with Ashley after Henry retired in 1925) indicated one strategy. Employers with means were retreating from the field. Ashley slowly moved out of the hunting business and into the role of outfitter. In 1826, he sold his interest in the Rocky Mountain Fur Company to Smith, David Jackson, and William Sublette. Stationed in St. Louis, the general continued to use his connections to secure credit and trade goods for the company, but he let his former captains assume the risk and the hassle of actually hunting. The company would undergo several more reorganizations after Smith's death in 1831 and as partners continued to join and drop out. Eventually, Robert Campbell took a turn as an owner.

The scramble at the top of the Rocky Mountain Fur Company reflected the desire of fur-trade entrepreneurs to perfect a timely exit. Quitting determined who rose or sank in the fur trade. The winners converted western pelts into eastern properties, businesses, and opportunities: real estate, mercantile stores, steamboats, or political careers. The trade encouraged expansive investment strategies built on short-term commitments. This included management of human resources. The bosses put up with small-scale mutinies from the rank and file because they needed loyalty only from a select group of top-tier employees. A central cadre of trustworthy leaders—men like Smith, Jackson, Sublette, Campbell, and Jim Bridger—operated the business in the field. These captains managed hunting parties; probed rival Mexican, British, and Indian territories; and brought back pelts after enduring (and meting out) violence and hardship. They rode herd on a rotating cast of nimrods. The grunts came and went, and their transience suited everybody. The owners didn't want to feed and protect them, and the workers didn't want to be treated like soldiers or servants. Both sides created a labor system that looked sloppy but functioned well. In less than twenty years, the Americans denuded the West of beaver, and a few greenhorns clambered up the bales of dead animal furs to enter respectable society.[19]

In 1835, Robert Campbell retired from market hunting. He teamed with William Sublette to open a dry-goods store in St. Louis. They specialized in outfitting western ventures: trapping gear for the beaver trade and provisions for overland travelers. Campbell purchased real estate, including a hotel, and invested in steamboats. He accumulated money and power, and regular citizens recognized his stature by calling him "Colonel" and telling stories about his success. Campbell, they said, rose from humbling and treacherous circumstances. "The privations and perils endured by Col. Campbell," wrote Fayel, echoing the common wisdom, "doubtless laid the foundation for his prosperous business career." His achievements as "a merchant banker . . . widely known throughout the Far West," whose "credit stood high and unimpeachable," sprang from his youthful dalliances with chronic undernourishment.[20]

But how did this work? Why did it seem "doubtless" to Fayel that starvation led to the development of business acumen? Environmental Americanism linked physical health with national and economic development. Campbell traveled west in the first place on his doctor's advice. An "invalid," he was "pale and subject to hemorrhages of the lungs." The Rocky Mountains offered a cure. The dry air healed "consumptives"; young male easterners returned from their adventures "restored to health and as hearty as bucks." The place bred strength and vigor, and Fayel followed the worn path from medical theory to national expansion, placing an emphasis on capitalist success. James Beckwourth accomplished a similar feat with race. He displayed physical dominance by enduring privation, making his body register as American and white. Campbell grew brawny, too, but he used his new lungs to strike deals as well as to outdistance rivals and bark at masters. He accumulated capital. His altered body modified his class.[21]

Campbell's triumph appeared "doubtless" because environmental Americanism naturalized it. The fur trade rooted his dry-goods, real estate, and steamboat investments in the ordeals he suffered as a young man out west. The rough environment changed him, refurbished his health, refounded his nation, and replenished his bank account.

But Robert Campbell sang of progress from the small choir of field captains. These men did indeed endure privations, and a few capitalized on their western traumas to justify the fortunes they accumulated later in life. They represented the minority of fur hunters, however. More voices boomed from the chorus of disobedient workers, the rank-and-file nimrods who drifted in and out of the employment orbits of fur-trade companies. These men linked health and capitalism as well, but they eschewed nationalist story lines of upward mobility.

The earliest printed version of Glass's crawl told the tale through the fur-hunting obsessions of food and equipment. Glass's predicament— left for dead, injured, and "scarcely breathing"—reached epic proportions when his caretakers not only abandoned him but took "his rifle, shot pouch, and all appliances" as well. The tools defined Glass's humanity. Without them, he was at worst a thing, a corpse; at best a wounded animal. Technology produced sustenance, but in the right hands it did much more. It turned living organisms into calories and commodities. It transformed mere survival into capitalism. Without his gun, knife, and flint, Glass starved twofold. He grew hungry, and the loss of his gear forced him to devote all his labor to sustaining his body. Both forms of starvation pushed him further into the wilderness.[22]

When he awoke from the deep slumber that had convinced his burial party of his imminent death, Glass squirmed to a nearby spring. He lay there for ten days, sipping water and munching low-hanging berries. He recovered "by slow degrees a little strength," and began to shuffle toward Fort Kiowa, 350 miles away. Time and distance slowed to a creep. Only a fortuitous meal broke the monotony. Glass stumbled upon a pack of wolves harassing a bison calf. He watched the predators tackle a youngster, and when the mewling stopped and the flesh-ripping commenced, he burst from his hiding spot and scattered the wolves. He sank his teeth into the carcass and ate his fill. Refreshed, he "continued to crawl until he reached Fort Kiowa."[23]

James Hall ended the ordeal with that. In all, he spent one paragraph on the crawl. Given the attention other authors lavished on the wilderness adventure, his brevity seems curious. The crawl represented Glass's nadir—the lowest and loneliest he could go. A proud hunter, his injuries and nakedness reduced him to rooting for berries and scavenging other beasts' prey. He was ripe for reckoning. The wilderness scoured humans of nonessentials, freed them from the junk of everyday life. Distractions lifted, pilgrims discovered the truth of their existence in religion, family, love, nation, race, or manly vigor. But not Hugh Glass—at least not in Hall's version. He crawled out of the void, undaunted and undented. He entered the bushes annoyed; he emerged fuming.

Hugh Glass covered 350 miles, but his voyage of self-discovery went nowhere. Once out of harm's way, he immediately dived back into the fire, hitching a ride with the *engagés* bound for an Arikara ambush. He rotated in circles of anguish, injury, and loss. Unlike the Christian seekers before him or the romantic explorers after, Glass found neither redemption nor insight in the wilderness, and Hall didn't feel compelled to invent an epiphany for him. The spectacle of endless abuse served his purposes. The point of the crawl wasn't Glass's character development, but rather how his punishing experience altered the nation. Hall used Glass to dramatize the painful rebirth of America out West without exposing the citizens of the United States to actual discomfort. Glass suffered for the group and returned to his work. His redemption wasn't part of the story.

Blunt trauma worked for the mountain men, too. They gained stature as white American men simply by withstanding hardships. Hunters gritted their teeth, clenched their jaws, and powered through wilderness experiences. They didn't pause to glory in the wonder of creation. They endured. Yet manly toughness wasn't the only meaning of starvation. The physical experience of starvation helped dramatize the social condition of starvation. Hunger provoked mountain men to rebel, to make demands on their employers, and to buck the middle-class mores of respectable consumption. Hunger could lead to inappropriate as well as heroic behaviors.

In 1831, a clerk from a Pittsburgh mercantile firm explored the multiple definitions of fur-trade starvation. Zenas Leonard left St. Louis in

By February, they were eating the beaver skins. Frost seeped into their bones as their metabolisms waned. Men collapsed and despaired. One "Mr. Carter" sobbed and declared, "'[H]ere I must die.'" Only Leonard and a "large muscular man" named Hockday could still walk; Stephens, "amongst the weakest of the company," proved useless. Hockday and Leonard went in search of food and ran into a stray bison bull nine days after the company had eaten their last food. The meat of the bull rallied the party enough to follow their tracks back to the winter camp. The hard truths of snow, cold, and altitude trampled the dream of Santa Fe and its galloping ponies.[25]

The horse-buying expedition ended badly, but failure didn't prevent the employees of Gant and Blackwell from orchestrating some fun. They decided to pull a prank on the four hunters left behind in the cottonwood grove. Just outside of the huts, the backpackers crouched behind boulders and slipped beneath shrubbery. They sent three of "the worst looking men ahead." The survivors approached the campers, exchanged greetings, and talked for several minutes before recognition struck. The rest of the crew then burst from their hiding spots, and everyone laughed at the disfiguring magic of the wilderness.[26]

Leonard defined wilderness with some precision. For him, it wasn't the whole West or the entire space beyond civilized human habitation; it was the desolation, the place where the supplies gave out, the game disappeared, and the "piercing wind" chilled bones. The wilderness broke men, exposed their weakness and ignorance. It reduced some to infants and transmuted others into animals. Hungry men dropped to their knees and crawled through the snow blubbering, "almost insensible to their situation," while stout fellows like Hockday remained "hardy as a mule and resolute as a lion." Starvation brought inner flaws and hidden resiliencies to the surface. Wilderness distilled the essence of men.[27]

The starvation episode demonstrated how malnutrition revealed and obscured identities. The ordeal changed the men in two ways. The tough ones underwent an internal, metaphoric transformation. They looked the same, but they exuded the brawn and courage of mules and lions. The animal-men were market—rather than diet—starved. When

April of that year. A novice hunter, he followed his employe
Blackwell, into the West as the partners tried to break in
become a crowded field. Leonard was in for a rough ti
pened on Daniel Potts's 1825 expedition, the Pittsburghe
food along the Republican River. Several employees quit a
home. The discovery of bison herds farther west along the
ended this first stretch of "despondency and horror," but t
endured another starving time. The company split into th
parties. Captains led crews up separate watersheds in sea
dams. They would rendezvous in the spring and carava
market in St. Louis. Leonard followed Captain A. K. St
hunting veteran and geographic imbecile. The party n
Laramie River until October snows forced them to camp
Christmas and New Year's passed, and the men ate we
valley-bound bison, elk, bighorn sheep, and antelope.
however, suffered. The men had built their squat "houses
of cottonwood trees with their horses in mind, believing
the trees would sustain the animals through the cold, gr
But when they tried to feed the bark to the herd, the hors
partake. The trappers had chosen the wrong species of co
"bitter" rather than the "sweet" kind horses liked. One b
mals died. The men ate their transportation, but the mea
as the tree bark. The campsite mistake would cost mone
lives.[24]

Stephens hatched a plan. Years before, he had travel
where horses were plentiful and cheap. A party of vo
backpack to Santa Fe, use beaver pelts to purchase ne
return in April, in time to haul the rest of the crew and
lated furs to their summer rendezvous. Leonard headed
teen men (only four stayed behind at the winter camp
hundred miles over the spine of the Continental Divio
the teeth of a Rocky Mountain winter. They didn't go far.
carried them through the plains and into the mountain
increased with the elevation, and soon the hunchback p
man carried a pack with bedding, a rifle, and nine beav
to a crawl. The hunters finished their last jerked bison

they reconnected with supply lines and exchange networks, their youthful sojourns in the West would propel their careers and advance their reputations. They would become seasoned capitalists, men of substance who had shed their green horns. Some, like Zenas Leonard, would turn their experiences into commodities by publishing them.

The truly emaciated men followed a different path. Their radical weight loss severed the connection between their appearance and their character. Surface and interior fell into confusion, which embarrassed but also enlivened them. Starvation turned the weakest employees of Gant and Blackwell into comedians. They took the stage and performed the slapstick of mistaken identities while the men with the mule and lion hearts hid and giggled. The biggest losers capped the anecdote; they made it worth telling. Without their shame, Leonard wouldn't have had a story to sell.

Environmental Americanism valorized altered bodies. So did mountain-man narratives. The difference between the two genres came down to distance. The nationalists admired and insisted upon the separation of home and wilderness. Men remade by nature traveled to the far West on behalf of all Americans, and they stayed on the frontier while their stories drifted home. Mountain men welcomed the attention environmental Americanism gave them, but they violated their restraining orders, hauling their skinny bodies into St. Louis restaurants and Taos saloons. Mountain-man narratives described out-and-back journeys that redefined the extremes of pain and pleasure. The return trips these men made radicalized the comforts of home just as their wilderness forays pushed the limits of human suffering.

Old-time fur trappers knew how to party. Hugh Glass probably wouldn't use this frat-boy language to describe his spending and drinking habits—"partake a snort" seems more frontier—but a beer-soaked animal house seems an appropriate setting for the later years of his career. Glass resembled the fraternity brother who never graduated, the one who lingered by the keg too long and grew old but never grew up. Fur hunting was a young man's occupation. Strong, lithe bodies could take the abuse of the work, but the youthful orientation of the business went beyond physical pragmatism. A trip out West under a contract to a fur-trade company gave adolescent males a wild adventure before they yoked their passions to stable families and sober careers. They tasted frogs and lizards. They starved and hurt. The privations educated them in middle-class values of hard work and delayed gratification. Hardships prepared young hunters for leadership positions and successful ventures back home.

This story line worked for some. Fur hunting propelled Robert Campbell into a future in retail. Zenas Leonard followed a similar trajectory. After Gant and Blackwell folded, he joined Captain Benjamin Bonneville's ill-fated expedition, to plant an American fort near the headwaters of the Columbia River as a counter to the Hudson's Bay Company's power in the region. The writer Washington Irving gave the whole affair more attention than it probably deserved when he published a book based on notes and documents Bonneville supplied him. After much scenery and drama, Leonard returned to Clearfield, Pennsylvania, in 1835, to the surprise of his family. Though literate and an avid journal keeper, Leonard never bothered to write his parents while he was gone. They thought him dead. The clerk-turned-hunter put away his rifle, settled in western Missouri to keep store and operate a boat. He married, had three children, and died "prosperous and apparently contented" in 1858. The Santa Fe boondoggle fell into the opening chapter of a long life story. He recalled the starvation episode to the newspapers in 1835 and published it in a book in 1839. The horror and despair he witnessed in the mountains seasoned him, but even as he proved that he belonged in the West, his maturity destined him for civilized success.[28]

There was no looking back for the likes of Hugh Glass. He kept spinning between the poles of starvation and intemperance. When he finished telling Willard the tale of his remarkable comeback, Willard asked the hunter about his future. "'I am old,' Glass said, "but I thought I would go out once more Doctor, but I think it will be my last.'" The "last" resting place of Hugh Glass was the wilderness, not St. Louis. The knowledge colored Willard's perception of their final moments together. As the caravan neared Taos, Glass ran ahead, reaching the liquor first.

When the doctor finally arrived, he was soused and extremely sociable. Glass grabbed Willard and tried to hoist him onto his shoulders. The physician, he slurred, had protected him from cholera on the trail. He owed his life to Willard, a favor worth three cheers and perhaps a couple rounds, if the doctor would spot the cash.[29]

PART III

AFTERLIVES

SIX

COLD LIPS SAY WAUGH!

In the summer of 1836, the former Hessian army officer and aspiring Texas land speculator Friedrich Wilhelm von Wrede waded into the Mississippi rabble to save on expenses. He purchased steerage tickets for himself and his grown son on a steamboat headed for St. Louis. His wife remained behind in New Orleans. Had she come, he would have most likely sprung for a semiprivate above-deck cabin to protect her sensibilities (and her senses) from the Americans' filthy clothes, their malodorous bodies, and their vile fondness for spitting tobacco juice on the floors, the walls, and the communal hearth fires. The steerage was a sickly environment, and the noxious fumes soon overwhelmed the son. He fell ill, and his father nursed him as best he could in the squalor. That's when Hugh Glass showed up.

Unlike his working-class mates, Glass looked good. His muscles rippled and his eyes darted. His stout body proclaimed his membership in "that class of the human race making up the restless flood of immigrants which surged over a thousand miles into the territory between Missouri and Oregon." He "loved" danger and enjoyed "overcoming deathly perils." Nothing thrilled him more than "searching for the fierce bear and buffalo in the hunting grounds of the Blackfeet Indians in the Rocky Mountains." Glass pulled up a seat and dazzled the father and son with stories of white bears, treacherous friends, and bloodthirsty savages. The fact that he was dead made his performance truly fantastic. An Arikara war party had killed Glass in 1833. His remains had been moldering for years when von Wrede ogled his "powerful build."[1]

The German didn't need to summon a ghost to hear Glass's legend.

A subscription would have sufficed. James Hall had freed the story of Hugh Glass from Glass himself eleven years earlier. After he published "The Missouri Trapper" in 1825, people could lift the survival drama from numerous reprints in books, magazines, and newspapers. At home, von Wrede perused American frontier literature for immigration tips and investment opportunities. He had read Crockett's autobiography, and he may have run across Glass in Hall's *Letters from the West*. Certainly, Hall's fingerprints were on von Wrede's Glass. Abandoned on the plains, the German's hero munched "buffalo berries" like Hall's. Both he and Hall called Glass a trapper instead of a hunter (dogs accompanied hunters; trappers worked alone, pushing them even further away from civilized society). Anger fueled both versions: Glass endured pain, hunger, and solitude for the chance to wring the necks of the "perfidious . . . wretches" who had left him. But in the end, von Wrede's Glass lectured his enemies rather than slaying them, as had Hall's.[2]

A rehash of someone else's material, von Wrede's story rightfully belonged to Hall, yet his borrowing raised questions beyond plagiarism. Why did he bother with Glass at all? Why did a German offering travel and business advice in German to Germans celebrate an environmental American? Glass's example seems more repellent than inviting: come to America and you, too, could feel the crush of bear incisors, the sting of abandonment, and the burn of obsessive rage. Von Wrede dragged a loquacious casualty to his son's sickbed convinced that his European readers would share his fascination with the scarred storyteller. His attraction to Glass underscored the transnational appeal of environmental Americanism. Before they appropriated him and his tale for their own designs, authors from the United States, Germany, and Great Britain wanted to meet Glass, inspect his features, and hear him speak. In this sense, talk really was Glass's revenge. For some reason, his appropriators needed Glass to say the words before they could steal them.

The compulsion for an auditory encounter reached back to Hall. He incorporated an outburst of verbosity near the end of "The Missouri Trapper." Following Glass's last hairbreadth escape from the Arikaras—the one when the Mandans swept him to the safety of their fort and he "sallied forth" in the night for another monthlong hike to Fort Kiowa—Hall recorded Glass's speech: "'Although,' said he, 'I had lost my rifle and all my *plunder*, I felt quite rich, when I found my knife, flint, and steel in my shot pouch. These little fixens,' added he, 'make a man feel right *peart*, when he is three or four hundred miles *from any body* or *any place*—all alone among the *painters* and wild *varments*" (Hall's emphasis). The phonetic misspellings and working-class hunter slang lent the dialogue an aura of authenticity, but Hall never set eyes on Glass, much less heard him talk. A soldier at Fort Atkinson, supposedly present at the final confrontation with Fitzgerald, handed him the legend. Hall's "informant" said that Glass offered the "gaping rank and file of the garrison" an "astounding," "wonderful narration." By lapsing into mountain man–ese, Hall simulated Glass's oral performance, bringing his readers within earshot of a man he never heard.[3]

And this was a critical distance. Civilized Americans had to approach within range of a well-aimed utterance to claim the exceptionalism the mutilated, talkative Glass conferred. Hall outlined how storytelling transmitted frontier racial enmity into the national character in "Indian Hating." Initially, immigrants became western and uniquely American by experiencing and witnessing violence. Indians attacked frontier dwellers, and their trauma changed some backwoodsmen into vengeful berserkers. In time, however, when the Indians died off or left, stories replaced murder as the triggers for revenge. Indian hating spread through the oral remembrance of atrocities. Older generations of westerners naturalized their offspring with bloody recollections. Injured mountain men served the same purpose. To complete the transfer of environmental Americanism from western casualties to eastern consumers, writers sought out hunter/storytellers and recorded their recitals. They preserved dialects, physiques, gestures, and dramatic flourishes. And when their subjects refused to act their parts, or their stories fell flat, or their accents lacked the requisite amount of color—or they died before they could tell their tales—these writers imagined the requisite speech into being.

The afterlives of Hugh Glass spun out in a series of command performances. Authors dug him up, pried open his mouth, and waggled his tongue for him. They strummed his vocal cords to produce an idiom of "fixens" and "painters." The fairness of their approximations of Glass's actual voice was, of course, not the point. Writers like Hall and von

Wrede proved miserable archivists of the spoken word, which shouldn't surprise us too much; authenticity wasn't their game. They invented an argot of low-class funny talk to conjure the physical experience of listening to men remade by nature. The literati appropriated Hugh Glass's language and bent it to their will. They needed the breath from his body to complete the transfer of environmental Americanism from the fringe of society to its core, and they preserved the illusion of his corporeal presence in fantasies of uttered words.

The bipolar impulse to hear, smell, and converse with Glass while keeping him far away on the frontier reflected Americans' ambivalence with their western heroes, and this need for intimacy felt at a distance opened the door to European poachers. Foreign writers nabbed environmental Americans and inserted them into multinational discussions about human bodies, the North American environment, and the fitness of the United States to straddle the continent, which is why von Wrede carefully distanced Glass from the American nation. The "restless" hunter and his fellow "immigrants" surged into the disputed territory beyond the state of Missouri. The British claimed the Oregon country, while the Spanish and then the Mexicans patrolled the borders of the Louisiana Purchase. Glass, according to von Wrede, searched for buffalo and bear on the Blackfeets' land. Consequently, his body grew strong and resilient outside the United States. The Americans in the steaming armpit of the steerage had lost their battle with their environment. Gaunt, shaky, and slobbering, they represented the true health of the United States. Glass, that international man of misery, represented the vigor and wildness European men might taste out West.[4]

George Frederick Ruxton could sympathize with the von Wredes. The Mississippi environment turned his gut as well. Ruxton survived warfare in Spain, forays into the Canadian wilderness, exploration disasters in tropical Africa, and tours of the North American interior in the midst of the Mexican-American War only to be felled by an intestinal parasite in downtown St. Louis. In August 1848, the muggy landscape killed the twenty-seven-year-old Englishman before he could reach the Rocky Mountains. During his previous trip to the West—when he discovered

American fur hunters and their language—Ruxton fell off a mule and landed on either a stump or an Indian tepee picket depending on the whims of his storytelling. The accident bruised his spine and ruined his health. His mother begged him to stay in England, but Ruxton thought a campfire high in a mountain valley was what would heal him.

Dysentery upset his recuperation plans. Even had he managed to escape the lowlands, it's hard to imagine how lengthy jaunts on horseback followed by nights spent sleeping on the ground would soothe his back. Ruxton's convalescent nirvana seemed a chiropractor's hell. The journey made even less sense when you factor in his narrative choices. The mule and stump (or picket) handed Ruxton an invitation for literary self-exposure—his very own western injury. Yet he minimized his presence in the serialized reports he filed for the Scottish *Blackwood's Magazine* (in 1849, a New York publisher packaged and sold the articles as *Life in the Far West*). Unlike Hall, who invented a greenhorn alter ego that roamed the Illinois frontier looking for men remade by nature, Ruxton erased his authorial self. He lingered in the background, eavesdropping on the mountain men's inner circle. Through their campfire speeches, he traveled with them into scenes and situations he couldn't have witnessed. Listening to their "waughs" and "fixens" brought him and his international readers closer to the new race of frontiersmen and their wilderness transformations and transgressions than Hall and his American readers dared or desired.

The third son of John Ruxton, Esq., and Anna Maria, daughter of Colonel Patrick Hay, George Ruxton was born a social universe away from the denizens of western campfires. The descendant of the noble houses of Errol and Tweeddale, however, displayed an antiauthoritarian streak a grouchy hunter might appreciate. Young Ruxton punished teachers and school officials for boring him. Today, his behavior would have earned him therapy sessions and a Ritalin prescription, but the nineteenth-century British upper class had other techniques for dissipating the energies of their third sons. Since they would inherit neither title nor property, excess male family members could join the military and wreak havoc elsewhere. At fifteen, Ruxton did just that. He volunteered his services to the Spanish Crown and won a medal at the three-day battle at the bridge of Belascoain in Navarre. The queen granted him the "cross of the first class, of the National Order of San Fernando" for his valor. Upon his return to Britain, he accepted the commission of ensign in the 89th regiment in the British Auxiliary Legion. Stationed in Ireland and then upper Canada, Ruxton's attention drifted from his military career. He began writing about his outdoor leisure activities. The Canadian woods, Indians, and animals reminded him of the "admirable romance" in the novels of James Fenimore Cooper. Eventually, he left the army and took up Cooper's profession. He launched his literary career describing his own physical ordeals as a gentleman/hunter/scientist/adventurer, but the Rocky Mountains supplied him with more intriguing subjects. By the time of his death, Ruxton had found his Hawkeyes, and they eclipsed their author in his narratives.[5]

Ruxton stumbled upon his hunter protagonists in the Bayou Salade, a natural "park" near the headwaters of the Arkansas River. He based "Killbuck" and "La Bonté" on real trappers and swore to their "truth," though he admitted to "softening traits in the character of the mountaineers." Like so many people in this book, Ruxton had an elastic conception of truth, and the suppleness of his reality extended to his principal contribution to western literature: the mountain-man vernacular. As an author, Ruxton excelled at creating the appearance of verbatim dialogue, but his true talent lay in invention rather than transcription. His mountain men spoke in rambling, complex sentences and paragraphs. They strayed from their main topic and flashed back, verbally weaving like drunks after last call; and the content of their language read as false as its convoluted structure.[6]

Ruxton's protagonists used jarring racial and animal metaphors. The mountain men routinely compared themselves and one another to animals and African Americans. Ruxton hinted that they were only kidding, but their humor fell as flat as Crockett's winking knowingness. Ruxton's English upbringing deafened him to the implications of these similes. He grasped the connection between race and nationalism perfectly well; Great Britain was an aggressive colonial power, and Ruxton, a military officer, an explorer, and an ethnographer—a classic penetrator of dark continents and savage cultures—sauntered to the ends of the earth jollied by his Anglo-Saxon fabulousness. What he didn't get was the push and pull of U.S. natural nationalism. Ruxton cheered the

Americans' manifest destiny, and he saw western fur hunters as the exemplars of the spreading nation. Unlike von Wrede, however, he had no intention of dwelling in North America. Killbuck and La Bonté were summer dalliances, not countrymen or relatives, so why fret when they called each other "niggurs" and "critters"? Secure in his jodhpurs, Ruxton poured racial and species confusion from the throats of mountain men, confident that his British citizenship protected him from the toxic mixture's splash-back.

Linguists and historical reenactors should look elsewhere for sources of authentic nineteenth-century American working-class slang. Still, Ruxton recorded the social history of western fur hunting with greater clarity than most of his American counterparts. The semiprofessional regionalists overstated the whiteness and U.S. loyalty of the mountain men. Western fur hunting attracted a spectrum of colors, languages, genders, and nationalities. Beaver pelts and buffalo hides drew men, women, Indians, French Canadians, free blacks, slaves, mulattos, Germans, Spaniards, and Britons. Ruxton preserved the flavor of the "multi-West"—a region defined by the diversity of its multicultural, multinational, multilingual, multiracial, and multigendered cast of human beings. In capturing this reality, the Englishman stripped away the protective fictions regionalists and survival artists applied to their Westerns to safeguard the purity of the American nation and the privileges of their whiteness and humanity. Rambunctious survival artists like James Beckwourth troubled elites likes Francis Parkman, but even the gaudiest liar took care to safeguard his whiteness and his humanity. Ruxton's heroes, Killbuck and La Bonté, shirked both with casual disregard. The "multi-West" was real; so, too, were the social pressures that prompted Americans up and down the social order to hide this reality.

Ruxton's vernacular unsettled the barriers that prevented the horrors of the West—the physical torment, the onerous labor, all the species and racial confusion—from invading the East. Following the American regionalists, he insisted on the separation between savagery and civilization. However, he ignored the sanitation procedures American regionalists and survival artists deployed when they smuggled environmental Americanism across the divide. Instead of quarantining the new race of men on a geographic frontier or burying them in a distant past, he sometimes brought back monsters. His protagonists represented the "hardihood" of the "North American union," yet their vernacular betrayed them, sent them into a free fall of racial and animal transmutation that threatened the privileges that adhered to their bodies as white *Homo sapiens*.[7]

In *Life in the Far West*, Ruxton wasted no time placing his readers within hearing distance of men remade by nature. Without introducing himself, he locates a campsite on Bijou Creek in the Bayou Salade and turns the narrative over to Killbuck, the group's "elder." Tall and gaunt, Killbuck embodied the new race growing in the West—his face was "browned by twenty years exposure to the extreme climate of the mountains." Later in the text, Ruxton will translate the mountain men's stories for his readers, limiting his characters to brief incoherent outbursts like "Do'ee hyar now, boys, that's *Injuns* knocking around," or "Ho, Bill! what, old hos! not gone under yet?" But there is no one to save readers from Killbuck's opening soliloquy. He rambles for pages, disgorging a fog of slang, personal references, and obscure place-names. He wanders and digresses, remembering the time Black Harris traveled back to Liberty, Missouri, after three years trapping on the Platte River. Dressed "like a Saint Louiy dandy," he met a lady at a restaurant who asked about his travels. Harris, ever the "darndest liar," told her about the "putrified forest" he encountered in the Black Hills, complete with mineralized trees, leaves, grass, and songbirds. The "marm" pressed Harris to correct his vocabulary: "putrefactions, why, did the leaves, and the trees, and the grass smell badly?" But Harris insisted on the correctness of the phrase ("would a skunk stink if he was frozen to stone") as well as the truth of his discovery. The incompatibility of the English language and western nature stranded the hunter and the marm on opposite shores of the gulf that split West and East, nature and culture, men and women, savagery and civilization. Harris knew western nature even if his dialect crippled the transmission of this knowledge, while the marm, oblivious to the trapper's experience and his sense of humor, policed his language instead of checking his credulity. Harris's incoherence extended beyond his dandy costume and garbled diction, however. Ruxton confused his race as well.[8]

The marm triggered their conversation with a query: "Well, Mister Harris, I hear you're a great travler?" To which, Harris responds: "Travler, marm, this niggur's no travler' I ar' a trapper, marm, a mountain-man, wagh!" No tourist, he belonged to the mountains. He was a natural westerner, *waugh!*—a racially suspect, socially inferior, verbally outlandish, and more-than-a-little-scary environmental American. The lady represented civil decorum, Harris the obverse; and if his clothes and words could not be trusted, neither could his intentions. The sexual nightmare of the slave-owning United States—the despoliation of white women by predatory African American men—lurked in Black Harris. "Putrefaction" takes on a dark and unfunny meaning in this context. Instead of arresting decay, western nature spread maggoty rot. As a product of this environment, Harris stunk. The West had curdled his true being; it had turned him black.[9]

The mountain men's vernacular opened avenues for humorous misunderstandings in Liberty restaurants, but the blurring of humans and animals, whites and blacks, civilized and barbaric squelched laughter even as it encouraged situation comedy. According to Ruxton, the hunters habitually identified with horses, raccoons, deer, buffalo, sheep, "porkypines," beavers, and bears. They declared themselves varmints, children, "injuns," critters, and "niggurs." Black Harris was following the conventions of the vernacular when he deployed the N-word. In the same story, another member of the hunting party, Young William Sublette, used the term to reaffirm his whiteness. After examining the stone forest, Sublette affirms: "'Putrefactions,' says he, looking smart, 'putrefactions, or I'm a niggur.'" The noun slipped back and forth from derogatory to endearing. Killbuck and La Bonté colored themselves and their Indian enemies with the phrase. They also referred to each other as "white." In their use of the vernacular, the hunters slid in and out of black and white, animal and human, slave and master, prey and predator. And these shifts underscored the nature of the West: the place was supposed to change people. Onlookers questioned what the changes augured.[10]

The prevalence of "niggur" and "crittur" showed Ruxton's tin ear for the American caste system. His deafness stood out because, unlike von Wrede, he believed in the Americans' manifest destiny, even if he didn't understand the concept's limits. He targeted the relationship between market hunters' bodies and the rough western environment as

the source of the young nation's unique providence. The "hardy enterprise" of these "wild and half-savage" trappers prepared the continent
for "that extraordinary tide of civilization which has poured its restless
current through tracts large enough for kings and queens to govern."
The tough hunters represented the "real and genuine character" of the
American people: stripped of the "false and vicious glare," they alone
were "due the empire of the West—destined in a few short years to become the most important of those confederate states which compose
the mighty union of North America." The scion of Tweeddale puffed
the frontier origins of the United States with the gusto of Frederick Jackson Turner. Then his heroes spoke, and his expansionistic blather
veered off course. The United States might spread like a tidal force of
nature, but if Killbuck and La Bonté were the ones riding the crest, then
this would go down as one of the weirder tsunamis in history.[11]

The older, more experienced of the two, Killbuck was beyond saving.
He "didn't have the heart to leave the mountains" and required "space
to move." Settled life would smother him. La Bonté's heart, however,
beat for a white woman as well as a wild place. Though he killed Indians, endured severe physical hardships, and enjoyed the biracial couplings that defined fur hunting in the West, he longed for the gal he left
behind in St. Louis. Mary Brand kept La Bonté tethered to civilization,
and in the melodramatic conclusion to *Life in the Far West*, he aban-
dons the mountains and his partner to follow Brand and her family to
Oregon (after saving them from rampaging Indians).

Killbuck's dedication to the West made him less troubling than La
Bonté. He would die far from civilization. A surprise mule kick, a well-
aimed Arapaho bullet, or an unwise desert crossing would put an end to
him, and he—like the "old coon" that he was—would drift off to hap-
pier scrounging grounds. La Bonté's future looked rosier. His path led to
the comforts of home, including a marriage bed. He would strip off his
animal skins, put on overalls, and plow the earth until his loved ones
planted him there. He would expire with dignity, not in the bushes like
some "crittur." His path followed his nation's destiny. After a youthful

fling with the frontier, he would calm down, reproduce, and labor to build enlightened institutions—families, towns, schools, and democracies. La Bonté's age granted him this future. Killbuck had seen and felt too much. The violence and privation of the mountains had stained him to the core. La Bonté still had time to change his occupation, his skin color, and his species.

La Bonté spilled his biography in typical mountain-man fashion. Seated around a campfire after a long day's hunt, Ruxton prodded the "modest trapper to 'unpack' some passages in his wild adventurous life." It was 1825, he began; "that was the time this niggur first felt like taking to the mountains." La Bonté's self-referential racial slur was Ruxton's cue to take over the narration (which, of course, he controlled from the start). "Perhaps it will be as well," he lectures to his readers, "to render La Bonté's mountain language intelligible, to translate it at once into tolerable English, and tell in the third person, but from his lips, the scrapes which befell him in a sojourn of more than twenty years in the Far West." Thereafter, La Bonté waughs in the background while Ruxton provides the "tolerable" subtitles. La Bonté was born in St. Louis of mixed parentage: his father was French; his mother from Tennessee. As a boy, he reveled in the woods and would have followed his animal prey away from civilization but for the vivacious Mary Brand. His beautiful neighbor snagged him like "a thoughtless beaver-kitten" caught in a steel trap, until an act of violence broke her grip. La Bonté killed a rival beau in a scuffle during a corn-husking party. To escape the law and the noose, he signed up with William Ashley for the Rocky Mountains. Before he left, he said goodbye to Mary: "They're hunting me like a fall buck, and I'm bound to quit. Don't think any more about me, for I shall never come back." La Bonté entered the West a panicked animal rather than a conquering hero.[12]

Three milestones helped him shed his hunted past. First, he killed a buffalo. Dropping his initial bison thrilled La Bonté, but the true revelation—the knowledge that started the process of turning him from a greenhorn into a seasoned mountain man—occurred later that night. He witnessed the druggy heights a pack of trappers could reach with a ton of red meat. The men dined themselves senseless, gorging on the choicest parts of the animals. They munched raw hump ribs, tongues, and intestinal "boudins." La Bonté watched "the fleshy mass grow small by degrees and beautifully less, before the blades of the hungry mountaineers." He ate and ate and wondered "that nature, in giving him such grastronomic powers, and such transcendent capabilities of digestion . . . that after consuming nearly his own weight in rich and fat buffalo meat, he felt as easy and as incommoded as if he had been lightly supping on strawberries and cream." The buffalo feast introduced La Bonté to the delights of the carnivore's life, and he came to associate well-being with shoving animal flesh down his gullet. Happiness was a distended stomach.[13]

La Bonté's second initiation followed closely on the first: he scalped a Pawnee while out tracking bison. The Americans knew that their buffalo feasts angered the plains tribes, so La Bonté girded for a fight as soon as he spied the Pawnee hunting party and they spotted him. The group selected one warrior to attack La Bonté and collect his coup. The warrior charged and nicked the American with an arrow. He drew his bow again, but "the eagle eye of the white" spotted the move, and La Bonté countered with a tackle aimed at the horse's neck. The warrior, his grip on his bow instead of his mount, tumbled to the ground. La Bonté triggered his rifle and dispatched his foe. The noise attracted the Americans; the Pawnees, seeing the reinforcements, fled; and that night the mountaineers watched like proud parents as their greenhorn "lifted" his first "hair."[14]

The violation of the corpse indicated the sharp edges of the racial encounter. A manly fight to the death clarified the categories of "white" and "niggur." In another episode, Killbuck rallied his mule to charge a group of Arapahos with the inspirational slogan: "At 'em boy; give the niggurs h——!" The Arapahos, in turn, stoked one another's aggression with race as well. After one fight, "elated by the coup they had just struck the whites," they gathered "four white scalps to incite them to brave deeds." Still, even if the constant threat of violence hardened racial identities, La Bonté's third rite of passage forecast their dissolution. Per the custom of the country, he married several Indian and Mexican women. In contrast to Timothy Flint, Ruxton acknowledged the widespread practice of hunter, Indian, and Mexican unions. But he couldn't bring himself to portray them as carrying the potential of mutual benefit, much less love. According to the Englishman (and contrary to some historical evidence) the "seasoned" mountain men treated their Indian partners cruelly. They beat, traded, exploited, and abandoned them. Inured to the hardships of western nature, the men had also grown insensitive to the pangs of human affection.[15]

Except, that is, for La Bonté. The shell around his "sensations" never fully calcified. He "treated his dusky *sposas* with all the consideration the sex could possibly demand from hand of man." He refused to slap them, punch them, or bash them with lodge poles. "Often his helpmate blushed to see her pale-face lord and master" help with "female" jobs. Unlike his male counterparts—white or Indian—La Bonté gathered firewood, chopped trees, butchered buffalo, and helped cure hides. His labor feminized him; his Indian wives thought him funny. By showing kindness to his nonwhite mates, he committed a "sin unpardonable in hunter law." Gallantry counted as one of "his failings as a mountaineer," but his consideration also opened his path back to white society. His love for Mary Brand kept his heart warm and soft. In the end, he could return to her because affection prevented him from succumbing completely to the callous environment of the West. (Leaving the West meant La Bonté would also have to leave his Indian wives. Ruxton solves the problem of spousal abandonment tarnishing La Bonté's reputation for benevolence by having rival Indians steal or kill his wives, sparing the trapper and the author difficult breakup scenes.)[16]

The passion La Bonté harbored for Brand drew him back toward civilization even while his soft heart pushed him into interracial relationships based on compassion rather than disregard. His love for a white woman actually made him more susceptible to caring unions with nonwhites, marriages that undercut a caste system glorifying white womanhood. In the West, La Bonté forever teetered on the precipice of racial abomination. He could play the savior of a white civilization—the environmental American who came back to invigorate and democratize the nation—or he could be the monster that returned home to rip the place to shreds.

La Bonté's body expressed his dual potential. His inner softness warred with his "storm-hardened flesh." A survivalist, he had endured horrific physical hardship. Deserts burned his skin; frosts blackened his fingers and toes. He went days without water, fortnights without sustenance. The harsh environment reduced him to a skeleton covered in leather and jerky; it carried him to the brink of death, humanity, and whiteness. The scene that determined La Bonté's fate, race, and species affiliation occurred in the wilderness with his true life partner— Killbuck. However much his love for Brand simmered in the reaches of his soul, the young trapper belonged to the grizzled veteran. Their relationship reached a crescendo of intimacy in a crude shanty alongside a small mountain stream that fed the Columbia River.[17]

In the aftermath of an Indian fight that blew apart their large hunting expedition, Killbuck and La Bonté drifted in the Rockies looking for a pass that would lead them toward the Pacific and the hunting grounds of the Columbia headwaters. Winter loomed, and they ran low on ammunition, which worried them less than the absolute scarcity of game to shoot at. They killed and ate a skinny horse, then cut the rest of their mounts loose to die on their own. La Bonté built a hut, and Killbuck collapsed into it, feverish and exhausted. In desperation, La Bonté hunted "morning till night." Finally, in their grimmest hour, Killbuck pulled his friend close and whispered:

> Boy, he said, this old hos feels like goin' under, and that afore long. You're stout yet, and if thar was meat handy, you'd come round slick. Now, boy, I'll be under, as I said, afore many hours, and if you don't raise meat you'll be in the same fix. I never eat dead meat myself, and wouldn't ask no one to do it neither; but meat fair killed is meat any way; so, boy, put your knife in this old niggur's lights, and help yourself. It's "poor bull," I know, but maybe it'll do to keep life in; and along the fleece thar's meat yet, and maybe my old hump ribs has picking on 'em.

La Bonté declined Killbuck's offer. Tenderly, he told the "old hos" that he hadn't "turned niggur yet."[18]

Ruxton packed many cultural references into this moment. He combined Europeans' centuries-old fascination with New World cannibalism with reports of the 1846 Donner Party fiasco with the survival-artist tales of younger hunters outenduring a grizzled vet with the animal and racial minstrelsy he gleaned from the mountain men's vernacular. None of these tropes belonged together. The survival artists carefully separated their bodies from animals' to protect their status as free, white men. Outsiders repeatedly labeled mountain men beasts and mulattos. Perhaps the hunters tried to drain the poison from these slurs by making them into jokes they could fling at one another. But Ruxton played the cannibal scene straight. Killbuck and La Bonté weren't being cheeky. If the young hunter tasted his partner, he could never return to civilization and wed Mary Brand. The western environment would devour him, and he would follow Killbuck into a netherworld where whites turned into blacks, people into animals, lovers into brutes, and humans into meat.

The authenticity of the close encounter with cannibalism mattered less than the overpowering sense of metaphoric possibility emanating from Ruxton's concoction. In the space of four sentences, Killbuck shifted from a horse to a slave to a bull to a rack of hump ribs. He, à la Glass, even injected a lecture on wilderness ethics into the proceedings: his discourse on the consumption of "dead" versus "fair killed" meat. He absolved his friend from the moral constraints of both civilized society and "hunter law." Munching his mentor would free La Bonté of sin. The Christ imagery weighs heavy here, and the religious gravity of the situation may have compelled La Bonté's rejection of Killbuck's flesh. La Bonté turned down more than a life-saving meal. He refused the string of metaphors Killbuck (and Ruxton) deployed to help him over his distaste for eating another human being. In the end, he could no more wrap his imagination around Killbuck's transmutations than he could around his proffered hams.

Western American shape-shifting fascinated George Ruxton. As an author, he wallowed in metaphors of changed bodies. The West hardened people; it darkened and seasoned them. Humans leapt species boundaries. Ruxton played with bodies for literary effect, but he also sought physical transformations for his own medical reasons. After his mule accident, he hoped the West would alter him. He wanted the mountains to fix his back, and he expressed these hopes in the mountain men's language. The invented jargon connected literature and nature through an oral medium, but the dialect needed human voices to come to life. The vernacular infiltrated civilized ears on the unbrushed breath of environmental Americans, and the physicality of their words lingered in print through garbled syntax, strategic misspellings, and italicized keywords. The published versions of the mountain-man vernacular carried the promise (and horror) of the western physical transformations across oceans, nations, and social classes. English gentlemen could touch western nature—could feel the promised transformation—by roaring waughs at one another.

In his final letter to his editor at *Blackwood's*, Ruxton explained the reasons for his trip back to the American West:

> As you say, human natur can't go on feeding on civilised fixings in this "big village"; and this child has felt like going West for many a month, being half froze for buffler meat and mountain doins. My route takes me via New York, the Lakes, and St. Louis, to Fort Leavenworth, or Independence on the Indian frontier. Thence packing my "possibles" on a mule, and mounting a buffalo horse (Panchito, if he is alive), I strike the Santa Fe trial to Arkansa, away up the river to the mountains, winter in the Bayou Salade, where Killbuck and La Bonte joined with the Yutes, cross the mountains next spring to Great Salt lake—and that's far enough to look forward to—always supposing my hair is not lifted by Comanche or Pawnee.

The missive demonstrated Ruxton's eagerness to speak the vernacular. The letter also suggested that both he and his editor indulged in the jargon. "Human natur can't go on feeding on civilised fixings" was the editor's "saying." Just as hat or glove makers reworked western beaver pelts into apparel, Ruxton and his publisher styled the people, places, and language of the fur trade into commodities. They harvested the sounds, smells, and stories of laborers and turned them into salable representations. Ruxton approached his raw material with the intentions of a realist. To readers, he appeared more taxidermist than tailor. But this persona was a put-on. He took advantage of the distance between words and things to create art. He manipulated the Bayou Salade and man-handled Killbuck, La Bonté, the Utes, and the Pawnees, revamping them to serve his desires. All writers are guilty of this crime to some degree. Even if they desperately want their creations to mirror reality, language betrays them in the end. Assumptions, perspectives, and biases creep in to ruin the correspondence between signified and signifier. Ruxton's literature settled on the frontier between history and fantasy, and the mountain-man vernacular epitomized the murky half-truth of his writing.[19]

By co-opting, adapting, and popularizing a hunting jargon, George Ruxton became one of the foremost ventriloquists in western American literature. He fed lines to his heroes and his fiddling produced unreliable history, a less-than-shocking outcome considering his genre. Westerns promoted their authenticity through calibrated realism. Authors harvested the minute details of settings, costumes, accents, and habits. They dressed heroes in buckskins and villains in war bonnets. They painted awesome landscapes with monumental vistas, snowcapped peaks, endless deserts, and churning rivers. They collected a lexicon of western phrases and place-names: cañon, fandango, Black Hills, cache, Colter's Hell, teepee, the Great Salt Lake, and rendezvous. They recorded extreme acts of violence and survival—scalpings, bear maulings, and cannibalistic interludes. All these peculiar tidbits fed the illusion of regional distinctiveness. The details turned the territory to the west of the United States into *the West*. This explains the centrality of the travel narrative in nineteenth-century western writing. Authors dramatized their accumulation of frontier exotica. They showed themselves absorbing the sights of Devils Tower along the Platte or a Ute winter camp in the Rocky Mountains; they let readers see them participate in western rituals such as Indian fights and bison hunts; and they seated the book-buying public alongside them at campfire storytelling sessions to hear the tales of environmental Americans.

Watching, hearing, and reading may sound like passive forms of aggression next to scalping and cannibalism, but consumers thrust themselves into the conquest of the region through the Westerns they bought. Americans exaggerated the exceptionalism of the West in order to appropriate and incorporate it into their nation. The region promised to invigorate the body politic, balancing the collective's humors like a fresh breeze or a clean shower after a muggy day. The West kept the nation spry. Hemmed in by ancient boundaries, European countries grew decadent, old, and sickly. Forever young, always on the move, the United States of America radiated health, vitality.

At least, that was the hope. The medicinal boost westward expansion provided wasn't a sure shot. Free radicals contaminated the region—men with questionable habits, murky bloodlines, and uncertain loyalties. Americans needed a filter that let La Bonté in and kept Killbuck out. To stay democratic, inventive, and vigorous, the nation required infusions from the new races growing out West, but the body politic couldn't survive an influx of violent, shiftless, nonwhite foreigners. Culture solved the problem. The nation adopted the stories from the frontier, and the bodies of environmental Americans who had merged too closely with nature were left to rot. Killbuck stayed in the mountains and faded into the past, while La Bonté strode with Mary Brand to Oregon, gorged like a tick with colorful anecdotes.

Of course, Ruxton created La Bonté, so he belonged to the parasitical chain as well. His position, however, was a curious one: while he supported the territorial expansion of the United States, he stood outside the body politic. He never claimed to be an American. This explains why he neither whitewashed nor humanized his hunters. They could transmogrify into "niggurs" and "critters" with abandon; his British nationality protected him from their racial and animal confusion. Later in the nineteenth century, other European authors would tap the vigor of the American frontier through the idea of Anglo-Saxonism, but Ruxton seemed uninterested in transatlantic biological constructs. He didn't want to extend the American body politic as much as he wanted the dynamism of a people living close to nature to revitalize him.

"The history of a country is closely allied to its geographical location and its natural conditions. The character of a people is molded by the influence of climate, production, and environment, in physical as well as in spiritual matters, eventually evolving into a distinct and recognizable national trait." With this statement of natural nationalism, Friedrich von Wrede opened a June 1839 letter to his German relatives. Environments molded people, infusing their bodies and their souls with a collective personality. People carried nature and nation around in their guts. For von Wrede, the prospect of landscapes forming political bodies wasn't all hopeful. He wrote to alarm as much as to assuage. Texas, he reported, stood between two natural and national regimes. The hot blood of the Mexicans ran toward Catholic hierarchy and spiritual repression, while the influence of temperate English Protestantism drove the Americans toward "freedom and democracy." In 1839, independent Texas languished as a borderland dominated by absence. The place was "unpopulated, uncultivated, and politically dead, remaining a huge hunting reserve." An injection of freedom-loving "German Protestantism," sterner stuff than even the English brand, might eventually turn the waste into prosperous farms, but at present the environment best suited wild animals and the feral humanoids who chased them.[20]

Hugh Glass and the restless edge dwellers growing strong in dead zones just beyond the reach of nations would have loved Texas. Glass and his compatriots likewise helped von Wrede escape the philosophical implications of his environmental determinism. Friedrich von Wrede arrived in North America in 1836, hoping to purchase land in Texas, settle his family there, and sell farm plots to surround himself with right-thinking Germans. However, the Texas Revolution and the turmoil that followed bogged him down in New Orleans. His funds ran dry, and he traveled to St. Louis and Natchez with his son looking for work. His wife found a job to help support the family; she taught in a New Orleans girls' preparatory academy, while he launched a series of anemic business ventures and labored as a cashier and a janitor in a theater. Then, in the winter of 1838, his wife sickened and died. The loss wrecked Friedrich. "Take away the reassuring greenery of a tree," he wrote, "that has already lost its blossoms, and it stands leafless, wintry, and withered before you. That is how I stand nowadays with snow white hair, at the grave of my life's companion." The arboreal metaphor captured the Hessian's thought process: he interpreted the loss of his wife and his economic failures as natural disasters. The Mississippi environment weakened and destroyed bodies with ague and fever. The place was wicked, and its

malice invaded the souls of the residents who had grown too accus-
tomed to its twisted nature. The rot in native-born Americans showed
most brilliantly in their business transactions. The Americans lied to
von Wrede. They robbed and poked fun at him. They advertised falsely
and broke contracts. And they had the gall to shrug off these nefarious
practices as humbugs.[21]

A humbug, von Wrede explained to his German readers, was a
cross between a practical joke and a scam. Americans continually promised more than they could deliver, and when victims called them on
their deceptions, they laughed at the dupes and lectured them on the
merits of cunning. The best businessmen perpetrated the most humbugs while avoiding being conned themselves. The "cleverness" of the
native-born Americans drove von Wrede berserk. To him, they were false,
dishonorable, and obnoxious. Far from ingenious or witty, they perpetrated "rascality."[22]

Humbugs and microbes nearly ruined von Wrede. He survived his
wife's death and New Orleans's hucksters and found his way to Texas,
but "the land of his hopes" let him down. He returned to Germany in
1843 and published his journals and letters. Later, he traveled back to
Texas to help his son manage a settlement of German farmers. Indians
killed and scalped him outside Austin on October 24, 1845. The Hessian perished in circumstances reminiscent of his steamboat ghost's
death (the Arikaras scalped Hugh Glass, too, after they murdered him
in 1833). Von Wrede, however, stayed buried while his book continued
his dialogue about the American West. As far as promotional literature
goes, von Wrede's *Sketches of Life in the United States of America and
Texas* underwhelms. Von Wrede never mastered the American art of
slinging bullshit; he plied ambivalence instead, which may have suited
his audience better. He inspired quite a few dour German Protestants to
follow him to the territory of lukewarm possibilities.

He saw potential in America, especially in the continent's "uncultivated" spaces. But he heaped so much personal disappointment on the
pages that his anguish weighed down the landscapes he intended to
boost. "I seem to be sitting," he opened one entry from Nacogdoches,
Texas, weeks after the burial of his wife, "in the midst of this world where
contrasts are sharper and more overwhelming than Germany—where

nature has such strong mastery over the human that he is compelled to fight and strive, to work and produce with his hands and feet in a calm resigned spirit . . . Here," he concluded, "it is either life or death." Von Wrede ruminated on the Texas environment, the harsh world outside him, to express his inner turmoil. America had stolen his beloved and broken his dreams. His land of hopes had dissolved into a world of sorrows populated with confidence men and killer fevers. The brutal nature of America compelled all human beings to "fight and strive," and von Wrede equated this struggle with labor. Nature commanded perspiration rather than inspiration. Immigrants would have to give up their notions of square deals and intact families and lash their spirits to their grunting bodies if they hoped to survive.[23]

People often invoke a higher power when grief hammers their psyches. They hand themselves to God, alcohol, twelve-step programs, or jogging. Von Wrede experienced his emotional trauma miles from home in a county that seemed giddy to thwart his plans. The environment and inhabitants of the Mississippi Valley had ravaged his life. Texas might heal him, but only if he could reform his thinking, discipline his mind to numb his misery. The land put his body to work, and von Wrede muffled his higher faculties, reacting to environmental stimuli with his cerebral cortex, his lizard brain. The stark landscape reduced decisions to simple binaries: fight or die, work or die, live or die. He calmed his spirit with the tonic of bare necessity.

Perhaps that's why the German immigrant dreamed of Hugh Glass. Von Wrede introduced the hunter as a paragon of emotional detachment. Of his "own free will," Glass "severed all connections with the civilized world" "to seek out the hardships and dangers of the wilderness." His "class of men" found happiness not in the bonds of human affection, but "in the excitement of saving their lives from or overcoming deathly perils." Glass lived to survive; "danger" was his sole "passion." To a husband and father trapped in an equally dangerous environment, though diseases and scam artists imperiled him rather than irate bears and marauding Blackfeet, Glass looked impressive. He appeared invulnerable: his body tough, his spirit bold. Isolation strengthened him. Sometimes he cohabited with Indians (savages he could never truly love), but most of the time he wandered in nature alone. Glass had journeyed beyond worry and heartache. In a world of sharp contrasts, where decisions boiled down to fight or flight, Glass discovered bliss in the rapid fire of basic instincts in his cerebral cortex. Still, lizard kings ruled puny domains. Glass freed himself from care, but he wasn't free. Just as Texas bossed von Wrede—put him to work—the western environment barked orders at Glass. The higher questions of romance, philosophy, or religion found scant purchase in a head consumed by survival. To be an environmental American was to be a puppet—a body jerked around by the caprice of nature.[24]

In the hands of the international writers, Glass cut ties with his employers, his family, his nation, his civilization, his race, and perhaps even his humanity to become a slave to his surroundings. Both unencumbered and tethered, Glass's wild servitude proved irresistible to foreign nationals on the hunt for literary material. Von Wrede spectacularly resurrected the old hunter, while George Ruxton picked him up to illustrate the ferocity of grizzly bears. "A hug" he wrote, "at close quarters is anything but a pleasant embrace, [the bears'] strong hooked claws stripping the flesh from bones as easily as a cook peels an onion." The image of the onion stuck with Ruxton. At the end of the tale, he has Glass declare that he felt "'as slick as a peeled onion.'" Food also surfaced in the second of the three direct utterances Ruxton allowed Glass: "'Harraw, Bill!'" he shouted to his partner as the she-bear launched her attack, "'we'll be made meat for sure as shootin'!'" The culinary metaphors underscored the bears' dreadfulness: they could flip the world upside down, turn protein-guzzling mountain men into dinner.[25]

Yet despite his references to peeling flesh and human entrees, Ruxton actually restrained his metaphorrhea when retelling the Glass saga. He buttoned up the region's premier escape artist—the trapper who "had seen, probably, more exciting adventures, and had more wonderful and hairbreadth escapes, than any of the rough and hardy fellows who make the West their home." Compared to Killbuck or La Bonté, Glass was mum. That's not to say Ruxton didn't show Glass talking. Indeed, he emphasized Glass's telling of the survival story over the actual survival. Glass crawls back from the brink out of sight, off the page. The bear mauls him and the men leave, taking his clothes, his gun, and his narrative with them. Months later, Glass appears "much altered" outside the gate of Fort Kiowa. The hunters invite him in and crowd "round to hear from his lips, how, after the lapse of he knew not how long, he had gradually recovered." Readers stand with them, listening to Glass recount his ordeals. But Ruxton doesn't let him speak in his own voice. The Englishman summarizes the action.[26]

Ruxton's treatment of Glass underscored his literary authority. Ruxton decided who spoke, what they said, and who got to hear them. This power corrupted his oral history. He abused his artistic license and faked the mountain-man vernacular. As far as we know, Glass held forth like a lyceum orator rather than a rootin'-tootin' gargler of grammar. But his diction died with him. Ruxton's patois, however untrue, marked a turning point in Glass's afterlife. When the mauled environmental American reappeared in twentieth-century poems, novels, and major motion pictures, he spoke with the tongue of a British writer/adventurer suffering from a bad back and terrible case of dysentery who desperately wanted to heal.

———— • ◦ • ————

The time has come to kill Hugh Glass. I've been delaying the inevitable to bring home a point: Glass lost control of his story and his body long before he died. An Arikara war party finally took his life, but their trespasses merely capped a series of appropriations that began when his friends absconded with his gun and clothes after the she-bear attack. For an independent cuss, Glass collected a remarkable array of masters: a judge from Illinois, a St. Louis newspaperman turned State Department bureaucrat, a retired trapper holed up in the Napa Valley, an American fur-company boss, a German land speculator, an English explorer/ethnographer, and a cavalry officer in the U.S. Army, among others. These authors pulled his strings and fed him lines. They tossed him into debates over nature and nations and enslaved him to stark environments. They circled his body, ogled his scars, and grinned when he declared that he felt "right peart." Their versions of Glass crawled into the future while the man drifted away, looking for work. Hence, culture devoured biography.

Still, just as Glass started out somewhere, he ended up someplace, too. He was murdered along with Edward Rose and a trapper named Menard as they crossed the frozen Yellowstone River in the winter of 1833. The Indians stripped the bodies and scalped them. A few months later, four Arikara men entered an American encampment to trade. The Americans noticed that their visitors wore and carried items belonging to Glass, Rose, and Menard. Johnson Gardner, the hunters' leader, ordered the Indians seized. One pleaded ignorance, and they freed him. The others found no mercy. The Americans sliced off their scalps and burned them alive. That summer, at Fort Union, Francis Chardon sold one of the Arikaras' scalps to Prince Maximilian of Wied-Neuwied, a German potentate touring the American West for thrills, scientific enlightenment, and literary acclaim. He kept a journal, publishing it back home in 1840 as *Reise in das Innere Nord-Amerikas*. An English version, *Maximilian Prince of Wied's Travels in the Interior of North America, During the Years 1832–1834*, appeared in London in 1843. A wonderful example of European science and leisure mingling with the working-class culture of fur hunting, Maximilian's writings chronicled the twilight of the beaver trade.[27]

Declining fur prices and animal populations set the stage for Glass's last acts. He appeared in the records of the American Fur Company, supplying meat for the company's post at Fort Union and joining at least one expedition to round up horses and liquor for the fort. Glass also trapped beaver on his own. Records described him as a free trapper. Working without a contract with a single firm, his unemployment "freed" him to sell his pelts to the highest bidder. However, only a few companies— most of the time only one, the Rocky Mountain Fur Company—sent goods to the annual summer rendezvous where the independent hunters gathered to cash in their hauls. In 1828, the free trappers sent Glass to Fort Union to plead with Kenneth McKenzie, the post's commander, to send American Fur Company traders and merchandise to that year's rendezvous in order to break the monopoly and foster better deals. The choice of Glass may have reflected the esteem in which his fellows held him or their appreciation of his knack for showing up at his intended destination no matter who bit, shot, or denuded him along the way. Whatever the rationale, he didn't succeed. McKenzie wanted the skins to come to Fort Union. When the steamboats reached the fort in 1831,

the post would become the hub of a new fur trade centered on bison robes rather than beaver pelts.[28]

Capitalism squeezed Glass as capitalism tends to do. A lowly supplier in a mammoth enterprise that shipped the remnants of western ecosystems across the globe, Glass hustled to keep his footing. But he was a nimble guy with a limited horizon. He didn't have a family to feed or shareholders to please. He could have killed bison for a while, then maybe guided American farmers through the mountains when the Oregon country beckoned. Desperation from another quarter foreclosed these possibilities: the Arikaras had hit bottom. The Americans and British armed their Indian rivals while driving the game from their hunting grounds. In the winter of 1823, the Sioux destroyed the Arikaras' villages on the Missouri River, killing "thirty or forty men" and breaking the nation in two. Half of the survivors went to the plains to hunt bison, while the other half planted one last maize crop. By 1833, John Sanford, the American Indian agent for the upper Missouri River, could no longer find the nation: "the Arikaras have abandoned the Missouri last fall and where they are gone to, or where they are at present I am unable to say." Up until this point, farming and villages had been the hallmarks of the Arikaras' subsistence. The abandonment of both signaled the bleakness of their situation.[29]

The Arikara men had separated into packs. They ambushed their rivals to salvage their honor as their world crumbled. Martial display seems to have been one of the motivations for killing Glass and his comrades. Glass, Rose, and Menard set out from Fort Cass at the mouth of the Bighorn River on a frigid morning. Rose and Menard were on the job. They "belonged" to the American Fur Company, and their boss had dispatched them to Fort Union. Glass, "a free man, a veteran trapper," joined them for protection. His destination was "a camp of white hunters some short distance below" Fort Union. The Arikaras "fell in" with the three just below where the Bighorn met the Yellowstone. They "treacherously killed" and "scalped them and left part of the scalps of each tied to poles on the grounds of the murder." Reading the strands of hair from a distance of more than a century and a half is tricky. Whites and Indians took and kept scalps to possess their enemies, to hold their spiritual powers or own them as keepsakes or commodities. Leaving the hair behind at the murder scene, the Arikaras behaved provocatively, and the scalps on the poles, whatever their precise meaning, did elicit an immediate response: "A party of Crows went in pursuit of them the same evening or next day but could not overtake them." The first group to try to avenge Hugh Glass—the ultimate environmental American— was a posse of Indians.[30]

Fittingly, Glass died so that others could make a statement. The Crows followed the Arikaras to settle another score. Edward Rose belonged to them as much as to the American Fur Company. "The son of a white trader and a half-breed woman, mixed Indian and Negro blood," Rose lived with the Crows for a number of years. He learned their language, and several fur-trade expeditions hired him to serve as their interpreter. Ashley employed him; remember, it was Rose who sneaked into the Arikara village with Stephens the night before the firefight on the beach. Incidents like this, along with his mixed race and his intimacy with Natives, raised hackles among some of the Americans. Joshua Pilcher called him "a celebrated outlaw." Washington Irving dug deeper into his thesaurus. To him, Rose was "a dogged, sullen, silent fellow with a sinister aspect and more of the savage than the civilized man in his appearance." Colonel Henry Leavenworth thought more highly of him. In the aftermath of the Arikara debacle, he granted Rose a commission in the army, recommending him "as a brave and enterprising man, well acquainted with the Indians. He had resided for about three years with them; understood their language, and they were very much attached to him." The Indians fond of Rose at the time Leavenworth wrote? The Arikaras.[31]

Edward Rose, observed Irving, "seemed to have neither kin nor country." He belonged to so many races, nations, and families that he appeared to belong to none. This appalled Irving, but the multiple loyalties of American mountain men attracted other writers. George Ruxton celebrated the mutability of fur hunters in the vernacular he had them speak. An unreliable linguistic source, Ruxton captured in his faux pidgin the crosshatched intricacy of the social relations that underwrote the fur trade. He even tried to harness the physical power of the spoken word to heal his own body. Friedrich von Wrede latched on to one mountain man for similar reasons. Hugh Glass radiated health in a sickly environment. He represented the good American, which, given von Wrede's distaste for them, meant he retained only the slightest connection to the nation of his birth. He wandered the geographic fringes, growing strong in the spaces between nations. Outside his country, Glass discovered a stark land that emboldened him instead of cut him down. He communicated this nature to von Wrede. As he talked through the night on the muggy, foul steamboat, Glass refreshed the environment. His stories lifted spirits and cured ills. The old ghost was a boon companion to a lonely, distraught immigrant.[32]

Ruxton and von Wrede could nab American mountain men because American writers held their environmental champions at arm's length. "Neither kin nor country" sounded like an invitation rather than a rebuke. Thus, foreign nationals served as the midwives for Hugh Glass's afterlife. It's entirely fitting, then, that a non-American took possession of the last piece of him. Prince Maximilian purchased two scalps at Fort Union. The first belonged to the Arikara who Gardner said participated in the winter murder; a shred of hair and skin hung from one of the poles. The second was Glass's scalp, which he placed in a trunk filled with animal pelts, Indian costumes, and western gewgaws.

I want to write this ending: On a warm day three summers ago, I sat in an air-conditioned archive in Wied-Neuwied, stroking Hugh Glass's hair. But I can't. Glass didn't make it to Germany. Maximilian's collection burned in a keelboat fire on the homeward journey. Glass drifted through his final environment on a puff of smoke.

SEVEN

I WILL SURVIVE

A horse fell on Charles Swin and pushed him through a hole in time. Out working his ranch by himself with a plow team, Swin unhitched the tandems to walk them down a steep wash single file. The lead animal stumbled and rolled, grinding his boss into the dirt like a spent cigarette. The seventy-three-year-old "lay with a broken back in his lonely dugout on a wind swept range, 18 miles northeast of Vernal" for three days and nights. Instead of a twentieth-century Utah cowboy scrounging a living from a 320-acre dust patch near the Colorado border in 1949, he found himself the star of a western drama that screamed nineteenth century. He fought nature alone; no one could hear him yowl.[1]

The accident rearranged Swin's cosmos. His vertebrae popped, and the cold, unfeeling outside advanced on him. Distances lengthened; horizons stretched. The line between the interior stuff of personhood—mind, self, will, soul, character, identity, attitude—and the external world of scrub brush and coyotes shifted. The outside claimed his body. He could no longer count his muscles and his stomach, his eyes and his ears, as allies. His muscles shivered and cramped; his stomach growled. He hallucinated and daydreamed. He battled a wilderness that included parts he once considered himself.

T. Pearse Wheelwright, the reporter from the *Deseret News*, knew he had a story when word reached him of Swin's ordeal. He rushed to the recuperating rancher's bedside at the Latter-Day Saints' hospital in Salt Lake City. The old-timer was a good interviewee. Following the wreck that dislocated his spine "out an inch," Swin recalled, he belly-wriggled two hundred yards to a dugout carved in the side of the wash. He lay there for days, firing his gun at intervals to catch the attention of the Evans family, his nearest neighbors, a couple of miles away. On the third morning, Swin concluded that inaction would kill him. He inched toward the Evans place, collapsing around noon, two hundred yards from the house. He woke and called, but even at that range they couldn't hear him. The family found him passed out on their doorstep that evening.[2]

Wheelwright prodded Swin for an uplifting resolution. Did he have big plans for the life he rescued? "I recollect," Swin said, "I'll have my strength back in two, three days." Then he would head back. "I've fought the land for thirty years," he said, "and I reckon I'll hang on out until I die."[3]

Swin epitomized the indivisibility of body, land, and spirit. The rancher had scraped the hardpan for his meager existence for so long that his bones and his outlook had turned to hardpan as well. The commingling of outer nature and internal personality saved him. He endured because decades of labor had pounded him to grit and gristle. He was as tough and unyielding as the place he worked. And he had grown fond of the daily struggle. Bent by excruciating pain, he crawled toward the horizon in order to return to where he started.

Wheelwright turned the accident into a Sisyphean fable, and he expected his readers to embrace Swin and his philosophy of unending toil. The old guy may have been poor and alone (Wheelwright gave no indication how he would pay his medical expenses), but he embodied the simple nobility of Utah's laboring classes. His was "a story of sheer human courage told in the simple language of a man who has ridden as a top hand, run his own outfits, and for the last 30 years tried to eke out an existence on 320 acres of desert land." He was a survivor and deserved credit for hanging on when softer specimens would have let go.[4]

The Western novelist Frederick Manfred clipped the Swin article from the *Deseret News* while conducting his research for *Lord Grizzly*, his 1954 epic retelling of the Hugh Glass legend. The old cowboy's torment helped him imagine Glass's ordeal. Their broken bodies united the men; so, too, did their social marginality. Both Glass and Swin worked close to nature, and their labor exposed them to accidents that blurred the line between self and environment, turning their own bodies into foreign and hostile territories. Nature violated both men, and their responses to these invasions launched them into popular culture. Dangerous work gone horribly wrong turned them from grunts into founts, and narrative hunters rushed quickly to the site of their misfortune—their wrecked bodies—to collect their stories and bring them to market.

Manfred first encountered Glass years before in the Works Progress Administration's guide to South Dakota. The story stuck with him, and in 1952 he decided to write *Lord Grizzly*. Manfred understood desperation. He had published several semiautobiographical novels set in the contemporary West, but the royalties from these titles financed only the purchase of beans; they didn't pay the bills. The kids complained about their legume-heavy diet, while Fred and his wife, Maryanna, looked out for the one bad turn—the accident or the illness—that would sink them. Hugh Glass showed up in the nick of time.

Using the techniques of the novel as well as a smear of Freudian psychology—flashbacks, first-person dialogue (the idiom he borrowed from George Ruxton), hallucinations, id and ego conflicts—Manfred inserted readers into Glass's head. At long last, audiences could see the ripe plums that drew him to the streamside thicket that hid the bear; they could feel the milk and blood gush over him as he stabbed the mama monster over and over to keep her teeth and claws at bay; and they could enjoy the diabolical tickle of the maggots squirming in the open wound at the center of his back, just beyond a finger scratch as he crawled toward Fort Kiowa. In *Lord Grizzly*, Manfred turned the empty patches in the tale into smorgasbords of sensations.

The fully endowed legend drew readers. Upon publication in 1954, *The New York Times* reviewed the novel favorably, and *Lord Grizzly* entered that paper's bestseller list. The book established Manfred's career and name. He adapted his version of the legend for Hollywood. Although the studios rejected his screenplay, they produced another writer's. In 1971, *Man in the Wilderness* flitted across American movie screens. The film starring Richard Harris was a dud, but the cinematic experience furthered Glass's transition from a *far* western figure into an intimate companion. The novel and the film welcomed an environmental

American home; authors and audiences no longer felt uneasy in his presence. Indeed, they seemed eager to trade places with him.

Glass had indeed traveled a long way over the previous hundred years. In the nineteenth century, audiences distanced themselves from mountain men and questioned their honesty. Everyone assumed they lied; few people placed confidence in them. In the twentieth century, Glass gained credibility. In 1915, John G. Neihardt dug him up and placed him on the far side of the frontier. Glass remained distant from readers in Neihardt's epic poem *The Song of Hugh Glass*, but this separation was temporal rather than geographic. Frederick Manfred collapsed the distance entirely in *Lord Grizzly*. Then an even stranger thing happened: Hugh Glass ended up ahead of Americans. He waited for them in the dystopian future.

His latest resting place is in survivalist media. Glass still lingers in popular renditions of desolation and woe, but he now belongs to a tribe of cannibals; a club of highly publicized, extreme pro-lifers who swig urine, hole up in animal carcasses, amputate their own arms, and, on occasion, eat their dead friends in order to stay breathing, on earth, in their bodies. Glass has become a role model for enduring catastrophe.[5]

A recent coinage, the term "survivalist" popped up in the 1970s to define a particular social type: wilderness kooks who stockpiled gold, canned goods, automatic weapons, and *Soldier of Fortune* magazines for the coming apocalypse. Of course, not all survivors are survivalists. Survivors merit admiration for their grace under pressure and indomitable spirits. Survivalists invite a wide berth and perhaps an ATF raid on their compounds. Yet, for all their differences, survivors and survivalists inhabit similar imaginative environments. They both live in post-cataclysmic dreamscapes where human beings under extreme duress unlock and contemplate the secrets of human existence. If the plane crashed, if the government collapsed, if the volcano blew, if the storm hit, if the plague descended, who would survive? Exemplary individuals like Hugh Glass. He and his ilk wouldn't panic or lament the disappearance of their former lives. They absorbed hard facts, stared down the truth.

From this perspective, the workplace accidents of Charles Swin and Hugh Glass gave them an opportunity to discover their innermost strength. Crappy luck exposed the cores of their souls. And the arrangers of survivalist compendiums collected tales like these to "guide" readers toward an educated relationship with nature. They taught consumers how to react when environments suddenly broke through the barriers protecting them from forces beyond their control. That both the marketers and their consumers assumed there were barriers separating the chaotic outside from their treasured insides showed the vast differences between them and people like Glass. He probably wasn't all that surprised that nature invaded him. Environments flowed into humans in the 1820s, either ruining or bolstering their health. The survivalist books, movies, and television programs reacquainted modern readers with old-style humoral nature, and laboring people like Swin and Glass served as the conduits to times and circumstances that bred revelatory calamities.

The survivalist media completed the reorientation of Hugh Glass. Instead of occupying a position far away or back in time, Glass ended up in front of Americans. He awaited them in the imaginative space of impending doom. Given the right (meaning horrendously bad) turn of events, anyone could land in his place. Glass became a person to emulate rather than cast away. He instructed pudgy, overcivilized weaklings in the art of enduring physical torment and environmental upheaval. He entered the twenty-first century a life coach for the end times.

However, before Glass could pull ahead, he had to be left behind— again. At the turn of the twentieth century, modernist artists borrowed Glass from international travel writers as well as apologists for United States expansion. These artists revised the meaning of the *far* West. Instead of isolating men remade by nature, moving them physically away from civilized society, the modernists quarantined environmental Americans back in time. Writers like John G. Neihardt consigned them to history. A fondness for western nature and vintage hunters united Fredrick Manfred and Neihardt, but they weren't friends. They quarreled over Glass. Neihardt claimed that Manfred stole his ideas, while Manfred accused Neihardt of oversentimentalizing the legend. The poet, Manfred wrote his editor at Doubleday, "missed it," which created an opening for him to "change the scene a little, the names also, and make it my own." Manfred traced his fascination with the story to the brief mention in the WPA's guidebook to South Dakota, not Neihardt's *The Song of Hugh Glass*. Their versions of the maul, the crawl, and the revenge were quite dissimilar. Neihardt invented new characters (as did Manfred) and used them to renovate the narrative. He introduced a greenhorn with flowing yellow hair and a borderline erotic attachment to Glass. "Jamie" (Jim Bridger?) finds Hugh's mangled body, and his search for Glass—rather than the bear fight—sets the stage for the betrayal. The legend's blood-gushing pivotal moment transpired out of sight. Manfred, in contrast, wallowed in the bear-on-man violence. The she-bruin and Glass, not Jim and Hugh, have the borderline erotic attachment, rolling on the ground, drenched in goo, trading breathless roars and waughs.[6]

Neihardt sat Glass between Mike Fink and Jedediah Smith in a cycle of five heroic songs that together told the epic history of the American West. Ashley's 1822 advertisement calling for "enterprising young men" kicked the saga into motion; the massacre of the Teton Sioux at Wounded Knee ended it. Neihardt designed the cycle to progress chronologically and spiritually. Ashley's men stood for "physical prowess" and "ancient needs and greeds." The conquered Sioux ghost dancers represented "spiritual triumph." Neihardt elaborated on this typology—rapacious whites versus mystical Indians—in his nonfiction work. In *Black Elk Speaks*, his best-known book, the poet melded ethnography and Euro-American romanticism to preserve Sioux culture and lambaste American colonization. American soldiers, reservation agents, and bison hunters destroyed the "sacred hoop," leaving the people and the environments of the Northern Plains shattered. Like Hall and the other nineteenth-century semiprofessional regionalists, Neihardt tracked down oral histories to compose his Westerns. Like them, he believed that spoken stories transmitted more than information. Talk changed listeners, turned them into Indian haters, or, in Neihardt's case, into a white spokesman for a dying Native religion.[7]

Age and youth, wisdom and enthusiasm, spirit and body, orator and listener: these were the primary ingredients in Neihardt's Westerns, and he applied them liberally in his song of Hugh Glass. Flaxen-haired Jamie loved "Mother Hugh" for his stories. Glass took a shine to Jamie after

the youth stood his ground during the Arikara fight. The two grew inseparable—"Graybeard and Goldhair riding knee to knee." At night,
after Glass returned from the day's hunt with meat for the expedition,
they huddled together, and Glass

> Summoned many a stirring story,
> Lived grimly once, but now shot through with glory
> Caught from the wondering eyes of him who heard—
> Tales jagged with bleak unstudied word,
> Stark saga stuff.

Jamie's attention "thawed" Glass's "gray mask." The adoration made
him suddenly vulnerable to emotions to which constant exposure to
danger and privation had numbed him. Jamie cracked Glass, got him to
smile. The bear and Jamie's depature broke the spell and rearranged
Hugh's face:

> A red gout clung where either brow should be;
> The haughty nose lay crushed amid the beard,
> Thick with slow ooze, whence like a devil leered.

Glass's "battered mouth" had healed into a permanent grin that
disguised his rage. He clawed his way back to Fort Kiowa to show Jamie
his new mask before he killed the youngster.[8]

Both Neihardt and Manfred exploited Glass's heightened emotional
state to penetrate his head. They fused hate, delirium, and western nature. The landscape, its animals, and Glass's fever and rage swirled into
a dream trance ripe for literary manipulation. The poet spun visions,
metaphors, and leaps of perspective, while the novelist fabricated mystical bears and flashbacks. Glass's madness jarred his time frame. Alone
in nature, he squirmed into a primitive space, a mythic nowhere of
perfect sympathy. Readers could access his mind because he was living
in his lizard brain, the instinctual zone all humans enter when desperation burns away the superfluities of fashion, history, and culture. Neihardt marked the passage into base humanity by having readers look at
Glass through animal eyes. Wolves, rabbits, crows, and gophers catch

glimpses of him and try to comprehend the weird "three-legged beast, bear-like, yet not a bear" in their midst. Glass's bruin-ness reaches a crescendo near the end of his crawl. A party of Arikaras pass him on a trail. Hidden in a patch of brambles, he watches them go by. Long after the main group disappears, an "old crone" shuffles past. Her vulnerability triggers Glass's bloodlust. He's tempted to jump from the bushes, murder her with his bare hands, and grab her flint and knife. But he can't. "Yet not a bear," mauling a defenseless human was beyond him.[9]

Neihardt's Glass overflows with emotion. He acts with deep purpose; his motives were unambiguous. This natural man has none of the obtuseness of his nineteenth-century forebear. Instead of vanishing, he sticks around and stays vivid, and we see all of him, ripped skin to torn psyche. These sharp, primitive feelings encased in language will cross the frontier boundary while Glass, with his torn body and violent temper, will remain behind. The clarity of Glass's emotions made his words as communicable as head lice. His words bore into listeners. He stumbled back to Fort Kiowa and spent months resting his body and working his jaw. The trappers cared for him and let him laze around; "the tale he told . . . were as gold / to bury a winter's comfort at the post." Glass's story shocked the men: "it seemed the deed was done / before their eyes who heard." His voice became his meal ticket and his primary weapon.[10]

Recovered, Glass hitched a ride upstream to unleash his oral vengeance on "Old Jules," the smooth-talking half of the duo assigned to bury him. Jules had tricked Jamie into leaving his beloved mentor by lying about an imminent Arikara attack and the certainty of Glass's demise. At Henry's fort, Glass cornered Jules and reduced him to a "pup" by the very fact of his presence. His mangled form proved Jules's deception, for if Glass fibbed, "then I lie both here and by the Grand [river, site of the bear attack]." A belittled and exposed Jules satisfied Glass; words satisfied him. Following Glass's discovery of the potency of his storytelling that winter at Fort Kiowa, he no longer needed to kill people. He punned Jules to death, made him a liar in the double sense: the thief spoke untruths, and only Glass's mercy prevented him from reposing in a grave. By this point in the song, figurative punishment was enough.[11]

Words had a powerful effect on Jamie as well. He heard the story of Glass's resurrection and left Fort Henry immediately to find him and

seek forgiveness. The two men missed each other several times, trudg-
ing and floating up and down the Missouri. Star-crossed chums in a
fur-trapper version of a romantic comedy, they yearned for one another
across the Plains and Badlands, ratcheting up the drama for the final
reunion. This coming-together happened in a Peigan teepee "North beyond Saskatchewan." Jamie is blind with fever. His guilt and hard travels
have wasted him: "A mass of golden hair / Falls round the face that sickness and despair / Somehow make old, albeit he is young." Jamie begs
his hosts to get him a priest. He wants to confess before he dies. They
bring him Glass. Confused, Jamie spills his guts to the "Black Robe."
"O Father," he asks at the end, "is there any hope for me?" Glass reas-
sures his "son." He's heard this story before, a young lad searching for an
old man, and it ends well. They find each other, "And both forgave—
'twas easy to forgive— / For oh we have so short a time to—" Then he
reveals himself: "O Jamie, Jamie, Jamie—I am Hugh! / There was no
Black Robe yonder—will I do." Male bonds restored, the curtain draws
closed, and assuming the greenhorn rallied, the pair lived happily ever
after.[12]

Neihardt adapted the bear legend into a transgenerational love
story. Glass and Jamie become fictive kin through a process that combined excruciating pain (physical and emotional) and storytelling. The
pair spend next to no time together in the poem. They go from being
coworkers to boon companions. Then Hugh's accident separates them.
They spend the crawl and initial revenge apart, only hearing of each
other. But whispers of news were enough to cement their relationship
as father and son.

Neihardt revered spoken connections; the words of old men were
his sole connection to the "saga-stuff of a country I knew and loved." He
grew up in northern Nebraska, "at the edge of the retreating frontier,"
where he befriended the neighboring Omaha Indians and communed
with the elderly "long-hairs." He repeated this approach with the Oglala
Sioux, seeking out "unreconstructed" old folks—Black Elk, for example—
to tell him "their thoughts, their feelings, their rich memories that often
reached back into the world of my *Cycle*."[13]

Their words brought the poet into contact with a lost world, but
time and colonization had whittled the connection down to speeches

and wistfulness. He loved well-aged Indians and trappers, but they inhabited the "farther slope of a veritable 'watershed of history.'" Their stories drifted down to him, but Neihardt stayed stranded in modernity, longing for epic heroes and Olympic Wests like a child yearns for the spry characters in the stories grandparents told of their youth. Talk was the place generations commiserated, and Neihardt exalted the feelings transmitted by oral culture. In Melville's terms, he was a nostalgia hunter, and he trusted some pretty flimsy chains of gossip to reach the old West. His conduit to the Ashley men, for instance, consisted of the "old men who had missed them, but had known men who knew some of them well." Two coots of separation stood between him and Glass. He heard the story from old-timers who heard the story from older-timers. This methodology guaranteed distortion, but Neihardt preferred talk over written sources. For him, spoken words carried emotional truths that scribbled observations missed.[14]

In many ways, John Neihardt was the prototypical regional modernist. He drew sharp lines between past and present, frontier and twentieth-century West, assimilated Indians and "long-hairs," crusty storytellers and greenhorn listeners. He stressed barriers in order to highlight the oral histories that he smuggled across them. The frontier line was both clearly drawn, formidable, and porous. Neihardt constructed topographies of watersheds and basins in which his poems and ethnographies acted as reservoirs of dying wisdom and spirituality. He manned the head gate. Time had diminished "the great mood of courage that was developed west of the Missouri River in the nineteenth century," but readers could raise a glass to the passing of the heroic age from their post on the downside of the summit.[15]

Neihardt pioneered no new ground with his western nostalgia. Frederick Jackson Turner, Theodore Roosevelt, and Owen Wister had been noting (and bemoaning) lost American frontiers for decades by the time he poeticized Glass. The far-back West of the twentieth-century modernists also resembled the faraway West of the nineteenth-century nationalists. Like the frontier modernists, the part-time semiprofessional authors appropriated western stories while keeping their distance from those stories' sources. The modernists simply replaced geography with time. This swap changed the emotional tenor of the

passage of men remade by nature from the periphery to the core. Sadness
overtook suspicion. The far away isolated western heroes whereas the far
back neutered them. Crazy Horse, Jedediah Smith, Sitting Bull, and
Hugh Glass could mingle in Neihardt's cycle because history had
eclipsed them all. None of them belonged in the modern West; their
racial, national, and cultural incongruities paled next to their shared
deadness.[16]

The far back gave frontier modernists a way to regret national expansion without opposing it. Neihardt criticized the United States's
conquest of the West. The extermination of the bison and the decima-
tion of Native religions upset him greatly. However, since colonization
stopped with the closing of the frontier, there was nothing he could do
to reverse the outcome of the "great fight." The onslaught of history
limited his activism to chatting with survivors and writing down their
memories. He responded to the inevitable spread of "Indo-European"
populations across the globe with ethnography. As Indians and white
old-timers passed from the scene, he recorded and rewrote their stories,
styling himself a troubadour "singing about a time and a country that
I loved."[17]

Frederick Manfred thought Neihardt's mournful attitude cloying
and wrongheaded. He rejected the poet's sentimentality and ditched
the modernists' pathos. Hugh Glass was neither far away nor far back to
Manfred. He pulsated nearby. He was all tissue, whiskers, and clotted
blood—a pumped-up musky man who raged and bucked at the universe. He fought with the Arikaras, the bear, and Colonel Henry, but
mainly he warred with himself. Manfred offered a Freudian Glass. He
organized the novel around groups of three: wrestle, crawl, showdown;
Glass, Bridger, Fitzpatrick; id, ego, superego. Manfred's triangulation of
the legend dislodged Glass from the binaries of the West depicted in
manifest destiny and frontier modernism. By giving his hero a transhis-
torical psychology, the novelist opened a pathway into his mind. Readers viewed the world through his often deluded vision. Manfred's
first-person reclamation of Hugh Glass prepared the hunter for his appearance in the survivalist media. In order to learn from and follow the
mountain man's example, consumers of survival how-to books and compendiums of desperation and woe needed him close by. Manfred reeled

him in with the id. Survivalists relabeled this psychological drive in order to harness it. They admired and tried to emulate Glass's "will." But Manfred had a crazier mainspring in mind when he wrote *Lord Grizzly*.

The drama in *Lord Grizzly* arose from Manfred's celebration of Glass's epic impulsiveness and the requirement—which the novelist adhered to—that Glass forgive his betrayers. Who or what would rescue him, and thus Fitzpatrick and Bridger, from the primal urges unleashed by the bear? How could Glass stay rebellious and repress his anger by letting the cowards go? Was he a wild man or a milquetoast?

Sex and money lurked in Manfred's thoughts as he researched and planned his novel. Desperate for a big seller, he selected the Glass legend because it lacked obvious eroticism. He had just failed to sell to Houghton Mifflin a book titled *The Rape of Elisabeth*, which one in-house reviewer dismissed as "too much Kinsey report." In letters to his agent and his editor at Doubleday, the press that published his early autobiographical novels, Manfred promised that "The Grizzly Bear" would have "no sex in it." "I want to write a first rate book that can also be read by very religious people and also young folk," he noted. "I don't really have a book that they can read. I think I can write one that for once will keep out 'hot' passages. I've got enough of them sprinkled through my other books." Glass did stay cool throughout *Lord Grizzly*. Solitude and grievous injuries minimized his chances for romantic entanglements. Yet while he kept Glass celibate, Manfred couldn't stop his propensity for "yeastiness" from infiltrating the text. In bringing the West close to readers, he also snuggled them in tight with western bodies. He composed a physical novel steaming with desires of all kinds.[18]

Manfred opened the story on the sandbar outside the Arikara village the night before the fight with Ashley's men. Glass stood guard while the younger trappers snoozed off "their day-long orgy with the pennyskinned Arikaree maidens." Too old for "sparking," Glass had watched the "boys" make love with the Indian women. Overheated, the Americans dropped to the ground once they struck their bargains and writhed in the open. The two sides seemed amicable. The Americans traded "mirrors, ribbons, vermilion, and such" for intercourse; the Arikaras assigned braves to police the exchanges. But Glass sensed trouble. He detected menace in the braves' "chokecherry eyes." That night, one of the "lads" lingering in the village pushed his luck too far, and Glass heard his dying scream from his sentry post. By morning, groans of pain supplanted moans of delight on the bar.[19]

In the publicity for *Lord Grizzly*, Manfred described the mental and physical regimen he endured to access Glass's world. He read more than eighty books, consulted experts, traversed the historical landscape by car and on foot, and strapped a board to one of his legs to feel the mechanics of Glass's post-bear lurch. The research showed in the Arikara fight set piece. Bullets perforated Gardner; Clyman floundered in the river until Gibson pulled him out; Larrison hid in his dead horse. Ashley yelled at the cowardly boatmen, but the "pork-eating neds" refused to join the fight. Glass showed his courage. He rallied the greenhorns and organized the covering fire for their retreat. He acted the part of the vet, the father who stood his ground while the "boys" scattered. After the fight, Glass continued to hold the Americans together. He spoke up at the mutiny scene, rallying support for Ashley. He talked of race, freedom, sex, and dinner: "I admit I've sometimes thought of makin' tracks back to white diggin's again, where the beds is soft and the wimmen white and the red niggers only a dream in the night . . . but then I remember fresh fleece from a buffler's hump, young cow at that, and sweet boudins just barely crimped with fire, and still sweeter beavertail." The rest could scram if they liked; Glass was sticking around for the meat.[20]

Oh, the carnivorous delights that awaited the lucky few who joined him. Manfred started *Lord Grizzly* after the main orgy at the Arikara villages. Readers on the hunt for titillation had to make do with Glass's memories of the bacchanal. Nothing separated those with prurient dietary inclinations from the mountain men's barbecue scene. In the homosocial setting of a traveling hunting expedition, food stood in for sex, and the Americans devoured the "piles of meat, fleece, tongue, ribs, boudins [that] lay on the blood-streaked buffalo skins" with unbridled lust. "They swallowed; they chocked back laughs; they swallowed so mightily their eyes sometimes closed." Knives flashed, and blood flew. They stomached loins, livers, and intestines by the yard, and as their bellies grew, so did their articulateness: "First there were groans of ecstasy, then grunts of pleasure, then fine eloquent social belches, and at last a few remarks." The heights of post-meal expression could be stunning. Jim Anderson proclaimed his meal the "best darn grub" he had "ever stuffed down [his] meatbag." They licked the grease off their fingers and wiped their gory utensils on their shirts. Manfred concluded the evening with the smell of their buckskins. Smoke and burnt wood mingled with "odors of other times too—the scent of love-making with musky Ree maidens, fired gunpowder, Kentucky whisky." Scratch the shirt of an Ashley hunter, and you'd catch a whiff of manliness that would make Clint Eastwood swoon.[21]

The meat orgy signaled the differences between the narratives that sprung from Manfred's Siouxland and the nationalist Westerns in his source materials. He borrowed the supper scene and most of his vocabulary from nineteenth-century travel writers. He didn't hide his debt; indeed, he flaunted his research. He scoured old texts, collected plants and roots from the site of Glass's crawl, and even ate an ant to approximate the taste of utter desperation. Steeped in the physical details of the past, Manfred stowed the information he had acquired and wrote from his gut. He described the process in a 1964 series of televised interviews with John R. Milton, the chair of the University of South Dakota's English department: "[W]hen it comes time to write, I turn my back on my more obvious knowledges . . . and I try to find the inner truth of what I am getting at." Manfred associated this core truth with the subconscious. He often dreamed of his characters at night and wrote about them during the day. He skimmed Freud's *Interpretation of Dreams* in an effort to decipher their nocturnal visitations. But he thought Freud "got everything backwards." Instead of trying to plumb the depths of human psychology from "today's scientific prejudices backwards," people should work from the bottom up. They should familiarize themselves with humanity's deep nature, what Manfred called "the Old Lizard. Or the Old Leviathan." *Lord Grizzly* sprang from his dialogue with his inner reptile.[22]

Manfred's barbaric yawp sent Freud's concepts of shame, repression, denial, guilt, and displacement to quiver in the corner. He venerated the id and equated unbridled human ebullience with personal freedom, creativity, and being American. The members of the nation rose from the primitive, he conjectured, and artists had to access the id's energy and truth to produce good stuff. He explained the process to Milton:

> You should always begin with blood and tissue and flesh and instinct and sensuality, and if something in you, the Old Lizard in you, wants to talk about that stuff, he knows there is meaning behind it there which, if you will pursue it in your writing, by the time he gets to the end of the book that meaning will pop through.

Sneaking theories and symbols into novels was a fool's move. Readers could sniff out counterfeit abstractions, and they hated authors—even if they didn't admit it—for tricking them. Themes emerged naturally from the subconscious as artists wallowed in physical details. They discovered universal truths through nature and the lower functions of the body. Forget philosophy, Manfred exhorted, and drop to the ground. The "worm's point of view," not the vista from the mount, revealed the transcendent.[23]

Few literary figures tapped into the perspective of creeping things better than Hugh Glass. He spent most of his epic on his stomach, and in his dilapidated state, he often slipped from consciousness. Manfred used the blackouts to introduce his wife and children and to blend them—through delirium—with Fitz and Jim. Glass's fever dreams solved the problem of *Lord Grizzly*'s final act. Manfred had to explain why Glass forgave his betrayers without turning him into a role model for Christian charity and moral self-restraint. He wanted the id to win. The id animated Glass, the Siouxland, the Old Lizard, and America. It was the hero. But the climactic group hug that ended the legend seemed a textbook example of the superego bringing the id and the ego to heel, just as the charity-toward-thy-enemies message seemed obviously religious. Manfred hadn't crawled around with a board strapped to his leg and swallowed bugs to wind up with a meek, Sunday-school Odysseus.

Glass's charitableness had to emanate from the same source as his anger, and Manfred turned to George Ruxton to keep the id his star.

During his crawl, Glass collapsed from exhaustion and Manfred had him slide into a Ruxtonian dream. He saw Jim, "his lad," crouched by him. I'm dying, he said. "And, boy, if you don't raise meat pronto you'll be in the same fix I'm in." Meat's meat, he reasoned. "Dip in, lad, and drink man's blood." The mention of cannibalism disturbed Glass. He admitted to Jim that he had tasted human flesh ("I did onct. One bite"), a crime he denied only seconds before ("I've never et dead meat myself, Jim, and wouldn't ask you to do it neither. But meat fair killed is meat anyway. So, Jim, lad, put your knife in this old nigger's lights and help yourself"). Soon the dream changed, and Mabel, the wife he left behind with two sons, clawed at his back, calling him "a worthless bum. A soak who couldn't stick to a job. A poorpeter who was always getting into fights with his bosses." She ripped him like the she-bear, belittled him. She ordered their sons to execute their worthless father. Jim— Glass's fictive son—materialized alongside his real ones. Old Hugh explained why he had betrayed his family: when civilization snared a man, he could run or submit. "If you make the littlest move," Glass said, "you just entangle yourself all the more in the law. No, lad, do like I did. Run off with the net and all." Thus, in the netherworld of his mind, Glass confronted his sins. He ate some people and betrayed others. He was no better than the bear or Jim. He shared the hunger, pride, wrath, and fear as well as the instincts for self-preservation that led to maulings, thefts, and abandonments. It all came from the id. Glass's orneriness made him a hero and a heel, a man tough enough to survive the wilderness and pitiful enough to abandon his family.[24]

Humans and animals, greenhorns and old-timers, avengers and rascals: everyone sailed in the same boat with the Old Lizard at the rudder. Glass forgave Jim and Fitz when he recognized the sameness of his love and hate. All intense, worthwhile emotions—the feelings that led animals and humans to maim, kill, and devour but also cherish, protect, and self-sacrifice—merged together. Glass put aside the law of the mountains, the code of the hunters, and embraced the moral ambiguity of his subconscious: "Turned tame, this child has. Passed through such a passel of things he don't rightly recollect wrong from right no more." In his final act, he rebuked authority one last time. Rules gave him such a fit that he scuttled the one he traveled two hundred miles to enforce. He cut Jim and Fitz and his id loose.[25]

Lord Grizzly sold well and received some glowing publicity. The novel spent sixteen weeks on the bestseller list, William Carlos Williams called the story "phenomenal," and Sinclair Lewis predicted that Manfred "may become one of the most important novelists in America." Reviewers latched on to the "reality" and "freshness" of his vision. They didn't show Westerns like this on television. J. Donald Adams praised Manfred in his "Speaking of Books" column in *The New York Times* for presenting Indians as human beings rather than "red devil" stereotypes. Manfred's psychological West drew praise, but his personal saga caught imaginations as well. Reviewers latched on to the similarity between Manfred's return from literary obscurity and financial ruin and Glass's crawl to Fort Kiowa.[26]

Before *Lord Grizzly*, Manfred had published under his Frisian given name—Fieke Fiekema. He thought about changing it as early as 1951, asking his editor at Doubleday what he thought about Fred Friskner. By 1954, when *Lord Grizzly* appeared, the renaming story had grown into a yarn about an impromptu man-on-the-street survey conducted at a busy Minneapolis intersection. Eager for success, according to the tale, Manfred canvassed a random assortment of passersby to see which name would sell the most books. They picked Fred Manfred.[27]

The truth of the story (Manfred did the survey, but he had been experimenting with noms de plume for years; the public didn't decide the issue one day on a street corner) mattered less than the populist sentiment it expressed. Through the name change, Manfred communicated his willingness to meet his readers halfway. He would trim the autobiographical content of his writing and trade in his unpronounceable name for a best seller. Instead of another regional novel about young male Iowans coming of age in twentieth-century rural households, he would offer a regional novel about a primitive ancestor common to all Americans. Manfred considered Hugh Glass one of the progenitors of his Siouxland and the birthplace of American independence. The mountain men, Indians, and cowboys of the nineteenth century belonged to the same history as his Dutch immigrant family. Manfred used the metaphor of a "long mural" to describe the seamlessness of Northern Plains history. He reached back to the 1800s—"when the white man hit" the region—to fill in the background of his later characters. When he died, Manfred could look back on his hall of fiction and see the Siouxland unwind from himself back to Glass, Jedediah Smith, Mike Fink, and Crazy Horse.[28]

The unitary theory of history, fiction, and region brought Manfred back to the id. Novelists did a better job "soaking up" the past than historians who were enslaved by details instead of freed by them. Novelists absorbed the "bare essentials" of stories and turned them into semiconscious myths. Like historians, they gathered the same information, pillaging memoirs, travel narratives, diaries, newspaper clippings, and court records, but when it came time to write, they put aside "obvious knowledge" and dug deeper into their own minds to "find the inner truth" of places and people. The truth of Glass wasn't the miles he crawled or the ants he ate, but his ideological self-propulsion:

> Hugh Glass was a hero for larger reasons. He didn't do it for money. He didn't do it because he was ordered by a commander . . . He didn't do it because his wife told him to do it. Or a minister of religion. He did it for the sake of an idea. The idea was at first a bad one, hate, but it was an idea. Then later on hate became love, or compassion, which was a still greater idea. You see, if you are doing something for the sake of an outside idea . . . someone telling you to do it, or if you are a member of a religious organization and do it for the cause of the organization or a society, well, you have that to sustain you when you are really down.

Glass pioneered South Dakota for self-starting free agents everywhere. He owned his courage. His ferocious commitment to life came from his subconscious, and since all human beings shared this deep, inner truth, post–World War II book buyers could tap this independence. The American past, the Siouxland, and Hugh Glass survived in the psyche.

He resided in the id, and if people listened to themselves instead of their bosses, spouses, and ministers, they might, in the quiet of their own heads, pick up the rumble of Glass's waughs across the buttes of time.[29]

Manfred tied his vision of American history and personal freedom to a particular time and landscape, but the rebellious spirit of the Siouxland extended seamlessly across the divides of modernity, geography, and personality. The Old Lizard squirmed in the back of everyone's consciousness; special circumstances could usher him forward. Glass learned to follow his own lead on a political and natural borderland. The United States had yet to extend its power over the Northern Plains, and the river bottoms still teemed with wild creatures and men. The place was unfixed, nebulous. The dry air and brilliant skies warped sight lines, sending nearby landmarks into the distance and bringing far objects close. Mirages appeared out of nowhere; false calls and whispers carried on the wind. The sensory dreaminess of the landscape eroded the boundary separating mind and nature. Manfred's Freudian Western (maybe we should term it Freud-inflected Western; he revered unruliness too much to adhere to a single theory with any kind of discipline) reproduced the porous human/nature relationship of nineteenth-century medicine. He replaced humors with hallucinations, black bile and pus with psychological projections and ids. Minds and landscapes crawled into one another in the Siouxland. This invasiveness created problems when Manfred tried to capitalize on *Lord Grizzly*'s success. Americans loved Westerns in the 1950s, but would they buy tickets to see one without clear boundaries?

Frederick Manfred internalized environmental Americanism. Hugh Glass represented the wild streak of a rascally nation, and rather than cool his heels in quarantine on the geographic or historical fringes, he resided in the cerebral cortex of all freedom-loving people. He was the Old Lizard, the primal urge. He migrated across space and time, a boundless, and therefore an intimate, western hero.

Instead of an empty vessel, Glass brimmed with motivation. His deep-seated inability to heed authority compelled his anger and his forgiveness. Yet even as Manfred's psychoanalysis cleared up old mysteries, his demolition of frontier boundary lines churned up new complications. The reviews of *Lord Grizzly* hinted at the problems. Critics applauded the book's "freshness," but they measured its vibrancy against television programs and movies as much as other books. In 1954, Americans *watched* Westerns. *Lord Grizzly* gained popularity, and Manfred began to feel the gravitational pull of Hollywood. He contemplated the job of turning Glass inside out. How do you witness a psychological transformation from the outside? Will people buy tickets to watch an actor grimace and grumble to himself for the eternal second act of the crawl? Without a gunfight, how could you end the picture? Audiences would want to see why Glass forgave Jim and Fitz, but *Lord Grizzly* buried the change of heart within Hugh. Manfred hoped the dreamy, Freudian atmosphere of the novel would lead readers automatically to his conclusion. They would accept the nonviolent climax because Glass's decision conformed to the trippy environment. He tried to reproduce this subconscious journey with visual cues in his screenplay. To represent Glass's undulating state of mind, Manfred enlisted the psychedelic nature of the Siouxland. He trusted the Great Plains environment to upend the senses and guide audiences toward a truly novel Western, but in the end, he inserted a *deus ex bruin* to pull off the show.

In his 1964 screenplay, Manfred encouraged the director to make the action "seem continuous, like a flowing stream, like consciousness itself." Languid shots would nudge viewers into the rush of existence and heighten "sudden movements" like the bear attack. The director could exploit location shooting in the Siouxland to manufacture the experience of seamlessness. Light flooded the high plains even in the late afternoon, making shadows appear more substantial than trees, horses, bears, or men. "The shadows do it," Manfred wrote; "they alone exalt the far deeps of the perspective." If the director could see the plains through his eyes, the camera would erode the line between perception and reality. The "'hants' (mirages)" would appear "as real as reality itself." And Glass, his injured body, and his mental turmoil would seem trancelike. "If this is consistently and imaginatively shot, Hugh's act of forgiving 'the boys' will be accepted as a true thing. And—we shall have on our hands a movie that will make the viewer think he has been caught up in an experience as overpowering as a lover's dream."

The breakdown of external landscape and internal perception would pull off the ending.[30]

But Manfred couldn't follow his own advice. He inserted a "hant" bear into a closing scene to symbolize the power of forgiveness. After lecturing Bridger, Glass went after Fitzpatrick. At night, on the trail to Fort Atkinson, he encountered a "great male bear." The animal hunted him down, forcing a desperate Glass to hide underneath the she-bear skin he still carried as a memento from his mauling. Instead of eating him, the bear snuffled under the hide until he found the seeping wound in Glass's back. The gouge had refused to heal and maggots filled the hole. The wound fixated the bear. He snorted excitedly and stuck his massive tongue into the gap. The bear's licking tickled Glass "horribly," but he kept still and accepted the cleansing. When he was through, the bear galloped away. Glass sat up in amazement and spoke to the camera: "By the Lord! Slick and clean. All the maggots and the crust gone. (doesn't quite break into hysterical laughter) The old bustard had a sweet tooth. . . . 'Twas the grizzly way of making up for a bad thing done me by one of their own kind." When Glass finally caught up with Fitz, he remembered the bear and forgave the "lad." "Well, damnation," Manfred had him say, "if a dammed grizzly can play at bein' a Jesus Christ, and offer to make up, why Old Hugh sure as hell can." And he did. Roll credits.[31]

William Froug, a producer at Screen Gems Studios, optioned the novel and Manfred's screenplay. He negotiated with the Walt Disney Company, but it eventually passed on the story with the Jesus/bear ending. No other studio picked it up. Manfred blamed the failure on producers' fear of audiences growing tired of watching one actor on screen by himself for "at least a half hour." The crawl, he thought, doomed the movie. The troublesome finale, however, seemed a more likely culprit. A dab of peanut butter might convince a trained bear to lick an actor's back easily enough, but would audiences really buy this tongue-lashing as their payoff for enduring Glass's ordeal? Could bear saliva soothe a man bent on revenge and convince viewers to accept a nonviolent conclusion to a Hollywood Western?[32]

Seven years after Manfred submitted his treatment of the Glass legend, Warner Bros. produced another screenwriter's script. Manfred considered *Man in the Wilderness* a rip-off of his novel. He threatened to sue, and the filmmakers offered him $25,000 and agreed to alter the script so that it resembled *Lord Grizzly* less. Manfred gave up the lawsuit: "[T]he movie is not the Hugh Glass I envisioned. Nor is it the vision of the country that I had in mind." (Convinced that they had actually stolen Glass from him, ninety-year-old John G. Niehardt actually did sue.) And the film was different—on many levels. Richard Sarafian, the director, and Jack DeWitt, the screenwriter, altered the names of the main characters and inserted a nautical theme. Captain Filmore Henry (John Huston) commanded a boat on wheels. A team of twenty mules dragged his ship filled with beaver pelts across the Northern Plains. Zach Bass (Richard Harris) hunted meat for the crew. An independent cuss, he was the only man Henry respected. The captain was an obvious reference to Melville's Ahab. Huston directed the 1956 film *Moby Dick*, and he seems to have borrowed Gregory Peck's epic hat from that movie. Henry's obsessions drove his men to the brink of insanity and ruin. He represented the crazed ambitions of American "fathers" who sacrificed young men to foreign quagmires. Henry looked like Ahab, but he was also General Westmoreland.[33]

The movie's last scene completed the Vietnamization of Hugh Glass, or Zach Bass. After a prolonged immersion in western nature, Bass caught up with the boat, stuck axle deep in the mud of the Missouri floodplain. (The river was a mere trickle; the ship useless.) An Arikara war party, which had been shadowing the Americans the entire film, arrived at the same time. They attacked the trappers, and the melee engulfed Bass. The Indians had nearly killed him when their chief called off the assault. The chief had seen this white guy before—gurgling blood on the banks of the Yellowstone River. He spared Bass then, even prayed over his body; then he granted Bass his revenge. He waved him toward Henry, smiling. He wanted to see the hunter impale his employer with the homemade spear he had constructed in the bush. Instead of killing him, though, Bass limped past his patriarch. He was done with war and male authority figures. A newborn son waited for him back at home. He fought through the wilderness to return to his child. He will be a different kind of father, a loving and available one—more Dr. Spock than Ahab.

Hitting theaters in 1971, *Man in the Wilderness* flowed with the current of popular culture, which meant it countered the conventions of the Western genre. Like *McCabe & Mrs. Miller* the same year and *Little Big Man* the year before, the film critiqued American politics and the poor judgment of the wise men who led the nation into misadventure in Southeast Asia. Glass's eternal struggle against bosses fit the mood of the times. He had potential as an anti-Western leading man. But Zach Bass was no Jack Crabb. *Man in the Wilderness* flickered and died, having failed to immortalize its hero. This raises a question: Given the obscurity of the last gasp of Hugh Glass in American popular culture, why is he still with us? Greeted with a frown or an indifferent shrug by critics and moviegoers, *Man in the Wilderness* should have mortally wounded Glass, but, true to form, he got up and crawled somewhere else. Instead of in Westerns, or even anti-Westerns, he found a home in American survivalism.

To reach his final resting place, Glass had to take a conceptual leap. He initially rose to prominence in a time when a young nation was building a sense of itself through a combination of vast social and geographic distances. Americans celebrated working-class men remade by nature, but they quarantined them on geographic frontiers. They took their stories of suffering and endurance and left their bodies to rot in the boonies. Later, they indulged in campfire fantasies, imagining themselves seated next to Glass while he waxed and waughed, but no one dreamed of assuming his place—of becoming him. Glass remained on the edges of the United States because his geographic location mirrored his social status: he was a marginal fellow. A chewed-up, impoverished old man with no family, no property, and eventually no scalp, he was no role model.

Then the world turned. The United States invaded the West and consolidated its power. The army defeated the strongest Indian militaries and imprisoned them on reservations. Railroads, mines, irrigation, and cities remade the environment, plugging extractable resources into distant markets. The West quickly became one of the nation's most urban, industrial, and multicultural sections. By the time Charles Swin broke his back near Vernal, the United States had bloomed into a superpower. The cowboy's fellow Utahans could point to the mushroom clouds kicked up by the test bombs detonated in their deserts as proof of their country's might. The weak and ineffective national body politic that stumbled west in the 1820s had gone steroidal. The United States strode the planet as a colossus. Indeed, people worried that the nuclear giant might destroy the earth. Instead of enduring nature, Americans seemed bent on ending it.

Survivalism grew in the fallout of mutually assured destruction. Adherents accepted the Strangelovian premise that consummate power bred paranoid, insane, and suicidal nations. The United States was bound to fall. Theorists on the left and the right disgorged any number of rationales for the nation's demise—high taxes, affirmative action, fascist militarism, sexual permissiveness, corporate malfeasance. Whatever triggered the apocalypse, survivalists agreed on the aftermath. The remnants of humanity would enter a new wilderness, battle hordes of savages (mutants, robots, welfare recipients), and flirt with the demon ideas that led to the meltdown (usually in the form of a rogue military outfit or a demented socialist commune) only to reject them for some sort of nuclear family. Survivors emerged into mildly optimistic futures filled with huts, New England–style town meetings, and lots of gardening.

The science fiction of apocalyptic survivalism dovetailed with the preparedness industry. Guidebooks instructed doomsayers and weekend pessimists in the art of hedging their bets. Both genres offered elaborate tips for outlandish scenarios. They told readers how to jump from a moving train without breaking their ankles or what brand of sardines tasted better after thirty years in storage. Glass even popped up in a guidebook containing instructions on how to emerge unharmed from an encounter with Bigfoot. Yet, for all their elaborate advice, the manuals presented a simple equation for ultimate survival. Life or death, they said, often boiled down to a tug-of-war between individual will and cruel nature. Bodies acted as the rope. Disaster-proof people exhibited the right attitude when the cosmos turned against them. They endured hostile environments by denying their bodies' calls for food, water, and comfort. They pushed through pain, drove past breaking points. This kind of resolve is hard to communicate to human beings reading books with their feet propped up in La-Z-Boy loungers, so authors stockpiled pulsating examples: endurance athletes, prisoners of war, mountain climbers, accident victims, and working stiffs with nasty jobs.

The preparedness media lured audiences with the promise of the inevitable catastrophe. Disasters, the texts implied, rained equally on the just and the wretched, the poor and the pampered. Dumb luck was an equal-opportunity afflicter; happenstance was democratic. Rich people got cancer, died in car crashes, and fell and hit their heads on sidewalks. Indeed, the twentieth-century gang of celebrity survivalists Glass fell in with included numerous examples of wealthy individuals financing their way into tight spots. They hired Sherpas to guide them into high-altitude "death zones" or built hot-rod balloons to race around the globe, only to crash in forlorn stretches of desert. They sailed their yachts into hurricanes and tumbled into the rapids of gold-medal trout streams clutching thousand-dollar fly rods. Glass's misadventure and resurrection won him a spot in a survivalist hall of fame that ignored pesky details like class. He emerged from the specific cultural, animal, and social environments that nourished and propagated his bear story to join a roster of imperiled souls that spanned time periods and social circumstances. These humans shared a profound commitment to biological viability as well as a stoic imperturbability in the midst of the worst maelstroms; otherwise, they could arrive from any walk of life.

After establishing that wrecks and crashes could happen to anyone, the survivalist genre asked readers to imagine their responses. What would you do if an avalanche engulfed you, or the zoo fence caved in and you toppled into the lion pit, or you had to escape a hotel fire by jumping into a Dumpster? American survivalism worked by means of voyeurism and reassurance. Authors exposed readers to dismal situations and then gave them instructions (often in the form of catchy acronyms like SAFE or ALERT) on how to escape. They peddled the contradictory notions of cosmic bedlam and individual vigilance: anything could happen to anyone at any time, but an arbitrary selection of couch potatoes could survive detached limbs on an African veldt or subzero descents of K2 with the right attitude and a teaspoon of savvy.

Glass, Charles Swin, and insurance adjusters might quarrel with the democracy of survivalism. Not everyone assumes the same risks when they rise from bed in the morning. Coal miners have a better chance of finding dire straits than caterers. Occupational differences matter; so do distinctions of race, class, gender, geography, and nationality. Danger stalks the vulnerable; accidents happen in social, political, and physical contexts that imperil some more than others, and human decisions and activities—bigotry, war, poverty, drug trafficking—sculpt these contexts along with random nature. Swin crawled through a wilderness created by his poverty and isolation. At the age of seventy-three, he labored in a dangerous profession (agriculture, where the need for traction exposed him to the volatility of large animals and machines) by himself. Certainly, the rough physical landscape contributed to his troubles. But Swin ranched in the dry country outside Vernal, Utah, because that's the land he could afford. He worked alone because he had no family labor to muster and no cash to pay for wage help. He was desperate before the horse fell on him.

Frederick Manfred collected the Swin story to better understand a desperate struggle with nature that happened more than a hundred years earlier. Manfred believed in the seamlessness of time. Freudian conceptions of ids and primal lizards nudged him toward ahistoricism, but geography also pushed him there. He conceived of himself as the artistic spokesperson for the grasslands and Badlands of the northern Great Plains. He grew up on the edge of this expanse in Doon, Iowa, the son of immigrant Dutch Reformed Calvinists. Despite moving to Minneapolis and away from his religious upbringing, he still felt rooted to this landscape and chose his literary subjects from that region. The poetry of place connected him to them. Along with collecting newspaper articles, he traveled the region searching for pathways into his characters.

In the fall of 1952, Manfred convinced his publisher to advance him two hundred dollars so that he could take a road trip through the Siouxland, Manfred's name for his birth region. He traced his route in advance on a Rand McNally road map of South Dakota, using red pencil. His plan: run down Hugh Glass in a Ford V8. On October 7, Manfred's wife, Maryanna, wrote a postcard home to their daughter, Freya: "[W]e've been riding the range . . . its really the wide open spaces. Nothing but hills & hills with a cowboy or Indian here & there . . . Dad found his Hugh Glass and followed the trail he took after the grizzly got him, all the way, so he's happy. See you soon, Mom." Like Swin, Glass had merged with the land. Manfred could unearth and own him by following his long-gone tracks.[34]

Manfred hiked Glass's path, "taking notes and collecting bits of fauna and dirt and rock." He filled in the gaps of legend with shards of modern nature. Through a novelist's commitment to a western place, Americans finally witnessed the scenes Glass's oral culture and poor sources obscured. But these insights came at a price. Manfred aided Glass's passage into the purgatory of survivalist media by establishing a first-person connection through nature. He used his empathetic understanding of the Siouxland to nuzzle up to Glass, but he had to play down the many differences between 1820s working-class hunters and 1950s consumers of popular literature to bring the environmental American home.

The single most dramatic asymmetry between the time periods was power. Calamity preyed on Glass because he was vulnerable. His employer and his nation couldn't protect him. He never established the alliances with the Indian leaders that safeguarded previous generations of European traders in the West. He bet his life on a poorly conceived scheme: the Americans thought they could sneak into the region, harvest furs with their own labor, and get out before the Native inhabitants punished them for their trespasses. This strategy worked for some— William Ashley emerged golden—but the majority of employees and free trappers slogged through the majestic scenery gaunt, scarred, and busted. The West beat them to pulp, and their stories communicated their impotence.

Environmental Americanism revised tales of desperation and woe into narratives of conquest. Instead of victimized castaways, mountain men emerged as spearheads of empire. Their workplace accidents became symptoms of domination. Their altered physiques staked the United States's claim to the West; their strength invigorated the collective body. Restyling crack-ups and sad defeats into heroic fodder is an

American narrative. Embarrassing displays of weakness often preceded "triumphs" of assertiveness (the Alamo, Custer's Last Stand, Pearl Harbor, 9/11). But I didn't write this book only to bemoan what nationalist hacks, modernist twits, and survivalist wackos did to Hugh Glass.

I'm far more intrigued by what he might have done to them.

CONCLUSION

What could a busted old man do to American history? Hugh Glass displayed a remarkable talent for hanging around, but loitering, even when performed at the highest of levels, seems more a hobo activity than a heroic accomplishment. A barnacle on a ship of fools rather than captain of his own destiny, Glass was a loser by most measures. Estates and fortunes evaded him. He appears to have impressed people with his physical endurance and storytelling skills, but there's no evidence that his confidants loved or admired him. He stuck with Ashley after the Arikara fight, but he proved disloyal on other occasions. He contributed a stellar legend to American folklore, but he couldn't say he authored it. Overall, he offered a weak case for commemoration. Yet the dude abides. Hence the paradox of Glass: How do you explain the astonishing sticking power of a historical wisp who grabbed headlines for withstanding occupational hazards?

The answer begins with nationalism. Americans built their nation on the margins. They trolled subordinate groups—Native and African Americans most prominently but also working-class people of all races— for symbols, costumes, and rituals that distinguished theirs from their parent society while preserving the European cultural endowments they wished to keep. By targeting the weaker segments of the populace, the nationalists hoped to pull off the bait and switch of exceptionalism: they wanted their differences to signal their superiority. They hid the paleness of their colonial imitations beneath blackface, buckskins, or Indian garb and declared the resulting oxymoron a natural aristocrat. They stole from the fringes in order to strut for the metropole, and for the most part they pulled it off. The frontier became a wellspring of American identity.[1]

Bodies, however, prevented the con of exceptionalism from achieving maximum effect. Cultural predators targeted faraway physiques for their exoticism and nativity. Indians, slaves, servants, and hunters merged with American environments. Their flesh, bone, and skin proved they belonged to North America. By grabbing their marginal bodies, mainstream Euro-Americans could seize the continent. The nationalists sought imagined qualities, not lower-class partners. They envisioned a cultural transfer, accomplished through stories, performances, and symbols. Artists, therefore, rigged the exchange. They took what they wanted and ditched the bodies at a distance. Slaves stayed on plantations down the river, Indians vanished along with the wilderness, and hunters backed into the woods. They endowed the nation with greatness even as they melted into the scenery.[2]

The Hugh Glass legend upended the disappearing act. A naturalized American, Glass scrambled back after being robbed and left for dead. He was the working-class body that wouldn't go away. And upon his return, he seized the narrative. He talked, giving his account of his adventure in nature, and after telling people what he went through and what he thought of them, he walked away triumphant. He crawled through hell to deliver the last word. Hall, Yount, von Wrede, Ruxton, Neihardt, and Manfred glorified a legend that critiqued the abuses of glorification. They made big productions out of a story that satirized the production of American nationalism.

I like to read the story this way. As a writer and a historian, I consider myself on a prolonged expedition to see how much I can get away with in the company of somber academics. I believe that history should be fun, sly, challenging, and artful. An egghead with antiauthoritarian tendencies, I picked a biographical companion who suited my personality. Was Hugh Glass truly a storytelling pirate, a clever performer who knew what audiences wished to hear and messed with their expectations through a self-aware survival tale, or am I letting my imagination run wild to satisfy my own desire to partner up with an outlaw?

I'm tainted with bias for sure, but I also think I'm right. Orneriness and mercy are twin recurrences in the many versions of the legend. These constants fit the immediate context of the legend, and they provide the basis for interpreting the story as a rebuke of cultural authority. The story originated among hunters on a mission gone haywire. The Americans had advanced up the Missouri to gather furs and get rich, only to watch the river sink their boat and the Arikaras thin their ranks. Stung by the setbacks, they improvised and saddled up. The move to horseback exposed Glass to the bear-infested, river-bottom environments. The Americans didn't want to wander the bushes; they wanted to stay on the boats in the Missouri. But their impotence limited their options. Glass's poor attitude flourished in the atmosphere of chaos and mistrust engendered by the Arikara debacle. His orneriness grew from his bosses' inability to deliver on their promises to outfit and protect men of enterprise.

The Glass legend taught many lessons, but *mistrust authority* ranked first. When things fell apart, masters lost their sway over their environment along with the servants. Unless they exhibited a talent for quick thinking and adaptation, confused leaders doomed their followers. The grave yawned equally for every class, creed, and color. Hunters observed that independent cusses endured the mayhem better than loyal employees. Experts on survival echo this wisdom. In chaotic situations, rule breakers live longer than good soldiers. Survivors ask impertinent questions and think for themselves. In the classroom, they are the ones sitting in time-out for disruptive behavior. In tense situations, they are the ones walking away while the panicked herd dashes over the cliff. Knee-jerk respect for the American chain of command in the 1820s was a dead man's response to a messed-up situation.[3]

To borrow a term from the nineteenth-century runaway ads, rascals escaped the wilderness while gentlemen and their dependable servants perished. Before Buckwheat, Alfalfa, and Spanky turned "rascal" into synonym for lovable scamp, the word accumulated a bounty of negative meanings. "Rascal" meant scumbag, camp follower, and cannon fodder. Rascals were human garbage and dishonorable thieves. According to one definition, rascals adored trickery and mischief; they made fun of people, embarrassed as well as robbed them. Another meaning associated rascals with animals. Sickly, young, or enfeebled, rascals were creatures too puny to rank as game. They became objects of pity; sportsmen didn't waste bullets on them.[4]

Masters used the rascal insult to separate worthy underlings from rotten ones and to prevent runaways from taking advantage of the fluidity of rivers and markets. Rascality inhered in individuals. You couldn't shirk or obscure it. Indeed, trying to hide one's rascality was a sure sign that one was a rascal. Rascals were incorrigible offenders, and authorities policed them relentlessly with the assistance of the community and the state. Upright citizens hunted rascals down, chained them up, and placed them under strict supervision.

In the West, the behaviors and attitudes that steered insubordinate servants toward jail increased their chances of survival. Skilled runaways adapted to their surroundings. The ads highlighted scars, skin color, and clothing to combat runaways' skill at blending in. The wilderness rewarded quick, independent thinkers. Adapters who recognized and shifted their outlook to match new realities thrived. James Beckwourth belonged in this category. The chameleon quality that led Francis Parkman and others to denounce him as a rogue served him well in the West. So did his tendency to fib. A sense of a humor and a playful disposition aided survivors. Laughter was a symptom of adaptability. Poking fun at dire scenarios helped cut them down to manageable proportions. Gallows humor acknowledged the pain and turmoil of laboring in the West but kept a muzzle on the emotions—despair and fatalism—that led to paralysis. The constant ribbing of the greenhorns not only educated the newcomers but also reminded experienced hands that their lives depended on their wits as much as their guns.

Hugh Glass matched the profile of a "survival personality," and the same quirks that carried him two hundred miles on his hands and knees may have aided his development as a cultural critic. If anyone could stand outside and comment on the process that turned injured workers into icons of natural nationalism, he could. Above all else, the unruly early American West rewarded self-awareness. Survival artists developed a twinkle in their eyes to combat the powers that imperiled them. They poked fun at deluded masters, aggressive bears, and clueless greenhorns. During the height of the beaver trade (1820–40), humor, improvisation, and flexibility defined successful American mountain men. They shifted loyalties, traded identities, and retooled their races to better suit their environments. The physical hardships of their work, their rambunctious personas, and the vibrancy of their campfire story-telling endeared these survival artists to pen-and-paper artists. Part-time semiprofessional regionalists, foreign travel writers, and even a few skep-tical literary leviathans like Herman Melville appropriated the back-woodsmen and preserved them like mashed flowers in the pages of books.

The Americans' gamble to equip bands of their own hunters and send them west to kill beavers was a disaster for the men contracted to do the job. They entered a region organized to serve the needs of others—among them bison, grizzly bears, buffalo-hunting nomads and their horse herds, and French-speaking traders with long-standing family ties to Native partners. They struggled to feed, clothe, and protect them-selves. Stories like Colter's run and Glass's crawl hinted at their bewil-derment and communicated their shared sense of powerlessness. The tales celebrated pain and endurance, and they survived long after the Americans secured the West and organized the place to serve their needs. The stories lingered because they dovetailed with the goals of national-ism, but they also persisted because of their survivalism. They presented a vision of hostile nature peculiar to a disempowered United States that resonated with members of a superempowered one.

Hugh Glass continues to inspire survivalist awe. In September 2004, the writers of *Outside* magazine included his bear adventure among their "Top Wilderness Survival Tales." He shared the honor with pilots, policemen, skiers, and hikers who escaped crashes, broiling deserts, ava-lanches, and volcanic eruptions. His epic jaunt fit nicely with the stories of the Labrador retriever who soloed for months in the Alaskan back-country and the fly fisherman who severed his own leg after being pinned by a rogue boulder. Indeed, Glass could be seen as the forefather of a trendy and lucrative literary genre: traumas in the wilderness.[5]

In the 1990s, Jon Krakauer and Sebastian Junger published enor-mously popular accounts of bodies frozen on mountains and drowned at sea. In 2003, a shark bit off the left arm of the fifteen-year-old surfer Bethany Hamilton on Kauai's North Shore. Hamilton survived, recovered, and continued surfing at the highest levels of competition. She also generated tremendous publicity. Her memoir, *Soul Surfer*, reached the *Los Angeles Times* bestseller list, and she made appearances on *Oprah*, *20/20*, *The Tonight Show*, and *The Ellen DeGeneres Show*. The same year as Hamilton's attack, the rock climber Aron Ralston achieved similar notoriety. Ralston cut off his forearm with a pocketknife after a shifting rock smashed his arm and trapped him alone in Utah's Blue John Canyon. Following his escape, he penned a successful memoir and toured even more talk shows than Hamilton.[6]

Yet while they recalled his durability and his high pain threshold, neither Hamilton nor Ralston was the most direct of Hugh Glass's descendants to reveal him- or herself in 2003. That October, an Alaskan bush pilot discovered the remains of Timothy Treadwell, a semifamous and controversial grizzly bear advocate, and his companion Amy Huguenard. A bear had killed and partially devoured the couple, and Treadwell's mangled body was collecting as many "we told you so"s as flies. For more than thirteen years, he had traveled to Alaska in the summertime to live—in park officials' minds—dangerously close to bears. He documented his close encounters on video and in print. In 1999, he coauthored *Among Grizzlies: Living with Wild Bears in Alaska*, and his exploits landed him on TV. He appeared on CBS's *Late Show with David Letterman*, declaring that he felt safer with the bears than among the wild things in New York City's Central Park. In 2005, the film director Werner Herzog incorporated Treadwell's footage into a documentary that explored the environmentalist's muddled legacy.[7]

A key scene in the film dealt with the most troubling piece of documentation Treadwell left behind—a sound recording of his death taken from a video camera with its lens cap in place. On-screen, Herzog sits with the tape's owner, Jewel Palovak, Treadwell's writing partner and former girlfriend, and listens on headphones. Horrified, he tells her that she must never listen to it and should destroy the tape. Herzog keeps the morbid soundtrack from his audience. Instead, the coroner who investigated the attack recounts the couple's last moments.

By not playing the final tape, Herzog severed the connection between the man and his recording devices. A moral decision, perhaps, for he prevented Treadwell from being doubly victimized by his animal companions and his advanced technology. Together, the killer bear and the blacked-out camera proved the weakness of his theories and his body. He couldn't live with grizzlies; he couldn't save his girlfriend; he couldn't even direct the climax to his own video-infused life. But Herzog could orchestrate this last scene and he does, cutting Treadwell's final act out of the picture.

The earphone scene announces Herzog's takeover of Treadwell's obsessive self-documentation. He will dictate the meaning of Treadwell's footage and his death. Herzog disagreed with Treadwell's vision of nature. Treadwell revered bears and considered them his friends. He believed that he had discovered the secret to living among them and that this knowledge made him an honorary member of their society. While sympathetic to Treadwell's kooky passion and his impressive camerawork, Herzog goes out of his way to rebuke him. When he looks into the eyes of the bears Treadwell filmed, he sees "only the overwhelming indifference of nature . . . no kinship, no understanding, no mercy . . . only a half-bored interest in food." Treadwell had crossed the line: he trespassed blithely into a cruel nonhuman realm, and he paid for it not only with his and his girlfriend's lives but also with his romanticism. The killer bear took the first two; Herzog the second.

Only in turn-of-the-millennium America could a failed actor and reformed drug addict re-create himself as the ultimate friend of some animals and land a spot on national television and a posthumous movie deal. The remarkable omnipresence of media to record and edit experience separates contemporary wilderness traumas from those suffered by the likes of Hugh Glass. Before he severed his arm, Ralston took a video camera from his backpack and said goodbye to his friends and his loved ones. The appliance gave him the director's cut over his accident; he interpreted the senselessness of a massive boulder shifting at the exact moment he parked his hand next to it. No one who saw the bear rip up Glass—including Glass—wrote about the incident. Thus, instead of being the prototype for survival nonfiction, Hugh Glass represents an odd case. He seemed uninterested in turning his injuries into a marketable narrative. He let others profit from his injured body, and his reticence stands out conspicuously amid the flood of words and images generated by shark girls, bear men, and do-it-yourself amputees.

Measured against an age filled with the cascading roar of publicity agents, personal Web pages, and twenty-four-hour media, the print culture of nineteenth-century America produced a weak dribble. Glass couldn't run to a talk show with his scars. The American fur hunters were inaccessible in ways modern wilderness travelers with radios, satellite phones, and global positioning devices cannot comprehend, and this remoteness plausibly explains why Glass didn't—and perhaps couldn't—sell his tale.

Glass and his contemporaries didn't know the word "survivalist"; they had never seen a Boy Scout or heard their preparedness motto; and they could scarcely imagine the existence of a character like Bear Grylls, the British Special Forces soldier turned adventurer who "survives" deserts, jungles, mountains, and Arctic tundra every week on cable television. Glass and his colleagues didn't assume they could manage disasters or escape suffering. They didn't think they could overpower nature. They lived in a world without action heroes; instead of "survival techniques" and "extreme preparedness," they mouthed words like "endurance" to explain their conduct during fiascos.

Glass's social, cultural, and natural environments cocreated his nightmare. His bosses, the she-bear, the Arikaras, and the freaked-out vigil sitters cast him into the wilderness. His social rank exposed him to the abuses of power as well as the caprices of nature. His scars spoke of labor and survival. The two were inseparable.

Today, the marriage of technology and information obscures the links among status, work, and dramatic catastrophes. The circumstances that bring survivors to the wilderness melt away, and the struggle for existence in the presence of media takes center stage. The preparedness industry disavows context to manufacture intimacy. Authors and directors lure audiences into the illusion that humans can encounter a timeless and primal nature. They exploit readers' and viewers' assumptions that cameras, diaries, and journalists will be on site at even the most remote and desperate struggles. In a world filled with outrageous acts of self-documentation, we fully expect to hear the screams when the boat floods, the avalanche cuts loose, and the teeth snap the bone.

Glass's silence proves especially frustrating in a media landscape dotted with chest-thumping publicity darlings. Yet our disappointment in the hole he refused to fill shouldn't blot out the wisdom he scattered at the edges of his absence. Glass's survival as both a human being and a cultural artifact sprang from similar sources: rebelliousness and humor. He approached grizzly bears and bosses with the same disreputable grin, and his insolent chattiness lasted through the many retellings of his legend. He neither overpowered the future with his achievements nor overwhelmed the historical record with his literary output. He merely endured.

In the final reckoning, I'm mightily impressed by his epic loitering. As a human being at middle age, I can picture my environments swallowing me. Nature will decompose my body, culture will deconstruct my stories, and society will forget my contributions. I have published books and articles, composed innumerable e-mails, paid taxes, shot a series of shaky family videos, irregularly updated my Facebook status, and pitched in to raise two wonderful children. Yet nothing that I leave behind will escape the erosion of time. Eventually, even my well-documented existence will disappear. My late grandmother used to look to the nighttime sky for perspective on our inevitable descent into nothingness. "Look at all those stars, Jonny," she would say. "You're not as big a shit as you think." I believe Hugh Glass bestowed a similar comfort on all Americans.

NOTES
ACKNOWLEDGMENTS
INDEX

NOTES

AUTHOR'S NOTE

1. Bruce Barton, *The Man Nobody Knows: A Discovery of the Real Jesus* (1925; repr., New York: Ivan R. Dee, 2000); Wes Roberts, *Leadership Secrets of Attila the Hun* (New York: Warner Books, 1985); and Walter Isaacson, *Benjamin Franklin: An American Life* (New York: Simon & Schuster, 2004). Unlike these monumental figures recast as civic and business role models, Glass most resembled two other audacious and incomplete recent biographical subjects. See Paul E. Johnson, *Sam Patch: The Famous Jumper* (New York: Hill & Wang, 2003), and Scott Reynolds Nelson, *Steel Drivin' Man: John Henry, the Untold Story of an American Legend* (New York: Oxford University Press, 2006).

2. Henry David Thoreau, *Walden*, ed. Jeffery S. Cramer (New Haven, CT: Yale University Press, 2004); Aldo Leopold, *A Sand County Almanac* (New York: Ballantine, 1990); Rachel Carson, *Silent Spring* (New York: Mariner, 2002).

3. Many scholars have acknowledged the relationship between the American nation and nature. See Thomas Hallock, *From the Fallen Tree: Frontier Narratives, Environmental Politics, and the Roots of the National Pastoral, 1749–1826* (Chapel Hill: University of North Carolina Press, 2006); Perry Miller, *Nature's Nation* (Cambridge, MA: Belknap Press/Harvard University Press, 1967); Joyce Chaplin, "Nature and Nation: Natural History in Context," in *Stuffing Birds, Pressing Plants, Shaping Knowledge*, ed. Sue Ann Prince (Philadelphia: American Philosophical Society, 2003); and Lawrence Buell, *The Environmental Imagination: Thoreau, Nature Writing, and the Formation of American Culture* (Cambridge, MA: Belknap Press/Harvard University Press, 1996). Jared Orsi has shown how aspiring gentlemen like Zebulon Pike used frontier hardships to enhance their status. See Jared Orsi, "Zebulon Pike and His 'Frozen Lads': Bodies, Nationalism, and the West in the Early Republic," *Western Historical Quarterly* 42 (Spring 2011): 55–75. No one, as far as I know, has investigated how working people mediated nature and nation in the early nineteenth century. Many, however, have linked backwoodsmen and national identity. See Constance Rourke, *American Humor: A Study of the National Character* (New York: Harcourt, 1931), and Henry Nash Smith, *Virgin Land: The American West as Symbol and Myth* (Cambridge, MA: Harvard University Press, 1950).

4. For nations as inventions, see Benedict Anderson, *Imagined Communities: Reflections on the Origin and Spread of Nationalism* (New York: Verso, 1983), and David Waldstreicher, *In the Midst of Perpetual Fetes: The Making of American Nationalism, 1776–1820* (Chapel Hill: University of North Carolina Press, 1997). John L. O'Sullivan, "The Great Nation of Futurity," *Democratic Review* 23 (November 1839): 426–30. O'Sullivan carefully based his nation on a nostalgic vision of yeomen and artisans. Wage workers and other "dependent" laborers (women, prisoners, slaves, and children) stood outside the polity and had to fight to get in. White male workers were just leveraging their race and gender to gain entrance in Glass's lifetime. See David R. Roediger, *The Wages of Whiteness: Race and the Making of the American Working Class* (New York: Verso, 1991); David Montgomery, *Citizen Worker: The Experience of Workers in the United States with Democracy and the Free Market During the Nineteenth Century* (Cambridge: Cambridge University Press, 1995); and Sean Wilentz, *Chants Democratic: New York City and the Rise of the American Working Class, 1788–1850* (New York: Oxford University Press, 1984).

5. For a sampling of the extensive literature on fur trade multiculturalism, see Sylvia Van Kirk, *Many Tender Ties: Women in Fur Trade Societies, 1670–1870* (Norman: University of Oklahoma, 1980); Jennifer S. H. Brown, *Strangers in Blood: Fur Trade Company Families in Indian Country* (Vancouver: UBC Press, 1980); William R. Swagerty, "Marriage and Settlement Patterns of Rocky Mountain Trappers and Traders," *Western Historical Quarterly* 11, no. 2 (1980): 159–80; and Michael Lansing, "Plains Indians Women and Interracial Marriage in the Upper Missouri Trade, 1804–1868," *Western History Quarterly* 31 (Winter 2000): 413–33.

INTRODUCTION

1. Quote from Daniel T. Potts, "Letter from the Rocky Mountains, July 7, 1824, to Thomas Cochlen," Yellowstone National Park Museum Collection, Albright Visitors Center, Mammoth, Wyoming; James Hall, "The Missouri Trapper," *Port Folio* 19 (March 1825): 214–19. While scantily documented, Glass is far from an unexplored historical and literary subject. See John Myers Myers, *The Saga of Hugh Glass: Pirate, Pawnee, and Mountain Man* (Lincoln, NB: Bison Books, 1976); Michael Punke, *The Revenant* (New York: Basic Books, 2003); Larry McMurtry, *The Wandering Hill* (New York: Simon & Schuster, 2005); Hiram Martin Chittenden, *The American Fur Trade of the West, Volume II* (New York: Harper, 1901): 698–706; and Philip St. George Cooke, "Some Incidents in the Life of Hugh Glass, a Hunter of the Missouri River," *St. Louis Beacon*, 2 December 1830.

2. James Hall, *Letters from the West* (London: Henry Coburn, 1828), 304. Bullboats were a Native technology. Fur traders elongated their round design to carry more bales of beaver pelts. As a result, Glass's boats may have looked more like banana-split dishes than peanut-butter-cup wrappers.

3. For bodies and environments, see Conevery Bolton Valenčius, *The Health of the Country: How American Settlers Understood Themselves and Their Land* (New York: Basic Books, 2002), and Linda Nash, *Inescapable Ecologies: A History of Environment, Disease, and Knowledge* (Berkeley: University of California Press, 2006).

4. On the fur trade, see David J. Wishart, *The Fur Trade of the American West, 1807–1840: A Geographic Synthesis* (Lincoln: University of Nebraska Press, 1979); Rob-

ert M. Utley, *A Life Wild and Perilous: Mountain Men and the Paths to the Pacific* (New York: Henry Holt, 1997); and Eric Jay Dolin, *Fur, Fortune, and Empire: The Epic History of the Fur Trade in America* (New York: Norton, 2010).

5. Hall, *Letters from the West*, ix–xii.

6. Frederick Jackson Turner, *The Frontier in American History* (Tucson: University of Arizona Press, 1920; 1986 ed.), 4.

7. Hall, *Letters from the West*, 293.

8. Ibid., 5.

9. Ibid., 8, 10.

10. Ibid., 2, 7.

11. Historians have long noted the darkness and the ambivalence in the history of the American West and the frontier myth. See Patricia Nelson Limerick, *Legacy of Conquest: The Unbroken Past of The American West* (New York: Norton, 1987); Richard White, *It's Your Misfortune and None of My Own: A New History of the American West* (Norman: University of Oklahoma Press, 1993); Richard Slotkin, *Regeneration Through Violence: The Mythology of the American Frontier, 1600–1860* (1973; Norman: University of Oklahoma Press, 2000); Kerwin Lee Klein, *Frontiers of Historical Imagination: Narrating the European Conquest of Native America, 1890–1990* (Berkeley: University of California Press, 1997); and Richard White, "Frederick Jackson Turner and Buffalo Bill," in Richard White and Patricia Nelson Limerick, *The Frontier in American Culture* (Berkeley: University of California Press, 1994), 7–66. For the West and nineteenth-century confidence games, see Louis S. Warren, *Buffalo Bill's America: William Cody and the Wild West Show* (New York: Knopf, 2005), 68–81, and Andie Tucher, *Froth and Scum: Truth, Beauty, Goodness, and the Ax Murder in America's First Mass Medium* (Chapel Hill: University of North Carolina Press, 1994), 57.

12. See Don D. Walker, "The Mountain Man Journal: Its Significance in a Literary History of the Fur Trade," *Western Historical Quarterly* 5 (July 1974): 307–18.

13. Myers, *Saga of Hugh Glass*, 16–19.

14. See Stephen Ambrose, *Undaunted Courage: Meriwether Lewis, Thomas Jefferson, and the Opening of the American West* (New York: Simon & Schuster, 1996); Thomas P. Slaughter, *Exploring Lewis and Clark: Reflections on Men and Wilderness* (New York: Vintage, 2003); Richard M. Clokey, *William H. Ashley: Enterprise and Politics in the Trans-Mississippi West* (Norman: University of Oklahoma Press, 1980); William E. Foley and C. David Rice, *The First Chouteaus: River Barons of Early St. Louis* (Urbana: University of Illinois Press, 1983); Barton H. Barbour, *Jedediah Smith: No Ordinary Mountain Man* (Norman: University of Oklahoma Press, 2009); John E. Sunder, *Bill Sublette: Mountain Man* (Norman: University of Oklahoma Press, 1959); William R. Nester, *From Mountain Man to Millionaire: "The Bold and Dashing Life" of Robert Campbell* (Columbia: University of Missouri Press, 1999); and Stanley Vestal, *Jim Bridger Mountain Man: A Biography* (Lincoln: University of Nebraska Press, 1946).

15. John G. Neihardt, "The Song of Hugh Glass," in *The Mountain Men*, Vol. I of *A Cycle of the West* (Lincoln: Bison, 1915; 1953 ed.); Frederick Feikema Manfred, "The Making of *Lord Grizzly*," *South Dakota History* 15 (Summer 1985): 200–216.

16. *Man in the Wilderness*, Time Warner, 1971.

17. Ibid.

18. Howard Thompson, "Film: The Pioneer Spirit 'Man in the Wilderness'" *New York Times*, 25 November 1971, 53.
19. *McCabe & Mrs. Miller*, Warner Bros., 1971.
20. Rowland Willard, "Manuscript Autobiography," Rowland Willard–Elizabeth Willard Papers, MSS, Box 1, Folder 1, Beinecke Library, Yale University, New Haven, CT.
21. Ann Fabian, *The Unvarnished Truth: Personal Narratives in Nineteenth-Century America* (Berkeley: University of California Press, 2000), 29.

1. THE METAPHYSICS OF HUGH HUNTING

1. Charles L. Camp, ed., *James Clyman, Frontiersman* (Portland, OR: Champeog Press, 1960), 7.
2. *Missouri Republican*, 15 January 1823. James Clyman provided a account of the Ashley men's early years in the West. His writings have been tapped by numerous authors. See Bernard DeVoto, *The Year of Decision 1846* (Boston: Houghton Mifflin, 1942), and Barton H. Barbour, *Jedediah Smith: No Ordinary Mountain Man* (Norman: University of Oklahoma Press, 2009), 37–55.
3. See the *Missouri Gazette*, 13 February–6 March 1822, and *St. Louis Enquirer*, 26 February–23 March 1822.
4. For mountain men as expectant capitalists, see William H. Goetzmann, "The Mountain Man as Jacksonian Man," *American Quarterly* 15 (Autumn 1963): 402–15.
5. Smith quoted in Dale L. Morgan, *Jedediah Smith and the Opening of the West* (Lincoln, NB: Bison Books, 1953), 34.
6. Thomas Hempstead, Fort Lisa, to Joshua Pilcher, St. Louis, 3 April 1822, in Dale L. Morgan, ed., *The West of William H. Ashley* (Denver, CO: Old West Publishing Company, 1964), 3–4.
7. For an example of a descriptions of the Missouri River, see Lewis H. Garrard, *Wah-to-yah and the Taos Trail* (Norman: University of Oklahoma Press, 1955), 8–9.
8. Camp, *James Clyman*, 8.
9. Ibid.
10. Ibid., 7.
11. For references to Shakespeare in an iconic western, see Owen Wister, *The Virginian: The Horseman of the Plains* (New York: Fireship Press, 2009), 102, 112, 154. The thespian in the cow town has become such a cliché that satirists have targeted it. See the Lili Von Shtupp character in *Blazing Saddles*, DVD, directed by Mel Brooks (1974; Los Angeles: Warner Bros., 2004); and the Jack Langrishe character in *Deadwood: The Complete Series*, DVD, created by David Milch (2006, season 3; Los Angeles: HBO, 2009).
12. *My Darling Clementine*, DVD, directed by John Ford (1946; Los Angeles: 20th Century Fox, 2004).
13. Hall's letter to Duyckinck was reprinted with editorial comments in David Donald, ed., "The Autobiography of James Hall, Western Literary Pioneer," *Ohio Archaeological and Historical Quarterly* 56, no. 3 (July 1947): 295–304. For a positive assessment of James Hall's life and literary career, see Randolph C. Randall, *James Hall: Spokesman of the New West* (Columbus: Ohio State University Press, 1964), and Edward Watts and David Rachels, eds., *The First West: Writing from the American Frontier, 1776–1860* (New York: Oxford University Press, 2002), 496–523. For a

less charitable view, see Richard Drinnon, *Facing West: The Metaphysics of Indian Hating and Empire Building* (1980; New York: Schocken, 1990), 191–215.

14. Donald, "Autobiography of James Hall," 297.
15. Ibid.
16. Ibid., 298.
17. Ibid., 299.
18. *Literary Cabinet and Western Olive Branch*, I (12 October 1833): 135; John E. Hall, Philadelphia, to James Hall, Shawnee Town, Illinois, 13 September 1827, Historical and Philosophical Society Library, Cincinnati; *The Hesperian* II (1828): 171.
19. Donald, "Autobiography of James Hall," 303.
20. For the communications revolution, see Daniel Walker Howe, *What Hath God Wrought: The Transformation of America, 1815–1848* (New York: Oxford University Press, 2007). For the contours and limits of this revolution, see Trish Loughran, *The Republic in Print: Print Culture in the Age of U.S. Nation Building, 1770–1870* (New York: Columbia University Press, 2009). For Melville's *The Confidence-Man* as a window onto American history in this time period, see Stephen Mihm, *A Nation of Counterfeiters: Capitalists, Con Men, and the Making of the United States* (Cambridge, MA: Harvard University Press, 2007), 4–19, and Walter McDougall, *Freedom Just Around the Corner: A New American History, 1585–1828* (New York: HarperCollins, 2005). For a critical literary treatment of the novel, see Jonathan Cook, *Satirical Apocalypse: An Anatomy of Melville's* The Confidence-Man (Santa Barbara, CA: Greenwood, 1996).
21. Herman Melville, *The Confidence-Man: His Masquerade,* Norton Critical Edition, ed. Hershel Parker and Mark Niemeyer (New York: Norton, 2006), 9.
22. Thomas Bangs Thorpe, "The Big Bear of Arkansas" *The Spirit of the Times,* March 1841, 43; for the affinities between Thorpe and Melville, see John Bryant, "Melville Essays the Romance: Comedy and Being in *Frankenstein,* 'The Big Bear of Arkansas,' and *Moby-Dick,*" *Nineteenth-Century Literature* 61 (December 2006): 277–310. Melville, *The Confidence-Man,* 16.
23. Johannes Dietrich Bergmann, "From the Original Confidence Man," *American Quarterly* 21 (Autumn 1969): 561. Of course, there couldn't be just one origin for such a slippery character. For a discussion of other possibilities, see Michael S. Reynolds, "The Prototype for Melville's Confidence-Man," *PMLA* 86 (October 1971): 1009–13.
24. Melville continued to write poetry. His last work, the novel *Billy Budd, Sailor,* was published after his death. See Andrew Delbanco, *Melville: His Life and Work* (New York: Knopf, 2005).
25. Melville, *The Confidence-Man,* 111.
26. Ibid., 130.
27. Ibid., 125.
28. Charles Wilkins Webber, "Metaphysics of Bear Hunting; An Adventure in the San Saba Hills," *The American Whig Review* 2 (1845): 174, 187. See also "The Metaphysics of Bear-Hunting," in C. W. Webber, *The Hunter-Naturalist: The Romance of Sporting; or, the Wild Scenes and Wild Hunters* (Philadelphia: Lippincott, Grambo, 1845), 343–80.
29. Webber, "Metaphysics," 171.
30. Melville, *The Confidence-Man,* 144.
31. For Hall and Melville and Indian hating, see Ronald Takaki, *Iron Cages: Race and*

Culture in 19th-Century America (New York: Oxford University Press, 1990), 80–107; William M. Ramsey, "The Moot Points of Melville's Indian Hating," *American Literature* 52 (May 1980): 224–35; Hershel Parker, "The Metaphysics of Indian-hating," *Nineteenth-Century Fiction* 18 (September 1963): 165–73; Drinnon, *Facing West*, 213–15.

32. James Hall, "Indian Hating," in *Sketches of History, Life, and Manners, in the West* (Philadelphia: Harrison Hall, 1835), 74.

33. Ibid., 75.

34. Ibid., 74–76.

35. Ibid., 76.

36. Melville, *The Confidence-Man*, 147.

37. Ibid., 156.

38. Hall, "Indian Hating," 82; Melville, *The Confidence-Man*, 161.

39. Camp, *James Clyman*, 15.

2. BORN TO RUN

1. Charles L. Camp, ed., *George C. Yount and His Chronicles of the West* (Denver: Old West Publishing Company, 1966), 197–207. For the Lafitte brothers, see William C. Davis, *The Pirates Lafitte: The Treacherous World of the Corsairs of the Gulf* (New York: Harcourt, 2005).

2. For captivity and adoption, see Daniel Richter, *Ordeal of the Longhouse: The Peoples of the Iroquois League in the Era of European Colonization* (Chapel Hill: University of North Carolina Press, 1992), 50–74; James F. Brooks, *Captives and Cousins: Slavery, Kinship, and Community in the Southwest Borderlands* (Chapel Hill: University of North Carolina Press, 2002), 1–19; and Brett Rushforth, "'A Little Flesh We Offer You': The Origins of Indian Slavery in New France," *William and Mary Quarterly* 60 (October 2003): 780–87. Camp, *Yount*, 198.

3. *Pittsburgh Gazette*, 23 April 1795. Advertisement quoted in Henry J. Kauffman, *The Pennsylvania-Kentucky Rifle* (Harrisburg, PA: Stackpole, 1960).

4. See David Waldstreicher, *Runaway America: Benjamin Franklin, Slavery, and the American Revolution* (New York: Hill and Wang, 2004); Waldstreicher, "Why Thomas Jefferson and African Americans Wore Their Politics on Their Sleeves: Dress and Mobilization between American Revolutions," in Jeff Pasley and David Waldstreicher, eds., *Beyond the Founders: New Approaches to the Political History of the Early Republic* (Chapel Hill: University of North Carolina Press, 2003), 79–103; Waldstreicher, "Reading the Runaways: Self-Fashioning, Print Culture, and Confidence in Slavery in the Eighteenth-Century Mid-Atlantic," *William and Mary Quarterly*, 3rd ser., 56 (April 1999): 243–72; and Jonathan Prude, "To Look upon the 'Lower Sort': Runaway Ads and the Appearance of Unfree Laborers in America, 1750–1800," *Journal of American History* 78 (June 1991): 124–59.

5. *Missouri Republican* (St. Louis), 26 March 1823.

6. *Missouri Gazette and Public Advocate* (St. Louis), 14 October 1820.

7. *Missouri Republican* (St. Louis), 25 September 1825; *Missouri Republican* (St. Louis), 4 October 1824.

8. For a sampling of skin-color descriptions, see *Missouri Republican* (St. Louis), 4 October 1824, 21 September 1826, and 10 May 1827. The ad for Lesseiur appeared in the *Missouri Republican* (St. Louis), 25 March 1828.

9. *Missouri Republican* (St. Louis), 17 April 1822.
10. *Missouri Republican* (St. Louis), 6 July 1826; *Missouri Gazette and Public Advocate* (St. Louis), 14 October 1820; *Missouri Republican* (St. Louis), 12 October 1826.
11. *Missouri Republican* (St. Louis), 23 September 1828 and 4 October 1824.
12. Timothy Flint, *Recollections of the Last Ten Years* (Boston: Cummings, Hilliard, and Company, 1826), 5–6. For nineteenth-century views on landscapes and health in the Mississippi Valley, see Conevery Bolton Valenčius, *The Health of the Country: How American Settlers Understood Themselves and Their Land* (New York: Basic Books, 2002).
13. Flint, *Recollections*, 132.
14. Valenčius, *The Health of the Country*, 79–80.
15. Flint, *Recollections*, 132, 137–38. Flint's stoic Indians were not peaceful. He explained Native American violence thus: so catatonic had Indians become that vicious passions—fighting, gambling, and drinking—overwhelmed their reason. They sprang into action like "whirlwinds" when "these excitements arous[ed] the imprisoned energies of the long and sullen meditation" (ibid., 139, 175, 178).
16. Ibid., 174–75. Flint tells his origin myth ibid., 161–62.
17. For Flint's aversion to racial amalgamation in the context of a multiracial frontier, see John Mack Faragher, "'More Motley than Mackinaw': From Ethnic Mixing to Ethnic Cleansing on the Frontier of the Lower Missouri, 1783–1833," in *Contact Points: American Frontiers from the Mohawk Valley to the Mississippi, 1750–1830*, ed. Andrew R. L. Cayton and Fredrika J. Teute (Chapel Hill: University of North Carolina Press, 1998), 324–25.
18. Flint, *Recollections*, 6–8.
19. Ibid., 97–98.
20. Ibid.
21. Ibid., 94–95.
22. Ibid., 16. For the myth versus the reality of boatmen's work, see Michael Allen, *Western Rivermen, 1763–1861: Ohio and Mississippi Boatmen and the Myth of the Alligator Horse* (Baton Rouge: Louisiana State University Press, 1990).
23. *Missouri Republican* (St. Louis), 25 October 1824; *Missouri Gazette and Public Advocate* (St. Louis), 31 October 1821 and 19 September 1821.
24. *Missouri Gazette and Public Advocate* (St. Louis), 2 January 1822; *Missouri Republican* (St. Louis), 12 July 1824 and 15 August 1825.
25. *Missouri Republican* (St. Louis), 11 July 1825.
26. *Missouri Republican* (St. Louis), 6 December 1824.
27. Richard Henry Dana, *Two Years Before the Mast: A Personal Narrative of a Life at Sea . . . with Journals and Letters* (Los Angeles: Ward Ritchie Press, 1964), 442–48.
28. Henry David Thoreau, "Walking" (1862), in *The Writings of Henry David Thoreau*, vol. 5 (New York: Houghton Mifflin, 1906), 217–18.
29. Ibid., 218.

3. THE NAKED AND THE DEAD

1. The Gardner letter is reprinted in Dale L. Morgan, *The West of William H. Ashley* (Denver: Old West, 1964), 31. The South Dakota Historical Society has the original.

2. Benjamin O'Fallon, U.S. Indian Agent, Upper Missouri Agency, Fort Atkinson, to William Clark, Superintendent of Indian Affairs, St. Louis, 24 June 1823, quoted ibid., 37.

3. For the Americans' precarious position in the 1820s, see Jeffrey Ostler, *The Plains Sioux and U.S. Colonialism from Lewis and Clark to Wounded Knee* (Cambridge, UK: Cambridge University Press, 2004), 32, and Richard White, "The Winning of the West: The Expansion of the Western Sioux in the Eighteenth and Nineteenth Centuries," *Journal of American History* 65, no. 2 (September 1978): 332–33.

4. See Kathleen Duvall, *The Native Ground: Indians and Colonists in the Heart of the Continent* (Philadelphia: University of Pennsylvania Press, 2006); William E. Foley and C. David Rice, *The First Chouteaus: River Barons of the Early St. Louis Fur Trade* (Champaign-Urbana: University of Illinois Press, 2000); and Richard Edward Oglesby, *Manuel Lisa and the Opening of the Missouri River Fur Trade* (Norman: University of Oklahoma Press, 1963).

5. *Dubreuil v. Lisa*, 32 Louisiana Territory (St. Louis Cir 1809), 1.

6. Ibid., 2.

7. Deposition of Augustin Dubreuil, 5 August 1808, Manuel Lisa Papers, Missouri Historical Society, St. Louis. The story of Drouillard is retold in Oglesby, *Manuel Lisa*, 4–6.

8. For a sampling of Lisa-inspired vitriol, see Thomas James, *Three Years Among the Indians and Mexicans* (St. Louis: Missouri Historical Society, 1916). On page 47 James blended race, nationalism, class, and rascality to denounce Lisa: "Rascality sat on every feature of his dark complexioned, Mexican face—gleamed from his black, Spanish, eyes, and seemed enthroned in a forehead 'villainous low.'"

9. John Bradbury, *Travels in the Interior of America* (Liverpool: Smith and Galway, 1917), 28–32.

10. Ibid., vii; Frederick Pursh, *Flora Americae Septentrionalis*, Vols. I–II, (London: White, Cochrane, and Co., 1814, 1816).

11. Ibid.

12. Bradbury's reticence contrasted sharply with the second-best source on Colter's run, Thomas James's *Three Years Among the Indians and Mexicans*. Like Bradbury, James heard the tale from Colter, but he published the story in the 1840s. By then the tale had acquired all the trappings of American exceptionalism. James subsumed Colter into the myth of the frontiersman: "He was about thirty-five years of age, five feet ten inches in height and wore an open, ingenious, and pleasing countenance of the Daniel Boone stamp. Nature had formed him, like Boone, for hardy indurance [*sic*] of fatigue, privations and perils." See James, *Three Years*, 58.

13. James P. Beckwourth, *The Life and Adventures of James P. Beckwourth, Mountainer, Scout, and Pioneer, and Chief of the Crow Nation of Indians* (Lincoln: University of Nebraska Press, 1872), 23–24.

14. Ibid., 24.

15. Ibid., 24, 29–30.

16. Ibid., 31. Francis Parkman scribbled the "gaudy liar" quip in his copy of Beckwourth's autobiography. Even if they disagree with Parkman, writers have hung the title around Beckwourth's neck ever since ever since. See Le Roy Hafen, *The Mountain Men and the Fur Trade in the Far West* (Glendale, CA: Arthur Clark, 1965), 37; Dale L. Morgan, *Jedediah Smith and the Opening of the West* (Lincoln:

University of Nebraska Press, 1964), 156; Jay Golden Taylor and Thomas J. Lyon, eds., *A Literary History of the American West* (Dallas: Texas Christian University Press, 1987), 85; and Elinor Wilson, *Jim Beckwourth: Black Mountain Man and War Chief of the Crow* (Norman: University of Oklahoma Press, 1981), 3.

17. Beckwourth, *Life and Adventures*, 37.
18. Ibid., 46.
19. Ibid., 47.
20. Beckwourth sprinkles his autobiography with examples of Ashley's respect and subservience. See ibid., 59, 60, 88. William Ashley, "Diary," Ashley Collection, Missouri Historical Society, St. Louis, MO.
21. Ibid., 76.
22. For slavery and animals, see Karl Jacoby, "Slaves by Nature? Domestic Animals and Human Slaves," *Slavery and Abolition* 15 (1994): 89–97; David Brion Davis, *Inhuman Bondage: The Rise and Fall of Slavery in the New World* (New York: Oxford, 2006), 2–3; *Missouri Gazette and Public Advertiser* (St. Louis), 22 March 1820.
23. Before scientific racism, the idea that a human being might shift races in new environments wasn't strange. See Linda Nash, *Inescapable Ecologies: A History of Environment, Disease, and Knowledge* (Berkeley: University of California Press, 2004); Matthew Fry Jacobson, *Whiteness of a Different Color: European Immigrants and the Alchemy of Race* (Cambridge, MA: Harvard University Press, 1998); and Joyce Chaplin, *Subject Matter: Technology, the Body, and Science on the Anglo-American Frontier, 1500–1676* (Cambridge, MA: Harvard University Press, 2001).
24. For discussions of Beckwourth's race, see Blake Allmendinger, *Imagining an African American West* (Lincoln: University of Nebraska Press, 2005); Laura Browder, *Slippery Characters: Ethnic Impersonators and American Identities* (Chapel Hill: University of North Carolina Press, 2000); and Quintard Taylor, *In Search of the Racial Frontier: African Americans in the American West, 1528–1990* (New York: Norton, 1999). Francis Parkman, *The Oregon Trail* (Garden City, NY: Doubleday, 1946), 106.
25. Charles Christy, "The Personal Memoir of Captain Charles Christy," *The Trail: A Magazine for Colorado*, vol. I (October 1908), 16.
26. For the Arikara fight, see "Extract of a Letter from General Ashley," *Missouri Republican* (St. Louis), 2 July 1823. Dale L. Morgan reprints two nearly identical letters from Ashley describing the scene in his *The West of William H. Ashley*, 25–31. See also the anonymous letter written by a member of the party to a friend in Washington, DC, ibid., 31–33. For a historical overview, see William R. Nester, *The Arikara War: The First Plains Indian War, 1823* (Missoula, MT: Mountain Press, 2001).
27. Charles L. Camp, ed., *James Clyman, Frontiersman* (Portland, OR: Champeog Press, 1960), 10–12.
28. Morgan, *The West of William H. Ashley*, 27.
29. John C. Calhoun, Secretary of War, to William Clark, Superintendent of Indian Affairs, St. Louis, 1 July 1822, quoted ibid., 17; Clark to Calhoun, 9 August 1822, quoted ibid., 18.
30. Benjamin O'Fallon, U.S. Indian Agent, Upper Missouri Agency, St. Louis, to Ramsey Crooks, Fort Atkinson, 10 July 1822, quoted ibid., 17.

31. William H. Ashley, aboard the *Rocky Mountain*, to Benjamin O'Fallon, Council Bluff, 4 July 1823, quoted ibid., 27; Anonymous to Washington, DC, quoted ibid., 33.
32. "To the Forty three men who Deserted Gen. Ashly," quoted ibid., 34–35.
33. Ibid., 34.
34. Camp, *James Clyman, Frontiersman*, 12.
35. Ibid.
36. Ibid., 3.

4. BEARS IN BLACK AND WHITE

1. Daniel T. Potts, "Letter from the Rocky Mountains, July 7, 1824, to Thomas Cochlen," Yellowstone National Park Museum Collection, Albright Visitors Center, Mammoth, WY.
2. Thomas Bangs Thorpe pokes fun at bears overheating in "The Big Bear of Arkansas," *Spirit of the Times*, 27 March 1841, 43.
3. Many writers have noted these similarities. See Bernd Brunner, *Bears: A Brief History* (New Haven, CT: Yale University Press, 2007), 1; Paul Shepard and Barry Sanders, *The Sacred Paw: The Bear in Nature, Myth, and Literature* (New York: Viking, 1985).
4. For an overview of hunting in American culture, see Daniel Justin Herman, *Hunting and the American Imagination* (Washington, DC: Smithsonian Press, 2001).
5. For a critical assessment of Crockett and Doggett and their place in American culture, see Constance Rourke, *American Humor: A Study of National Character* (New York: Harcourt, Brace, 1931); Richard M. Dorson, ed., *Davy Crockett: American Comic Legend* (New York: Spiral Press, 1939); Carroll Smith-Rosenberg, "Davey Crockett as Trickster: Pornography, Liminality, and Symbolic Inversion in Victorian America," *Journal of Contemporary History* 17 (April 1982): 325–50; Michael A. Lofaro, ed., *Davy Crockett: The Man, the Legend, the Legacy, 1786–1986* (Knoxville: University of Tennessee Press, 1985); J. A. Leo Lemay, "The Text, Tradition, and Themes of 'The Big Bear of Arkansas,'" *American Literature* 47 (November 1975): 321–42; and Richard Slotkin, *Regeneration Through Violence: The Mythology of the American Frontier, 1600–1860* (New York: HarperPerennial, 1973), 479–84.
6. David Crockett, *A Narrative of the Life of David Crockett* (1834; Lincoln: University of Nebraska Press, 1987), 68.
7. Ibid., 160.
8. Ibid., 161, 63. For race and hunting, see Stuart A. Marks, *Southern Hunting in Black and White: Race, History, and Ritual in a Carolina Community* (Princeton, NJ: Princeton University Press, 1992), and John M. Mackenzie, *The Empire of Nature: Hunting, Conservation, and British Imperialism* (Manchester, UK: University of Manchester Press, 1988).
9. Crockett, *Narrative of the Life*, 188–90.
10. Ibid., 167, 168–69.
11. Ibid., 207, 171–72, 198.
12. For the Crockett in the almanacs, see Michael A. Lofaro, "The Hidden 'Hero' of the Nashville Crockett Almanacs," in Michael A. Lofaro, ed., *Davy Crockett*.

13. Crockett, *Narrative of the Life*, 148, 207, 198.
14. Richard Boyd Hauck, *Davy Crockett: A Hand Book* (Lincoln: University of Nebraska Press, 1986), 129–30. Paul Andrew Hutton also revisits the grinning episode in his excellent introduction to Crockett, *Narrative of the Life*, xv.
15. Thorpe, "The Big Bear," 43.
16. Ibid.
17. Ibid., 44.
18. Ibid.
19. Ibid., 43, 44.
20. See Augustus Baldwin Longstreet, *Georgia Scenes* (New York: Harper, 1846); Johnson J. Hooper, *Some Adventures of Captain Simon Sugge* (New York: Irvington, 1973); and George Washington Harris, *High Times and Hard Times* (Nashville, TN: Vanderbilt University Press, 1967).
21. Thorpe, "The Big Bear," 44.
22. John Bryant, *Melville and Repose: The Rhetoric of Humor in the American Renaissance* (New York: Oxford University Press, 1993), 105.
23. Gary Brown, *Great Bear Almanac* (New York: Lyons and Buford, 1993), 21; Paul Schullery, *The Bears of Yellowstone* (Boulder, CO: Roberts Rinehart, 1986), 38.
24. For a discussion of the grizzlies' dominance hierarchy, see Stephen Herrero, *Bear Attacks: Their Causes and Avoidance*, rev. ed. (Guilford, CT: Lyons, 2002), 197–236, and Frank C. Craighead, *Track of the Grizzly* (San Francisco: Sierra Club Books, 1979), 31–48.
25. Craighead, *Track of the Grizzly*, 35–37, 45.
26. James P. Beckwourth, *The Life and Adventures of James P. Beckwourth: Mountainer, Scout, and Pioneer, and Chief of the Crow Nation of Indians* (Lincoln: University of Nebraska Press, 1872), 80–81.
27. Osborne Russell, *Journal of a Trapper*, ed. L. A. York (Boise: Syms-York, 1921), 12–13.
28. Beckwourth, *Life and Adventures*, 85–86.
29. Ibid., 88–89.
30. For slave- and dog-naming practices, see John Wood Sweet, *Bodies Politic: Negotiating Race in the American North, 1730–1830* (Philadelphia: University of Pennsylvania Press, 2003), 70.
31. Charles L. Camp, ed., *James Clyman, Frontiersman* (Portland, OR: Champeog Press, 1960), 18.
32. Ibid.
33. Dale L. Morgan, *Jedediah Smith and the Opening of the West* (Lincoln: University of Nebraska Press, 1964), 18; Camp, *James Clyman*, 18.
34. Scholars of the role of tattoos in homosocial communities have noted this practice of reading bodies and linked it to power inequities. The marks identified the men who bore them to other communities. See Simon P. Newman, "Reading the Bodies of Early American Seafarers," *William and Mary Quarterly* 55 (January 1998): 59–82, and Margo Demello, "The Convict Body: Tattooing Among Male American Prisoners," *Anthropology Today* 9 (December 1993): 10–13.
35. For grizzlies' propensity for attacking human faces, see Zenas Leonard, *Narrative of the Adventures of Zenas Leonard: Five Years as a Mountain Man in the Rocky Mountains* (1839; Santa Barbara: The Narrative Press, 2001), 15. For bear body language and facial attacks, see Herrero, *Bear Attacks*, 14, 18. For comparative bite

force, see Stephen Wroe et al., "Bite Club: Comparative Bite Force in Big Biting Mammals and the Prediction of Predatory Behaviour in Fossil Taxa," *Proceedings: Biological Sciences* 272 (22 March 2005): 619–25.

36. Elliott Coues, ed., *The Journal of Jacob Fowler* (New York: Harper, 1898), 41–42.
37. Ibid., 43–44.
38. Camp, *James Clyman*, 15.
39. Coues, *The Journal of Jacob Fowler*, 44.
40. Camp, *James Clyman*, 189.
41. Reuben Gold Thwaites, ed., *Original Journals of the Lewis and Clark Expedition 1804–1806* (New York: Dodd, Mead & Company, 1905), 2–4, excerpted in Fred R. Gowans, *Mountain Man and Grizzly* (Orem, UT: Mountain Grizzly Publications, 1992), 28, 37. For Joe Meek's adventures, see Frances Fuller Victor, *The River of the West* (Hartford, CT: Columbian Book Company, 1871), 86–94, 194–95.
42. James B. Marsh, *Four Years in the Rockies* (Newcastle, UK: W. B. Thomas, 1884), 117.
43. Ibid., 111–13.

5. JUST ANOTHER WORD FOR NOTHING LEFT TO CHEW

1. Rowland Willard, "Manuscript Autobiography," Rowland Willard and Elizabeth S. Willard Papers, 1825–1884, WA MSS S-2512, Box 1, Folder 1, Beinecke Library, Yale University, New Haven, CT.
2. Ibid.
3. Ibid.
4. Ibid.
5. Rowland Willard, "Manuscript Journal," Rowland Willard and Elizabeth S. Willard Papers, WA MSS S-2512, Box 1, Folder 14, Beinecke Library, Yale University, New Haven, CT; James O. Pattie, *The Personal Narrative of James O. Pattie, of Kentucky*, ed. Timothy Flint (Cincinnati, OH: J. H. Wood, 1831), 327–64.
6. Willard, "Manuscript Autobiography."
7. Lewis H. Garrard, *Wah-to-yah and the Taos Trail* (Norman: University of Oklahoma Press, 1955), 19.
8. Ibid., 29, 25.
9. Daniel T. Potts, Letter from the Rocky Mountains, July 7, 1824, to Thomas Cochlen, published in Dale L. Morgan, ed., *The West of William H. Ashley* (Denver, CO: Old West Publishing Co., 1964), 7.
10. Ibid.
11. Daniel Potts, Letter to Brother, Rocky Mountains, July 16, 1826, reprinted ibid., 8; Potts to Cochlen, ibid.,
12. Potts to Cochlen, ibid., 80.
13. See especially Richard White's discussion of "besoins" in *The Middle Ground: Indians, Empires, and Republics in the Great Lakes Region, 1650–1815* (Cambridge, UK: Cambridge University Press, 1991), 128–30; Mary Black-Rogers, "Varieties of 'Starving': Semantics and Survival in the Subarctic Fur Trade," *Ethnohistory* 33 (Fall 1986): 353.
14. "Enterprise," *St. Louis Enquirer*, 13 April 1822.
15. "Biographical Notice of Genl. William H. Ashley," *Missouri Saturday News* (St. Louis), 14 April 1838.

16. Kenneth Kamler, *Surviving the Extremes: What Happens to the Body and Mind at the Limits of Human Endurance* (New York: Penguin, 2004), 112–14.

17. William Fayel, ed., *A Narrative of Col. Robert Campbell's Experiences in the Rocky Mountain Fur Trade from 1825 to 1835* (1886), microfilm, St. Louis Mercantile Library, University of Missouri at St. Louis, 1.

18. Ibid., 8–9.

19. Competition between fur companies put a premium on less-capitalized firms to sell out at the right time. See David J. Wishart, *The Fur Trade of the American West, 1807–1840* (Lincoln: University of Nebraska Press, 1979), 148–66.

20. For Campbell's biography, see William R. Nester, *From Mountain Man to Millionaire: The "Bold and Dashing Life" of Robert Campbell* (Columbia: University of Missouri Press, 1999). Fayel, *Narrative*, 3.

21. Fayel, *Narrative*, 4.

22. James Hall, *Letters from the West* (London: Henry Colburn, 1828), 300.

23. Ibid.

24. Zenas Leonard, *Narrative of the Adventures of Zenas Leonard* (1839; Santa Barbara, CA: Narrative Press, 2001), 9.

25. Ibid., 23–24.

26. Ibid., 25.

27. Ibid., 23.

28. Washington Irving, *Adventures of Captain Bonneville* (London: Richard Bentley, 1837); Leonard, *Narrative*, 2.

29. Willard, "Manuscript Autobiography."

6. COLD LIPS SAY WAUGH!

1. Friedrich W. von Wrede, *Sketches of Life in the United States of North America and Texas*, trans. Chester W. Geue (Cassel, Germany, 1844; Waco, TX: Texian, 1970), 29.

2. For similarities, see James Hall, "The Missouri Trapper," *Port Folio* (Philadelphia), March 1825, 299; von Wrede, *Sketches of Life*, 31, 37.

3. Hall, "The Missouri Trapper," 303–4.

4. Von Wrede, *Sketches of Life*, 29.

5. For Ruxton's "schoolboy atrocities," Spanish medal, and romance quip, see Leroy R. Hafen, ed., *Ruxton of the Rockies: Autobiographical Writings by the Author of Adventures in Mexico and the Rocky Mountains and Life in the Far West* (Norman: University of Oklahoma Press, 1950), 4.

6. Quotes on veracity in "The Late George Frederick Ruxton," *Blackwood's Magazine*, November 1848; reprinted in George Frederick Ruxton, *Life in the Far West* (Norman: University of Oklahoma Press, 1951), 231–32. For an assessment of Ruxton's vernacular, see Richard C. Poulsen, *The Mountain Man Vernacular: Its Historical Roots, Its Linguistic Nature, and Its Literary Uses* (New York: Peter Lang, 1985).

7. Ruxton, *Life in the Far West*, 51.

8. Ibid., 116, 178, 7–9.

9. Ibid., 7.

10. For animals, see ibid., 10, 11, 12, 16, 30, 45, 49, 85, 168; for racial, animal, and

ethnic metaphors, 7, 9, 12, 31, 45, 79, 168, 174; Sublette quote, 9; references to whiteness, 18, 34, 71, 181.

11. Ibid., 51.
12. Ibid., 54.
13. Ibid., 62–63.
14. Ibid., 64–65.
15. Ibid., 33–34.
16. Ibid., 111.
17. Ibid., 109.
18. Ibid., 127.
19. "The Late George Frederick Ruxton," *Blackwood's Magazine*, reprinted in Ruxton, *Life in the Far West*, 232.
20. Von Wrede, *Sketches of Life*, 89.
21. Ibid., 69.
22. Ibid., 46.
23. Ibid., 75.
24. Ibid., 29.
25. Hafen, *Ruxton of the Rockies*, 253.
26. Ibid., 255.
27. They also illustrated the scene. Maximillian traveled with the Swiss artist Karl Bodmer, who produced some of the most striking images of Indians, nature, and trappers from the period. For the scalp, see Prince Maximilian's *Journals*, 14 June and 4 July 1833, cited in Barton H. Barbour, *Fort Union and the Upper Missouri Fur Trade* (Norman: University of Oklahoma, 2001), 79.
28. For Glass's Fort Union activities and the McKenzie episode, see John Myers Myers, *The Saga of Hugh Glass: Pirate, Pawnee, and Mountain Man* (Lincoln, NB: Bison Books, 1976), 216–17, and Barbour, *Fort Union*, 43.
29. John Sanford, Mandan Villages, to General William Clark, St. Louis, 26 July 1833, microfilm 42, Fur Trade Excerpts, National Archives, Washington, DC.
30. Ibid.
31. For Rose's mixed heritage and the Pilcher and Leavenworth quotes, see Capt. Reuben Holmes, "The Five Scalps," *Missouri Historical Society*, Volume V (January–March 1939): 3–4; Washington Irving, *Astoria; or, Enterprise Beyond the Rocky Mountains* (London: Bentley, 1839), 183.
32. Irving, *Astoria*, 183.

7. I WILL SURVIVE

1. T. Pearse Wheelright, "With Broken Back Rancher Crawls Two Miles for Aid," *Deseret News*, 21 June 1949.
2. Ibid.
3. Ibid.
4. Ibid.
5. Glass has appeared in a wide range of survival literature, including Edward E. Leslie, ed., *Desperate Journeys, Abandoned Souls: True Stories of Castaways and Other Survivors* (New York: Mariner, 1988), 265–91; David Alloway, *Desert Survival Skills* (Austin: University of Texas Press, 2000), 5–6; Samuel A. Southworth, *U.S. Special Warfare: The Elite Combat Skills of American Modern Armed Forces*

(New York: Da Capo Press, 2004), 142; David Borgenicht, Trey Popp, and Melissa Wagner, *The Worst Case Scenario Almanac: Great Outdoors* (Vancouver, BC: Quirk Productions, 2007), 83; David Dary, *Frontier Medicine: From Atlantic to Pacific* (New York: Knopf, 2008), 104–5; and Conrad Wennerberg, *Wind, Waves, and Sunburn: A Brief History of Marathon Swimming* (New York: Breakaway Books, 1974), 27–28.

6. I borrow this definition of modernism (as well as its application to Neihardt) from Phillip J. Deloria, "Historiography," in *A Companion to American Indian History*, ed. Deloria and Neal Salisbury (New York: Blackwell, 2004), 13–14; Frederick Feikema Manfred, Bloomington, MN, to George Shively, New York, NY, 24 September 1952, Frederick Manfred Correspondence, 1950–52, Anderson Library Manuscript Collection, University of Minnesota, Minneapolis, MN.

7. John G. Neihardt, *The Mountain Men: The Song of Three Friends, the Song of Hugh Glass, and the Song of Jed Smith* (Lincoln: University of Nebraska Press, 1949), vi–vii.

8. Ibid., 133–34, 131, 142.

9. Ibid., 169, 207.

10. Ibid., 222, 224.

11. Ibid., 236.

12. Ibid., 245–46, 253–54.

13. Ibid., vi, ix–x.

14. Ibid., x–xi.

15. Ibid., v.

16. See Frederick Jackson Turner, "The Significance of the Frontier in American History," in John Mack Faragher, *Rereading Frederick Jackson Turner* (New York: Henry Holt, 1994), 31–60; Theodore Roosevelt, *The Winning of the West*, Vols. I–IV (New York: Putnam, 1889–1904); Owen Wister, *The Virginian* (New York: Macmillan 1902).

17. Neihardt, *The Mountain Men*, v, xi.

18. Frederick Feikema Manfred, Bloomington, MN, to Alan Collins, New York, NY, 20 October 1952, Frederick Manfred Correspondence, 1950–52, Anderson Library Manuscript Collection, University of Minnesota, Minneapolis, MN.

19. Frederick Manfred, *Lord Grizzly* (1954; Lincoln: University of Nebraska Press, 1983), 1, 3.

20. See Jay Edgerton, "Novelist Lives 'Grizzly Story,'" *Minneapolis Star*, 26 September 1953; Manfred, *Lord Grizzly*, 15, 49.

21. Manfred, *Lord Grizzly*, 65, 68–69.

22. See "Lord Grizzly," *Featurescope*, undated transcript, *Lord Grizzly* Reviews, Frederick Manfred Papers, Anderson Library Manuscript Collection, University of Minnesota, Minneapolis, MN; John R. Milton, mod., *Conversations with Frederick Manfred* (Salt Lake City: University of Utah Press, 1974), 109, 42–43.

23. Milton, *Conversations*, 97–99.

24. Manfred, *Lord Grizzly*, 106.

25. Ibid., 281.

26. Williams Carlos Williams to Frederick Manfred, 1954, in *Lord Grizzly* Reviews, Frederick Manfred Papers; Lewis quoted in Joe Adams, "Details of Big 'Crawl' Make Your Stomach Follow Suit," *Indianapolis News*, 21 October 1954; J. Donald Adams, "Speaking of Books," *New York Times*, 28 October 1954.

27. See Robert J. Markson, "Author Rings Fiction Bell with New Name, Fine Novel," *The Sacramento Bee*, 10 February 1955.

28. For the name change, see Frederick Manfred, Bloomington, MN, to editors of Doubleday Books, New York, NY, 3 August 1951, Frederick Manfred Correspondence, 1950–52, Anderson Library Manuscript Collection, University of Minnesota, Minneapolis, MN; Milton, *Conversations*, 105.

29. Milton, *Conversations*, 107.

30. *Lord Grizzly*, unproduced screenplay by Frederick Manfred, 1964, Anderson Library Manuscript Collection, University of Minnesota, Minneapolis, MN, forward.

31. Ibid., 110, 116.

32. *Publishers Weekly*, 3 March 1967.

33. "Manfred Blasts Movie Maker, Wants New American Aristocracy," publisher unknown, September, 1972, Frederick Manfred Clipping File, Anderson Library Manuscript Collection, University of Minnesota, Minneapolis, MN.

34. Postcard from Maryanna Manfred to Freya Manfred, Minneapolis, 7 October 1952, Research Materials for *Lord Grizzly*, Anderson Library Manuscript Collection, University of Minnesota, Minneapolis, MN.

CONCLUSION

1. See Frederick Jackson Turner, "The Significance of the Frontier in American History," in John Mack Faragher, *Rereading Frederick Jackson Turner* (New York: Henry Holt, 1994), 31–60; Henry Nash Smith, *Virgin Land: The West as Symbol and Myth* (Cambridge, MA: Harvard University Press, 1950); Richard Slotkin, *Regeneration Through Violence: The Mythology of the American Frontier, 1600–1860* (Norman: University of Oklahoma Press, 2000); Richard White and Patricia Nelson Limerick, *The Frontier in American Culture* (Berkeley: University of California Press, 1994); and Kerwin Lee Klein, *The Frontiers of Historical Imagination: Narrating the European Conquest of Native America, 1890–1990* (Berkeley: University of California Press, 1999).

2. For cultural appropriation from the margins, see Philip J. Deloria, *Playing Indian* (New Haven, CT: Yale University Press, 1998), and Eric Lott, *Love and Theft: Blackface Minstrelsy and the American Working Class* (New York: Oxford University Press, 1993).

3. See Laurence Gonzales, *Deep Survival: Who Lives, Who Dies, and Why* (New York: Norton, 2003), and Al Siebert, *The Survivor Personality: Why Some People Are Stronger, Smarter, and More Skillful at Handling Life's Difficulties . . . and How You Can Be, Too* (New York: Perigree, 2010).

4. *The New Shorter Oxford English Dictionary*, Vol. II (Oxford, UK: Clarendon Press, 1993), 2479.

5. Jason Daley, "I Will Survive," *Outside* magazine (September 2004), www.outside online.com/outdoor-adventure/outdoor-skills/survival/I-Will-Survive.html.

6. Jon Krakauer, *Into Thin Air: A Personal Account of the Mount Everest Disaster* (New York: Random House, 1997); Sebastian Junger, *The Perfect Storm: A True Story of Men Against the Sea* (New York: Harper, 1997); Bethany Hamilton, *Soul Surfer: A True Story of Faith, Family, and Fighting to Get Back on the Board* (New

York: MTV, 2004); Aron Ralston, *Between a Rock and a Hard Place* (New York: Atria, 2004).

7. Timothy Treadwell and Jewel Palovak, *Among Grizzlies: Living with Wild Bears in Alaska* (New York: HarperCollins, 1997); *Grizzly Man*, DVD, Lionsgate, 2005.

ACKNOWLEDGMENTS

My heartfelt thanks go out to the colleagues and students who read parts of this book and shared their thoughts, their patience, and their good humor: Dan Graff, Paul Cobb, Gail Bederman, Erika Doss, Sandra Gustafson, John McGreevy, Ted Beatty, John Van Engen, Matt Salafia, Chris Osborne, Erik Peterson, Bryan Smith, Matt Grow, Craig Kinnear, Courtney Wiersema, Meredith Meagher, Felicia Moralez, the Notre Dame history department colloquium, and the members of the History and Biography University Seminar. I would especially like to thank Thomas Slaughter, Louis Masur, and John Mack Faragher for reading the entire manuscript. Their comments made the book so much better. I'm to blame for the worse parts.

The most excellent Dan Lanpher helped me corral the Willard documents. I would like to thank George Miles at Yale's Bienecke Library for leading me to them. I would also like to thank Barb Bezat and Cecily Marcus at the Archives and Special Collections Manuscripts Division of the University of Minnesota Libraries, and Freya Manfred, Ben Vander Kooi, and the members of the Manfred Literary Committee for granting me permission to view and photocopy items from the Frederick Manfred papers.

A remarkably game Thomas LeBien put his faith in me and Hugh. I appreciate his willingness to sign on to a project that at times sounded like a parody of the *Seinfeld* sitcom—a biography about nobody. I would also like to thank Dan Crissman and Dan Gerstle for all the work they put into the book.

Last but not least, I would like to acknowledge my family. Mom and CC, thanks for joining us in South Bend and proving that nuclear families spin better tucked in larger orbits of kin. I associate John and Cally Gilbert with rest rather than writing, but one doesn't happen without the other. Thank you for Cat Island and the fishing trips, for your open home and hearts. Harry and Louise: I appreciate you thinking (or pretending with conviction) that me writing another book was cool.

Annie Gilbert Coleman, thank you for putting up with the bad puns, the early wake-ups, and the vacant stares when I should have been listening to you but was thinking about marauding bears instead. They're gone; I'm back. I will get a dozen eggs; you look smashing in that outfit; the upstairs toilet's running days are numbered. As ever, this one's for you.

INDEX

Baker, William, 50

Baptiste, 112

Barnum, P. T., 34

Bayou Salade, 158, 169

bears, 3, 4, 6, 9, 10, 15, 37, 44, 96–124,
156, 174, 214; anatomy, 99, 110; attacks,
3–6, 12, 14, 42, 60, 96–129, 131–32,
169, 174, 214–15; black, 98, 100–109,
111, 120; blacks and, 101, 103, 105, 106,
112–15; brown, 98, 111; color, 111–12;
Davy Crockett and, 100–106; cubs,
111; Dawson attack, 118–20; facial
expressions, 117; fat, 120–21; Glass
legend, 3–6, 12, 42, 60, 96–97, 99, 101,
118, 119, 123–29, 131–32, 143, 174–75,
180–213, 215–17; grizzly, 3–6, 98, 100,
109–24, 126; hibernation, 104, 110;
human resemblance, 99, 101, 117;
humor, 100, 101, 108, 113–14, 115,
122–23; mating, 110; mother, 111;
mythical, 107–9; narratives, 6, 44,
96–124; parts and products, 120–21; as
pets and slaves, 112–14; size, 109, 110,
111, 115, 117, 120; Smith attack, 115–18;
social system, 110–12

Beatty, Warren, 13

beavers, 34, 44, 56, 70–71, 73, 76, 98,
113, 121, 125, 134, 142, 145, 146, 159,
212–13, 222n2; decline of, 176–77;
height of beaver trade, 212–13;
see also fur trade; hunters

Beckwourth, James Pearson, 79–88, 94,
112–15, 122, 123, 133, 140, 142, 159,
212, 228n16, 229n20; bears and,
112–15; white-hunter persona, 79–88

Beinecke Library, Yale University, 127

Bennet, Daniel, 50

Bible, 34

Biddle, Thomas, 113–14

Bigfoot, 203

Bighorn River, 177

bison, 4, 44, 98, 121, 130, 131, 133, 140,
143, 145, 146, 156, 159, 163, 164, 177,
185; extermination of, 190

Bissonette, Antoine, 74

Black Elk, 188

Blackfeet, 75–80, 91, 153, 156; Colter
escape from, 75–80

Black Hills, 160, 169

Black-Rogers, Mary, 136

blacks, 158, 209; bears and, 101, 103, 105,
106, 112–15; Beckwourth narrative,
79–88, 112–15; freemen, 24, 47, 49–50,
58, 159; mountain-man vernacular
and, 158–62, 164–65, 167, 170;
runaways, 45, 47–51, 85–87; skin color,
48–50, 114; vagabond uprisings,
58–60; see also slaves

blacksmiths, 49, 50, 80, 114

Blackwood's Magazine, 157, 168

Blazing Saddles (film), 224n11

boatmen, 3, 19–25, 28, 37, 105, 132;
cordellers, 23, 132, 137, 138; interracial
couplings, 53–54, 56, 164–65, 191–92;
Mississippi River, 19–20, 45–63, 101;
Missouri River, 22–25, 56, 67–95, 133,
136–38

boats, 3, 5, 22; bullboats, 4–5, 222n2;
canoes, 7, 9; keelboats, 22–25, 45, 89,
113, 132, 133, 137, 138, 179; sinking of,
3, 22, 104–5; steamboats, 31, 141, 142,
143, 153

Bodmer, Karl, 234n27

body, 5, 8, 9, 14, 16, 20, 52, 114, 115, 156,
161, 210; apocalyptic survivalism and,
203–4; of consumptives, 142; disease,
52–53; do-it-yourself amputations,
214, 215, 216; eye-gouging, 55, 56,
58; facial expressions, 117; feast and
famine cycle, 129–33, 136, 163–64;
frostbite, 102, 134; of Glass, 3–6, 45,
125–29, 131–32, 143–44, 153, 175, 187,
200, 215; humoral fluids, 5, 52, 99,
102, 133; identifying marks, 117,
231n34; manhood, 7, 8–9, 12, 20,
34, 72, 115, 116, 138; nakedness, 72,
74–80, 93, 94–95, 97, 144, 175;
runaways, 45–51, 55, 85–87; scars,
wounds, and hardships, 3–4, 9–10, 12,
15, 35, 39, 61, 62, 72, 102, 116–21,
126–49, 167, 206, 213; of slaves, 50–51,
85–87; starvation, 129–49, 166–67;
streakers, 74–80, 94–95, 97

Bonner, Thomas D., 80, 83, 84

Bonneville, Benjamin, 148

Boone, Daniel, 7, 37, 95, 228n12

AMERICAN PORTRAITS

EDITED BY LOUIS P. MASUR AND THOMAS P. SLAUGHTER

Published and Forthcoming Titles

Eric Arnesen on A. Philip Randolph

Mia Bay on Ida B. Wells

Jon T. Coleman on Hugh Glass

Philip F. Gura on Jonathan Edwards

Lori D. Ginzberg on Elizabeth Cady Stanton

Steven W. Hackel on Father Junipero Serra

Charles L. Ponce de Leon on Elvis Presley

*Darren Staloff on Alexander Hamilton,
John Adams, and Thomas Jefferson*

Camilla Townsend on Pocahontas